HOLY
BROTHER

HOLY
BROTHER

INSPIRING STORIES AND ENCHANTED TALES
ABOUT RABBI SHLOMO CARLEBACH

YITTA HALBERSTAM MANDELBAUM

JASON ARONSON INC.
Northvale, New Jersey
Jerusalem

Permission to reprint portions of Shlomo Carlebach's teachings, which appear at the beginning of each chapter, was kindly granted by: *The Holy Beggar's Gazette* (San Francisco).

The author also gratefully acknowledges permission to print excerpts from Aryae Coopersmith's work (forthcoming; untitled).

This book was set in 11 pt. Palatino by Alabama Book Composition of Deatsville, Alabama, and printed and bound by Book-mart Press of North Bergen, New Jersey.

Library of Congress Cataloging-in-Publication Data

Mandelbaum, Yitta Halberstam.
    Holy brother : inspiring stories and enchanted tales about Rabbi
    Shlomo Carlebach / Yitta Halberstam Mandelbaum.
        p. cm.
    Includes index.
    ISBN 0-7657-5959-4
    1. Carlebach, Shlomo—Anecdotes. 2. Rabbis—United States—
    Anecdotes. 3. Hasidim—United States—Anecdotes. 4. Pastoral
    counseling (Judaism)—Anecdotes.   I. Title.
    BM755.C2745M36 1997
    296.8'332'092—dc20
    [B]

                                                                96-33144

Printed in the United States of America on acid-free paper. For information and catalog write to Jason Aronson Inc., 230 Livingston Street, Northvale, New Jersey 07647-
1726, or visit our website: www.aronson.com

Dedicated to the blessed memory of my father,
Yiddish and Hebrew writer
Rabbi Laizer Halberstam
for whom Truth, above all, was paramount.

Rabbi Shlomo of Karlin said: "If you want to raise a man from mud and filth, do not think it is enough to keep standing on top and reaching down to him a helping hand. You must go all the way down yourself, down into mud and filth. Then take hold of him with strong hands, and pull him and yourself out into the light."

A father once explained sadly to the holy Baal Shem Tov that his son had abandoned God. "What shall I do, Rabbi?" he asked in despair. And the Baal Shem Tov answered, "Love him more than ever!"

One evening, several of Rabbi Chaim of Kosov's hasidim sat together in his House of Study and told one another stories about great tzaddikim of the past, and about the holy Baal Shem. And because both the telling and the listening were very sweet to them, they were at it even after midnight. Then one of them told still another story about the Baal Shem Tov. When he had ended, another sighed from the bottom of his heart. "Alas!" said he, half to himself. "Where could we find such a man today?"

At that instant, the hasidim heard steps coming down the wooden stairs that led from their rebbe's room. The door opened and Rabbi Chaim appeared on the threshold, in the short jacket he usually wore in the evening. "Fools," he said softly, "he is present in every generation, he, the Baal Shem Tov, only in those days he was manifest, while today he is hidden." Rabbi Chaim closed the door and went back up the stairs. The hasidim sat together in silence.

"When you tell stories about holy people, and you tell other people there are holy people in the world, it fills you with joy."
—Rabbi Shlomo Carlebach

Contents

Acknowledgments

No single volume could ever hope to encompass the essence, the spirit, or the magnitude of Rabbi Shlomo Carlebach. So, first and foremost, I would like to humbly acknowledge my own limitations, the limitations of time and space, and the limitations of this book. It should not be considered a comprehensive account by any means; instead, it should be viewed as a single superficial scratch on the surface of a remarkable man who stretched across worlds and whose spiritual riches are just beginning to be mined. This book is meant to be used simply as a kaleidoscope, offering fragments, facets, glimpses, dimensions, snapshots, and sparks. It is my greatest hope and most fervent wish that many more works about Reb Shlomo will follow, so that the world can truly know and benefit from his light.

Working on this book has been an intense and spiritually uplifting experience, a privilege, and a gift. I have had the honor of meeting the *chevra*—Shlomo's friends and followers—from all over the world, and I have been enriched by each one. They are shining examples of Shlomo's legacy: spiritual seekers who are thoughtful, reflective, kind, loving, generous, and sweet. I want to thank each and every one of them for their warmth, enthusiasm, and tremendous cooperation and devotion to this project. Without them, it could never have happened. There were hundreds, and I owe them all a great debt.

I especially want to thank those on the West Coast: Aryae Coopersmith, Janice Belson, Joy Krauthammer, Darlene Rose, Olivia Schwartz, Michael and Jill Elias, Michael Ozair, and Jeanette Goldberg. Midnight Music's Stuart Wax (who will certainly one day have a book written about him) is an amazing prototype of a new breed of Jew firmly taking root in Los Angeles. He is in the vanguard of the "Shlomo *Chevra*" on the West Coast, and he and his wife, Enny, were pivotal in many ways in helping me.

On the East Coast, no one was more dedicated to the mandate of this book and more generous with his time than Joey Greenblatt. Mayer Appel, Denise Sassoon, Rabbi Yehuda Fine, Rabbi Joel Dinnerstein, Rabbi Yaakov Haber, Penina Shram, Rabbi Howard Schwartz, Rabbi Yisroel Finman, Hadassah Carlebach, Rabbi Zalman Schacter, Lisa Mechanick, Charley Roth, Devora Davi, Raquel Schraub, Yaakov Braude, Rabbi Laizer and Michelle Garner, Menachem Daum, Rabbi Eliahu Klein, and Chaya Adler were also exceptionally helpful. Shulamith Levovitz, Shlomo Carlebach's older sister and the last remaining sibling of the Carlebach clan, was singularly dedicated, involved, and committed to the fruition of this project—living, breathing, and dreaming it with me. I am privileged to know her and call her my friend.

In Israel Dr. Joshua Ritchie, who has already established a "*Bais* Shlomo" outreach center and synagogue in the old city, was enormously generous with his time, as were Sharon Braun, Rabbi Itzik Aisenstadt, Faye Bloom, Rabbi Simcha Hochbaum, Rabbi Uzi Weingarten and Tuvia Heller.

Of all the Shlomo *chevra*, I have reserved my final and most heartfelt thanks for the man who, more than anyone else, served as my mentor, guide, and champion throughout the entire process: Rabbi Meir Fund, a talmid *chaver* of Reb Shlomo's and currently the spiritual leader of Brooklyn's inspiring Flatbush *Minyan*. Rabbi Fund is the ultimate example of someone whose own extraordinary inroads into uncharted Jewish territory and exemplary achievements with searching Jewish souls have been highly informed by Shlomo's teachings, and I am deeply indebted to him for the assistance he rendered to me so cheerfully, graciously, and generously, during the writing of this book.

There were also many other people who helped make this book happen. Brooklyn handwriting analyst Annette Grauman, an extremely gifted graphologist, was the first one to push me onto the path of writing a book, based on her analysis of my handwriting. Rabbi Joseph Telushkin, who genuinely exemplifies his teachings and is a true *mentsch*, took time out from his own writing—even as he was rapidly approaching a deadline—to help me when I was first starting. Yossi Toiv, a courageous and creative man, has published many of the controversial articles that I wrote for his magazine. Among those articles was a lengthy piece about Reb Shlomo, and it was the warm and enthusiastic reaction of the *heimishe* public to that piece that helped spur my decision to write the book. I want to thank Arthur Kurzweil, Vice President of Jason Aronson, who saw it as his personal mission to bring Reb Shlomo's light to the world, Pamela Roth, Associate Publisher, and Steve Palmé, Production Editor, for their expertise and editorial assistance. Kudos also to Elizabeth Hayes for her excellent copyediting, which greatly enhanced the book.

As Wordsworth said, "The child is father of the man," and I feel I must acknowledge a child's debt to an exceptional woman who nurtured a fledgling talent. Irene Klass, owner and editor of *The Jewish Press*, began publishing my articles on "The Children's Page" when I was eight years old, and then "graduated" me to the regular pages when I was eleven. Her effusive encouragement and warm praise still ring in my ears, and I will always be grateful for her exceptional generosity to me as a child. I also want to acknowledge my early mentors: Rebetzin Sara Freifeld and Rabbi Aryeh Kaplan of blessed memory, Rabbi Nathan Bulman, Rabbi Yehiel Perr, and Dr. Jean Jofen.

My most precious friends—Babshi Berkowitz, Bella Friedman, Yidis Frankel, Ettie Grossman, and Anna Dinnah—have cheered me on throughout the writing of this book, and I am grateful for their friendship. I count Raizy Steg as one of the blessings in my life. Was there ever a more loyal, devoted and stalwart friend? Her presence in my life has sustained me over the last nineteen years. I want to thank my in-laws, Rabbi Leib and Sima Mandelbaum, for their tremendous support all these years. My mother, Claire Halberstam, and my brother and sister, Moishe and Miriam Halberstam, truly rejoiced with me both when I began working on and when I sold the book. Their love, excitement and encouragement have been both heartfelt and heartwarming.

My husband, Mordechai Mandelbaum, comes from the hasidic world (as do I), where extremely capable women are expected to assume many roles, one of which continues to be the domestic one. He good-naturedly waived any expectations of my ever fulfilling that role in favor of my sitting at the computer, and it has been a long time since I last brandished a mop or threaded a needle. An unconventional, independent thinker, he has been the greatest champion and exponent of my work, and a continuous source of wisdom and encouragement. My sons Yossi and Eli cheerfully forgave me for my deficiencies as a mother during the year in which I immersed myself in this project, and I thank them for their love and tolerance. One of my bedtime rituals with little Eli consists of nightly stories, and for a year the only ones he heard were about Reb Shlomo! He patiently and indulgently listened to them all, and became so absorbed and inspired by them that he came to make the suggestion that I entitle this book "The Rabbi of Love"!

And finally, the person to whom this book is dedicated: My father, Rabbi Laizer Halberstam, of blessed memory. As a child it seemed as if he was always pulling my ear . . . in the direction of the non-fiction section at the children's library, even as I veered toward the fiction; in the direction of books, magazines, and newspapers that would instruct and educate, even as my eyes flickered hopefully over the toys stashed in the corner; and always in the direction of my little desk, where pen and paper awaited my childish scrawls and puerile poems. Oh, how he coaxed, cajoled, threatened and even bribed me to write ($1 a poem, $2 a story, a tidy sum in those days)! As a youngster, I greatly resented his intrusion into my life, but as an adult I couldn't be more appreciative or nostalgic. It seems that so much of what has endured in my life since childhood has been my father's legacy, and almost all of my values have been shaped by his. It was my father who introduced me to the two greatest spiritual influences in my life: Shlomo Carlebach, the subject of this book, and Elie Wiesel, the writer of its foreword. My father had guts; he was the only hasid in a long black coat and big broad-rimmed hat to participate in Shlomo Carlebach's concerts at Town Hall and The Village Gate in the '60s, and he always had me in tow. At that time, my father was such an incongruous sight that people used to point and stare. As a little girl I wished could wipe that moment into oblivion; today I treasure it.

It was my father's greatest dream that I write a book, but for many years, almost as a backlash to the enormous pressure he had placed upon me, I barely wrote at all. He would gaze at me sadly then and shake his head. *Tatta*, how I wish you were alive today, how I wish I could tell you the news. *Mazel Tov, Tatta!* Your dream for me finally came true! This book is a lovesong to Shlomo Carlebach but, *Tatta*, it's also a lovesong to you.

Foreword
by Elie Wiesel

Permit me to begin with a digression.

In 1948, in Paris, I met a rabbi, the son of rabbis, a man of great human qualities whose face shone with wisdom and warmth. Reticent, yet cheerful, a gleam in his eyes, he radiated an aura of nobility that made you lower your voice when speaking with him.

His name was Reb Laizer Halberstam.

We used to meet frequently at the editorial offices of a Yiddish weekly—*Zion in Kampf*—that reflected the ideology of the Irgun. Laizer would translate articles from the Hebrew with the flair of a true writer.

About his person, about his life, I knew hardly anything. I knew only that he was a descendant of the famous Rabbi Chaim'l Halberstam, the founder of the Zanz hasidic dynasty, and that he had endured the horrors of the German occupation. But he never spoke of that. We would speak rather of the situation in Palestine, of the future of European culture, of faith in God. I enjoyed listening to him.

The paper closed down in 1949. I didn't see Laizer again until the day I met him, several years later, in New York.

It is with great emotion that I think of him. And I'm thinking of him because I have just read a very beautiful book that his daughter Yitta, the heir of his talent as well as of his religious belief, has just written about Reb Shlomo Carlebach.

I knew him, too. I see him once again. Always in a good mood, his eyes and his face glowing, his guitar slung across his shoulders, his thirst for a life of singing and of hope. Traveling across the world in search of lost souls, he would sing of the love that everyone should have for his fellow man, for all of creation, and naturally for the Creator Himself. He attracted young people most of all, and they adored him. He made them laugh, dance, dream. He would help them overcome the bleak intoxications of daily life by modeling for them the spellbinding and mysterious worlds that every human being carries within himself. He would tell the hasidic tales, giving wings to their imagination. He would show them how to discover the beauty of prayer.

For him, all human beings were worthy of attention. He would suffer with those who suffered. A lover of loving, he would never offend the person to whom he was speaking. Where others might use argumentation and recrimination, he preferred praise. I never once heard him speak ill of another, even of those who cared a little less for him. It's all so simple. The very fact that a Jew was a Jew and a human being was enough to make him worthy of his warm affection. Did he not call the people with whom he came into contact "Holy Reb Shmuel" or "Holy Reb Yisroel"? For him, all the descendents of Abraham, Isaac and Jacob were saintly, that is to say Just Men.

All of this, and more, you will find in this passionate work written by the daughter of Reb Laizer: by telling the life story of Reb Shlomo, she does her father great honor.

—Translated from the French by Joseph Lowin

Introduction

"Holy Sister Yitta," he would beam whenever we met. "You're the sweetest. The holiest." It didn't matter that I had just heard him utter the exact same greeting to 300 people before me. His luminous countenance radiated unmistakable sincerity, and I felt suffused with the warmth of his unconditional love and acceptance. This he had offered to me and to tens of thousands of Jews like me and unlike me, Jews from all walks of life and all countries of the world, who for more than three decades had drunk from his wisdom, soared from his song, and scaled spiritual heights under his gentle tutelage. Whether seeking brief respite or long-term refuge, pilgrims always found a place under Shlomo Carlebach's sheltering, all-embracing wing.

The damaged and the dispirited, the scarred and the searching made their way to the doors of Reb Shlomo. Homeless souls, broken souls, yearning souls, lost souls—but ultimately what mattered most for Shlomo was that they were *Jewish* souls—alternately limped, staggered, and stumbled their way into his heart and embrace, looking for renewal and redemption. There were always failures of course, but many thousands of transformations took place at Shlomo's House of Love and Prayer in San Francisco (an outreach center for Jewish runaways and spiritual seekers), Moshav Modiin in Israel, and the Carlebach Shul on the Upper West Side.

If they didn't seek him out, he went out to hunt them down himself. A brave, lonely crusader, he ferreted them out from the most unlikely places, offering friendship, sanctuary, and a chance to become a Jew again. Shlomo Carlebach was in fact the true father of the *kiruv rechokim* (Jewish outreach) movement. Long before other organizations jumped onto the bandwagon, he went into the gutter and, mired with the mud, single-handedly began pulling them out, one by one by one.

He found lost sparks everywhere: in ashrams, moonie centers, yoga retreats, Village cafes, student union buildings, Grateful Dead concerts, the Fillmore West and the Fillmore East, and even Studio 54! He demonstrated a special affinity for college students. But young spiritual seekers were not the only ones filling the concert halls, college coffeehouses, and synagogue basements where Shlomo sang and taught. Everyone who made the pilgrimage to Reb Shlomo was searching for something, of course; he touched responsive chords in disparate groups of people who sought different things from him. Respectable, affluent, assimilated secular Jews from Scarsdale and Great Neck packed his Carnegie Hall and Town Hall concerts in the '60s, looking for the spiritual elevation that had somehow eluded them in suburbia, but which they found in his exultant *niggunim*. Young Orthodox Jews from Brooklyn, alienated from the stiff conventions of "NO" Rabbis crowded into his classes, seeking to experience the ecstasy of a *yiddishkeit* that said "YES!" And those fleeing or renouncing nothing and nobody, but who were on personal odysseys of growth found in his thinking and vision seeds of evolution and development, seeds that flowered on the fertile ground of his own wide-ranging creativity and genius. In rivulets, in streams, they flowed to him, in an ever-changing river of dreams, hopes, and life.

Shlomo saw the divine spark in every person he encountered and strove to ignite that spark until it burst into fiery flame. For those who had pursued nirvana with drugs, he offered the rapture of a transcendent *davening*; he infused holiness into the ordinary and made sacred the profane. He accentuated the positive in *yiddishkeit*, affirming and celebrating its beauty and joy. He was utopian in outlook, quixotic in his quest. In short, he was a religious fanatic.

The palpable love that pulsated from Shlomo, his trusting innocence and unwavering belief in each Jew's potential for *tikun*, and the powerful, stirringly beautiful melodies that sprang from his soul, created miracles. "Open the Gates," he would cry out to God during his concerts, "Open the Gates!" not realizing that he, as the agent of transformation, already had.

Who will open the Gates for us now? Those who found a spiritual connectedness to God through Shlomo's teachings and songs are truly bereft, for he had no peer. His *ahavas yisroel* (love for Israel) was legendary; his sense of duty to and responsibility for the collective welfare of Jews the world over was unparalleled. Every fiber in his being vibrated with another Jew's pain and suffering. As the conscience of the Jewish world, who could never say no to a Jewish cause, he was a ubiquitous presence at rallies, demonstrations, and protest marches. At a fast and furious clip (ignoring the pleas of his doctors and the ominous presence of his pacemaker), he fearlessly crisscrossed the globe several times a year, bringing *yiddishkeit* to far-flung, remote regions of the world, where few others dared to tread. His almost psychic ability to tune into where he was most needed came as a constant surprise.

Shlomo was a Visionary, a Trailblazer, a Spiritual Giant, and there were those who reviled him for it. He knew that certain segments of the right-wing community misunderstood and scorned him, and this breach saddened him to no end. But possessing the infinite moral courage that was his hallmark and the unwavering determination to fulfill what he saw as his personal *tafkid* (mission), he never faltered from his path. A favorite story that he repeatedly told at his concerts illuminates that resolve: "Reb Zishe, the brother of Rebbe Elimelech, constantly brooded over his concern about what would happen to him in the Afterlife. 'I am not worried,' he told his disciples, 'that I will be asked to explain why in my lifetime I was not Avraham Avinu or Moshe Rabeinu or the Rambam. I am terribly worried that I will be asked to explain why in my lifetime I was not Reb Zishe.'"

With his unique combination of talents, genius, charisma, warmth, idealism, sensitivity, and unconditional love, Shlomo Carlebach was a man made for his mission. Few in recent Jewish history have sacrificed and achieved so much for the Jewish people. He died almost penniless, a Holy Beggar, who gave all the money he made to *tzedakkah* (charity). The Jewish world was profoundly affected by his life and will be irrevocably altered by his death. The profusion of gifts he bequeathed us, both in terms of the thousands of heart-rending melodies he composed and the inspiring teachings he imparted, will have to console us in our wrenching loss. The tens of thousands of recreated Jews, whom we call *baalei teshuva*, also remain, as a testament to his enduring legacy.

Shlomo, move closer, let me tell you something so deep, so awesome, it's *mamesh* a *gevalt*!

Shlomo, you were a Tzaddik (Saint) and a *Godol* (Giant), a beacon of light in the darkness, a shining, radiant, celestial light, a light that gave us succor and strength, a light that pierced the hidden places of broken shards and scattered sparks.

Shlomo, open your heart and listen to the deepest of the deep: You were the sweetest, Shlomo.

And the Holiest.

Biography

RABBI SHLOMO CARLEBACH
(1925–1994)

Rabbi Shlomo Carlebach, one of the most influential and internationally renowned Jewish personalities in the twentieth century, died at the age of 69 on October 20, 1994, leaving behind hundreds of thousands of mourning fans and followers throughout the world.

Alternately known as "The Dancing Rabbi," "The Singing Rabbi," or "The Hippie Rabbi," Shlomo Carlebach was one of the most original and inspired Jewish personages of this century, probably second only to the late Lubavitcher Rebbe in his universal appeal and extensive international impact. Widely regarded both as the father of contemporary Jewish music (with over two dozen Jewish albums to his credit) and one of the original founders of the Jewish "outreach" movement, Rabbi Carlebach's name was a household word throughout the world. He was a bridge-builder and ambassador of love and joy, and his message of openness and inclusion spoke to Jews and non-Jews of all stripes and persuasions. His "hasidim" (followers) represented every spectrum of Jewry and included spiritual seekers of all faiths. He was a ubiquitous presence at ecumenical gatherings and conferences and a popular attraction at New Age retreats.

Rabbi Carlebach was a songwriter, musician, and recording artist who performed alongside Bob Dylan, Joni Mitchell, and Pete Seeger at "peace and love" concerts in the '60s. He rose to prominence in the "New Age" world when he established the famous "House of Love and Prayer" in San Francisco in 1967 to draw back young Jews who felt alienated by Judaism. Embracing the earliest visions of hasidism, with its call to serve God and reach other Jews through joy, Rabbi Carlebach brought a new creativity and spirit to contemporary Judaism, saved a generation of Jews from wholesale rejection of their faith, and initiated a movement that now extends worldwide.

An accomplished Jewish scholar and serious "maggid" (storyteller), whose reputation as a spellbinding raconteur received acclaim in New Age retreats, storytelling seminars, and concerts throughout the world, Rabbi Carlebach's message of love and joy permeated his tales. Everyone in the Jewish world knew Shlomo Carlebach for his music and storytelling gifts; this book reveals a side many suspected but far too few really knew: Shlomo Carlebach the "Tzaddik" (Holy Man), the *"Lamed Vovnik"* (Hidden Righteous Man), the Holy Beggar (who died penniless, having given all his money away to charity), and the Latter Day Saint.

———

Shlomo Carlebach was born in Berlin on January 14, 1925, to one of the most illustrious rabbinic dynasties in Germany, heir to an aristocratic lineage that traced its roots back to King David via eighteen different branches of the family. His grandfather, Rabbi Dr. Solomon Carlebach (after whom he was named) was in fact such a widely respected and revered spiritual leader in Germany that he merited a special mention by Nobel Laureate Thomas Mann in his book *Dr. Faustus*. A citizen of the German city of Luebeck where Rabbi Dr.

Carlebach also resided and reigned as Chief Rabbi, Thomas Mann wrote, "I have retained the impression that the long-bearded, cap-wearing Talmudist, Dr. Carlebach by name, far surpassed his colleagues of another faith in learning and in religious penetration."

In addition to his acclaimed Talmudic erudition and secular scholarship (he received his Ph.D in German Drama from the University of Tuebingen), Rabbi Dr. Carlebach was deeply involved in the affairs of the *kehillah* (Jewish community) and was often employed as its ombudsman to the government. Once, serving as an advocate for a worthy communal cause, Rabbi Dr. Carlebach sought and was granted an uncommon audience with Baron von Bleichroeder, personal banker to Emperor Wilhelm II. The Baron was known as an assimilated, self-hating Jew, and well-intentioned advisers had discouraged Rabbi Dr. Carlebach from seeking the appointment. An unusually optimistic man with a broad and positive perspective, Rabbi Dr. Carlebach was undaunted by his seeming lack of prospects with the Baron and persisted in his efforts to set up a meeting, which finally took place shortly before the outbreak of World War I. During the lengthy interview, Rabbi Dr. Carlebach won the admiration of the Baron, who later wrote, "I have never seen a Rabbi before in my life and I am happy that at my age I now have the privilege of looking at the face of such a distinguished one."

In the aftermath of this visit, the Baron drew closer to the Jewish heritage he had renounced and added a clause to his will, stipulating that "when I close my eyes Rabbi Dr. Carlebach of Luebeck is to be asked to deliver the eulogy. Should he decline to do so, no one else shall be asked to speak." Rabbi Dr. Carlebach did indeed officiate at the Baron's funeral, surrounded by the German crown prince, rulers of the various German dynasties, counts and barons, generals and dignitaries, the diplomatic corps, the intellectual and social elite of Germany, and the most prominent members of the Emperor's industrial and academic circles.

Rabbi Dr. Naftali Carlebach, the youngest of the twelve children of Solomon Carlebach, and father of Shlomo, inherited both his father's commitment to Torah and singular dedication to the Jewish people. In 1917, after he had assumed the rabbinate of the Passauerstrasse Synagogue in Berlin, a Jewish soldier from the south German town of Eschwege turned to him for assistance. A matzo baker by trade, the soldier—who had been forcibly inducted into the German army—desperately sought three months' leave in the spring so he could go home to bake his matzos in time for Passover. The sole breadwinner in the family, it was imperative that the soldier receive this leave, otherwise his family would be destitute. To advance the soldier's petition, Rabbi Dr. Naftali Carlebach traveled at great personal risk to Koepenick, headquarters of the High Command, and convinced the General in charge to release the young matzo baker for a period of three full months!

Shlomo Carlebach's mother, Paula Cohn, was herself the scion of a noble and distinguished rabbinic family. Her father, Osher Michael Cohn, was the Chief Rabbi of Basel, Switzerland, and a founder of Agudath Israel, a prominent international political and religious organization. She was as zealously committed as her husband to the ideal of implanting the principles of Torah, Avodah (service) and *Gemillat Chasodim* (good deeds) into her community, her society, and her family.

The birth of Shlomo Carlebach and his twin, Eli Chaim, was fraught with difficulty. In the early 1900s, the phenomenon of twins was an uncommon occurrence, and multiple deliveries were such dangerous and delicate affairs that both mother and babies were placed at great risk. At one point during the arduous, complicated, and long labor, Rebetzin Carlebach's physician confided to her wearily, "My dear, I don't know if I'll be able to deliver both babies alive!" Stricken, she begged to be left alone for ten minutes in order to pray. Later, she recounted to family and friends that, in addition to recitation of prayers, she had also made a silent vow to God. "*Rebonono Shel Olam* (Master of the World)," she pledged, "if both babies are born safely, I swear to you that I will consecrate them to a life of Torah and good deeds! I will immerse them in such intense spirituality, they will be a light unto the world!" Both babies lived, and news of their birth created a sensation in Berlin.

From infancy on, Shlomo Carlebach displayed boisterous high spirits and extraordinary energy. His sister, Shulamith Levovitz, recalls him walking at the age of seven months, and describes him as a lively and active child, always eager to explore his environment. Once, when he suddenly disappeared from his father's synagogue at the age of four and an alarm had been raised throughout the neighborhood, he was discovered hiding inside the sanctuary's Torah Ark, fervently clutching and kissing the Torah scrolls encased within.

Both Shlomo and his twin, Eli Chaim, were educated at home by pedagogues, private tutors, and Torah scholars. Shlomo demonstrated prodigious Torah ability at an unusually young age, having begun the study of *Chumash* and *Rashi* (Bible and Commentaries) at four, and *Gemora* (Talmud) one year later. All of the European Torah Sages who passed through the Carlebach household (in 1931 the Carlebachs had moved from Berlin to Baden bei Vien in Austria, a health resort renowned for its sulphur baths, which drew many Torah Giants) were much taken by Shlomo's *kop* (literally "head") and pronounced him an *ilui* (prodigy).

As the product of a *Yekki* (German Jewish) home, which typically placed a premium on advanced secular education, Shlomo's destiny would probably have been quite different had it not been for an unusual incident that occurred when he was thirteen. In 1938 Shlomo's entire family traveled to the Lithuanian city of Telz to participate in the bar mitzvah celebration of the son of Rabbi Yosef Kahaneman, the celebrated *Rosh Yeshiva* (head of the yeshiva) of Ponovezher Yeshiva. Although a brief trip had been originally scheduled, because of a series of successive accidents and illnesses that mysteriously befell the family each time they planned their departure, they were forced to stay with the Kahanemans for months instead. "This is what happened," Shulamith Levovitz, Shlomo Carlebach's last remaining sibling recalls. "First time around, just as we were bidding our hosts farewell and were almost out the vestibule, a trap door in the hall suddenly swung open, and my father fell down a flight of basement stairs, breaking his ankle. There was no way he could be moved from the house, and no way would my mother leave him, so we all stayed with the Kahanemans for weeks. Finally, when my father was pronounced healed by the local physician and declared well enough to travel, I suddenly fainted! I became terribly sick and was diagnosed with hepatitis. Well, obviously my parents wouldn't leave me alone, so again the entire family was forced to remain at the Kahaneman home for several more weeks. Then, just as soon as I showed signs of recovering, and my parents began to once again plan their departure, Eli Chaim became ill . . . twice . . . first with middle ear syndrome, then with his own bout of hepatitis. Some mysterious force seemed to be blocking our departure. All of our attempts to leave were stymied. At this point, my father turned to my mother and said, 'Something is not right here! Obviously, these messages are coming from God. Do you have any idea what they mean?' Suddenly, my mother remembered that shortly after the birth of the twins, she had made a *neder* (taken an oath) that both boys would be sent to Ponovezher to study. As soon as my father learned the source of the trouble, he convened, according to Jewish Law, a group of rabbis to *matir neder* (declare null and void) my mother's vow. After that, no one became ill again, and we were finally able to take leave of our gracious but exhausted hosts!

"Meanwhile, Shlomo—the only one to remain unscathed by illness—was enrolled in Ponovezher Yeshiva, an event that represented a major turning point in his life. Here, he was introduced for the first time to the *Litvish* (the analytic yeshiva method of studying Talmud) style of learning, which is dramatically different from German/Jewish. The Torah learning at Ponovezher Yeshiva was of the highest caliber and superior to anything else in Europe. Shlomo emerged from his months of study at Ponovezher with even more zeal for learning Torah than before. The experience was critical for him because it drew him into the nucleus of elite Torah scholarship, and redirected his energies."

In 1939 Shlomo's family arrived in the United States and immediately settled in the Upper West Side of Manhattan, where his father opened Congregation Kehilath Jacob, uni-

versally known as "The Carlebach Shul." Shlomo and Eli
Chaim were enrolled in Yeshiva Torah Vodaath of Brooklyn,
under the stewardship of Rabbi Shlomo Heiman, a famous
Torah Sage who took Shlomo under his wing and tenderly
nurtured his genius. When Shlomo was seventeen years old,
he was invited by Rabbi Aharon Kotler, the preeminent Torah
Sage in the United States, to join his rabbinical seminary,
Lakewood Yeshiva, which was then—and still remains to this
day—the most celebrated Talmudic academy in the United
States.

In the mid-1940s Shlomo became fascinated by the hasidic fervor and esoteric teachings of the neighboring Bobover
hasidim, who had transplanted a tiny portion of their deci-
mated European ranks onto the streets of the Upper West
Side. He began to frequent the Bobover Shul and participate
in the Rebbe's *tish* (literally "table," meaning ceremonial
meals and celebrations), often walking from Manhattan to
Crown Heights on Shabbos (the Sabbath), when the hasidic
sect moved its headquarters there. Later, he would become
equally attracted to the flavor of *Lubavitch*, and transfer to its
yeshiva.

In 1949 Shlomo Carlebach's destiny was irrevocably
altered when he received a summons (together with his friend
Zalman Schachter-Shalomi), from the *friehardiger* (literally
early, meaning previous) Lubavitcher Rebbe. "It was *yud tes
kislev* (the 19th of Kislev, in December)," Rabbi Schachter
recalls, "and Shlomo and I were inside 770 (Lubavitch headquarters), standing in the corridor near the Rebbe's study.
Suddenly, the door opened and Berel Hashin, one of the
Rebbe's assistants, waved us into the inner sanctum. 'The
Rebbe wants to talk to you both,' he whispered. The Rebbe
looked at us and said incisively, without preamble, '*kedei eir
zolt onheibein foran tzu colleges* (it's time for the two of you to
start visiting college campuses).' At this point in his life,
Shlomo had never done college outreach before, although he
had organized a learning group geared towards people of
limited Jewish backgrounds called TASGIG (Taste and See
that God is Good). I had done a little outreach work previously at Brown University, and also was teaching United

Synagogue Youth people, but we were both wet behind the ears. The Rebbe suggested Brandeis University for our first foray, and we collected thirteen pairs of tefillin (phylacteries) to distribute at a Chanukah party scheduled to be held in the campus cafeteria.

"I'll never forget that day," Zalman chuckles. "We walked up an icy stairway to the campus cafeteria where a 'Chanukah Dance' was in progress. When Shlomo and I walked in, laden with packages, the music came to a halt and everyone just stared at us, two Lubavitcher hasidim with yarmulkes, beards, and tzitzit. We divided up the cafeteria like two generals: 'you take the right side, I'll take the left!' and we started doing our thing. Shlomo began telling hasidic stories, and I started speaking about Jewish mysticism. Soon we were totally surrounded by enraptured listeners, and we didn't leave until two o'clock in the morning. As we prepared to depart the way we had come in—an icy stairway that had been transformed into a slippery slope—someone yelled after us 'Hey, there's an easier way out that isn't icy; you'll slip and fall and break your necks if you go down those steps.' For some reason, we disregarded the warning, and descended the steps easily, without incident. Watching our easy descent, a couple of kids tried to follow us, only to slip, slide, and topple down the icy stairs. 'Hey, how'd you manage to navigate the stairs without falling?' one student asked us in astonishment, after he watched his friends' precarious plummet. With a wink and a grin, Shlomo answered, '*Os Mein Halt Zich Oohn Oiven, Falt Mein Nisht Hinten*: If You Hold On To Above, You Don't Fall From Below.' Quintessential Shlomo!

"The Brandeis adventure marked the beginning of our outreach careers," recalls Zalman. "We had no doubt that we had been enormously successful because the University President warned us never to come back again. Obviously, by virtue of the fact that we had opposition, we knew we had been effective and accomplished much good!

"At this point, Shlomo only played the piano, and although he had started composing, his songs were very complex and difficult to follow. Once he began his outreach career, he switched to the guitar and less complex melodies.

The shift was clearly intended to appeal to and galvanize the masses through song," Rabbi Schachter notes.

In the 1950s Shlomo continued his outreach efforts (first as an emissary of the Lubavitcher Rebbe, later striking out on his own), coupled with a series of successive jobs across the United States in *chinuch* (Jewish education) and the Rabbinate. One of his first *shtellars* (pulpits) was a small synagogue in Harlem, where he cemented a lifelong affection and respect for blacks (he later would join Southern Baptists in civil rights demonstrations). He was also instrumental in single-handedly galvanizing the Sabbath observance of a large portion of the Jewish community of St. Louis, where he served as a day school Rebbe. "Shlomo asked the parents of his day school students, who were primarily not religious, to try to keep the Sabbath just for three hours each Saturday," recalls one St. Louis resident. "They reported to him that they found the experience very peaceful and spiritual. 'So how about four hours next Saturday?' he wheedled, until ultimately he brought them to complete Sabbath observance."

In 1959 Shlomo Carlebach released his first album—*Haneshoma Loch* (Songs of My Soul),—which was an instant hit (selling 5,000 copies the first week) and completely revolutionized Jewish music. "The first record caused a musical furor both in the Jewish and non-Jewish worlds," recalls musicologist Velvel Pasternak, the foremost authority on contemporary Jewish music in the United States. "Rather than the Eastern European gestalt that had characterized Jewish music up until then and with which American Jewish youth couldn't identify, Shlomo Carlebach's music was written in an American idiom. He seemed to cut completely with the past. His first record was arranged by Harry Belafonte's arranger, and appeared to bear the imprint of American folk music. His genius was that the ordinary guy on the street could relate to his music and sing it with passion. Thus his music became the cornerstone of American Jewish music, known to every single Jewish bandleader in America, sung in Orthodox synagogues, Conservative *havurot*, Reform summer camps, and hasidic *shtiebels* (synagogues). He was a musical visionary, very

advanced, and his influence on Jewish music has been im-
measurable and everlasting."

Following the extraordinary success of the first record,
Shlomo Carlebach began appearing in concerts throughout
the world, and in New York was most notably showcased in
Town Hall and The Village Gate. Art D'Lugoff, owner of The
Village Gate, recalls Shlomo playing a total of six concerts
there in 1963 alone, one of which drew Lenny Bruce. "Lenny
was performing next door at the Café Au Go-Go," reminisces
D'Lugoff, "and I invited him to come hear Shlomo. He loved
him!" Shlomo's message was "love," D'Lugoff reflects, "harmony to humanity. He had a lot of respect for different types
of artists and was eager to bring people together. He was very
well-respected by all of them."

Shlomo became the "troubadour of the Soviet Jewry
movement" in 1965, when he was asked by Yaakov Birnbaum
and Glenn Richter, leaders of SSSJ (Student Struggle for Soviet
Jewry) to compose a song for the struggle. The result was the
Carlebach classic *Am Yisrael Chai* (The People of Israel Live),
which became the anthem both for the Jews of Russia in
particular, and rallying cry for oppressed Jewish communities
in general. It was played and sung at thousands of worldwide
Jewish rallies and demonstrations held in the '60s, '70s and
even '80s, until the massive Soviet Jewish exodus was finally
effected.

In 1966 Shlomo Carlebach was invited to perform at the
"Berkeley Folk Festival" (which drew over 100,000 people)
alongside the folk greats of the '60s. This event drew him to
the Bay area for the first time, where he witnessed close-hand
the sight of thousands of Jewish hippies wandering the streets
of San Francisco in search of nirvana. Recognizing the intense
need, Shlomo Carlebach established the only Jewish presence
in Haight-Ashbury with his founding of "The House of Love
and Prayer," which served as the prototype for the *Chabad*
(Lubavitch college outreach) Houses that followed later. As a
result of his bold and original initiative, Shlomo Carlebach
sparked the "Jewish return" movement that continues, un-
abated, up until today.

In San Francisco Shlomo Carlebach was highly regarded

as a spiritual master, and was often invited to participate as a Jewish representative in ecumenical "Holy Man Jamborees" and "Whole Earth Expos." (In 1984 he would participate in the historic "East Meets West" Conference in Bombay, which also featured Mother Teresa and Swami Muktananda.) His coterie of devoted followers—which embraced spiritual seekers of all faiths—included Charismatic Catholics, Unitarians, and Sufis. Rabbi Moshe Shur, a folksinger and currently Hillel Director of Queens College, often played gigs with Shlomo in San Francisco, and recalls being especially intrigued by the spectacle of a strict Buddhist sect trailing Shlomo everywhere, serving as his ad hoc bodyguards. He once asked the leader of this sect, an elderly Buddhist, why Shlomo appealed to him so much and was told: "I come from Eastern Europe and was sent to concentration camp because of my beliefs. In concentration camp, I met some of the greatest hasidic Rebbes in Europe—few of whom survived—and had many long and earnest dialogues with them. Despite the evidence all around us, they continuously insisted that there was no evil in the world, only holiness. When I met Shlomo Carlebach, there was something about him that reminded me vividly of these Rebbes, and I therefore feel an obligation to protect him."

In 1977 Shlomo Carlebach closed "The House of Love and Prayer" and brought his hippie disciples to a settlement near Tel Aviv called *Moshav Modiin*, where they continue to live and perpetuate his teachings.

Shlomo Carlebach's travels and impact were worldwide and extensive; virtually every Jewish enclave dotting the globe—large and minuscule alike—hosted him at least once. In 1988 and 1989 he embarked on unprecedented concert tours of both Poland and Russia, playing at 21 sold-out concerts in the most famous music halls of Leningrad, Moscow, Kiev, and Vilnius, mobbed in theaters everywhere by Jews and Christians alike. (He would reprise his Poland tour, by popular demand, two years later.)

Darlene Rose, one of several Americans who accompanied Shlomo on both historic missions, recalls that hordes of television, radio, and newspaper reporters descended frenetically on Shlomo as he stepped out of the plane at Moscow

Airport. "Why are you coming to this Godforsaken place?" one journalist shouted at him. "My sweetest friend," Shlomo beamed, "if you have the power to destroy . . . you also have the power to rebuild!" This remark was broadcast all over Russia, and Shlomo was conferred with the status of a folk hero, followed everywhere by admiring throngs. "Please remember *chevra* (friends)," Stuart Wax, who organized the Russian tour, recalls Shlomo exhorting his entourage before embarking on the trip, "many of our Russian brothers have never smiled before; so few of them have known real joy. It is our mission to make them smile; it is our mission to bring them joy!" "My sweetest friends," Darlene recalls Shlomo telling both his Russian and Polish audiences at the beginning of each concert, "I came to tell you how beautiful you are!" Jolanta Galazka-Friedman, a Polish astronomer who attended one of Shlomo's concerts in Poland, declared, "I would say that Shlomo Carlebach—during only one hour of his concert—said more about love than I will hear for many years in church."

"Post-Holocaust, most Jews today maintain one of two different stances towards life," reflects Menachem Daum, a filmmaker who accompanied Shlomo on his Poland tour. "Either they circle the wagons and draw inward, or else they focus on universal concerns and, in the process, lose their Jewishness. Shlomo Carlebach was one of the rare individuals who brilliantly combined both.

"On the one hand, nothing was more important to him than *yiddishkeit*, restoring it, revitalizing it, renewing it. At the same time, he also took very seriously the mandate that Jews serve as a beacon of light for the nations, an obligation to fulfill a certain role in relation to the rest of the world. His mission, as he perceived it, was to bring light to all the dark places in the world."

"People asked me," Shlomo told *Talkline*'s Zev Brenner in one of the last television interviews before his death, "why am I going to Poland? Don't I know that 'Poland is a mecca of anti-semitism'? Okay . . . so Mazel Tov! Poland is a mecca of anti-semitism . . . what are you going to do about it?"

"The only antidote to hatred is joy," Darlene recalls

Shlomo telling his Poland entourage before their trip. "If you want to get hatred out of someone's heart, you have to fill him up with so much joy, there simply isn't room left anymore for hate!"

"Some people sleep until morning," Shlomo Carlebach was frequently heard to say. "Other people . . . bring the morning!"

1

The House of Love and Prayer

"Now I want you to know the deepest depths. Every person has a share in this world and a share in the world to come. We understand the concept of a share in the world to come, but what does it mean having a share in this world? Open your hearts. Having a share in this world means I know exactly what I have to do in this world. This is a very high level. If I know that if I don't do it, it just won't happen. Then I've just got to do it. This is my share in this world.

"Evil is always new. Imagine, if you do something wrong, you swear to yourself you'll never do it again, right? How come evil returns the next day? The answer is very simple. Evil has a newness. So how do you fight evil? With even more newness!"

"Abraham was the first Jew, the first messenger of God on earth. The first thing Abraham did was to open his house, in fact he took away the doors. Everybody was welcome. Abraham didn't preach to the sinners, 'Listen you dirty pagans, you are going to hell!' He just took them in and told them, 'This is my house and this is your house too.'"

—Rabbi Shlomo Carlebach

———

"Many people mistakenly believe that it was Bob Dylan who first invited Shlomo Carlebach to participate in the legendary 1966 Berkeley Folk Festival, but this is in fact a misconception," says Stuart Wax, an important figure in L.A.'s music industry. "The truth about how Shlomo Carlebach came to perform with the folk greats of the '60s is actually much more interesting.

"In 1966 Shlomo appeared at a concert in Miami, and a woman in great distress approached him at the end of the performance. 'Your music is so spiritual,' she told him. 'My daughter is a lost Jewish soul who could probably benefit just by listening to it. Can you help me?' Shlomo spoke with the woman at length and then gave her his card and a free album. 'Send them to your daughter,' he urged, 'you never know!' As it happens, the daughter lived in Berkeley and one night was playing Shlomo's record with the windows wide open. As it also happens, the organizer of the Berkeley Folk Festival (which drew over 100,000 people) lived right next door, and his windows were also open. Suddenly, she heard a pounding at her door, and the organizer stood on her threshold. 'What's that music? Who's that singing?' he demanded. 'This singer is awesome! This music is rapturous! I want to inject a little international flavor into the Festival, and these foreign language songs are perfect. What language is this? Who, who is this singer? I must contact him immediately.' As it so happens, the daughter had in her possession Shlomo's card that her mother had sent her, and the rest is history.

"The Berkeley Folk Festival brought Shlomo to the Bay Area for the first time, where he encountered a lost Jewish generation that was spiritually starved. His experiences at the Festival impressed upon him the need for a Jewish retreat and outreach center in San Francisco. As a result, he established the House of Love and Prayer, which was instrumental in catalyzing the Jewish renewal movement throughout the United States. All of this sprang from an album and a card. Instead of reclaiming one lost Jewish soul, the card and album that made its way from Miami to Berkeley ultimately reclaimed thousands. As Shlomo had originally told the woman, 'You never know!' You never know when the simplest act will have the profoundest effect."

———

In 1966, when Rabbi Saul Berman was spiritual leader of Beth Israel Synagogue, an Orthodox congregation in Berkeley, California, he met Shlomo Carlebach for the first time. "He knocked on my door one Friday morning and introduced himself," Rabbi Berman reminisces. "He said he was going to be performing at the massive Berkeley Folk Festival on Saturday night and was looking for an Orthodox family with whom he could share *Shabbos* (the Sabbath). Someone in town had directed him to my home. Of course, I immediately invited him to spend *Shabbos* with us and he gratefully accepted, exclaiming effusively, 'Oh, my sweetest friend, you're doing me the biggest favor of my life!' We spoke for a while and then, after several minutes of animated discussion, he bid me farewell and turned to leave. As he strode down the path, he called over his shoulder, 'Just in case I find a couple of lonely Jews who also want to taste *Shabbos*, would it be OK if I bring them with me?' 'No problem. Gladly!' I responded and went into the kitchen to advise my wife to prepare a little bit more than usual.

"The way the Festival organizers had structured the concert," Rabbi Berman recalls, "was that on the Friday preceding the event, all the performers were scheduled to do ten-minute gigs out on Sproul Plaza of the Berkeley campus as a kind of preview to what they would be doing the following night. From the moment Shlomo began singing, he had the crowd mesmerized. No performer before him had elicited the response that he did. He had them singing, clapping, and dancing in a way that was unbelievable! Everyone came to hear him, and before the ten-minute gig was over, he was playing to a mob of several thousand people.

"When the gig was over, Shlomo thanked the crowd and said in his characteristic expansive way, 'Anyone who is interested in continuing this experience and also would like to taste *Shabbos* is invited tonight to the home of Rabbi Saul Berman,' and he announced my address.

"Friday night, 400 people showed up at my door! Needless to say, my wife hadn't prepared for quite that many, and she ran to our next door neighbor, fortunately also kosher, for help. We pooled all our Sabbath food and chopped it into teeny little pieces and distributed it all around.

"There wasn't much food and there certainly wasn't much room, but nobody seemed to notice or to care, because what we did have in abundance was lots of *ruach* (spirit) and love to match.

"This *Shabbos* marked Shlomo's formal introduction to the Berkeley community, and developed within him a sense of connectedness to these people. One year later he opened the House of Love and Prayer in San Francisco."

———

"The Berkeley Folk Festival, which I attended in 1966, featured an impressive roster of the '60s greats," reminisces Dr. Aryae Coopersmith. "Pete Seeger; Peter, Paul, and Mary; Joan Baez . . . they were all there and accorded warm receptions. But of all the stars who performed at the concert, it was Shlomo Carlebach who elicited the greatest response. Everyone agreed, 'The Singing Rabbi' emerged as the undeniable hit of the entire show.

"When the concert ended, Shlomo had in tow hundreds of fans whose hearts he had opened during his performance. A virtual unknown at the start of the show, his charisma, warmth, and authenticity had instantly transformed him into a kind of Pied Piper of Judaism. When he left the concert, we pursued him onto the streets, where we followed him as he slowly walked towards his hotel.

"As we reached the entrance to the hotel, we felt disheartened that the moment to bid Shlomo farewell had arrived so quickly. We had heard that he was booked on a return flight to New York the next morning, and we wondered if we would ever see him again. Sadly, we began to approach him one by one for a last embrace.

"In the meantime, Shlomo stood framed in the doorway *shukeling* (swaying way and forth, in a prayerlike manner) intently, stroking his beard in a meditative way. It took only a minute for him to snap out of his reverie. '*Chevra* (friends),' he shouted joyously. 'Do you want to continue this experience?' We responded with a thundering 'Yes.' 'Then please wait out here a moment; I just had an idea,' Shlomo said, opening the doors to the hotel.

"Now the old Shattuck Hotel where Shlomo was staying," Aryae chuckles, "was probably one of the most staid and sedate hotels in the area, attracting an extremely conservative clientele. Nonetheless, Shlomo had no compunction about walking up to the desk clerk and saying, 'I'm so sorry to bother you in the middle of the night, but would it be possible for me to rent the whole top floor of the hotel for my holy friends?' The desk clerk was startled, but as it so happens, the top floor was indeed vacant, and he was therefore happy to comply with Shlomo's request. Luckily, he had not yet seen the hundreds of 'holy friends.'

"We were astounded by Shlomo's generosity. At his own personal expense, he booked us into the hotel for days, ordered food and drink, and proceeded to give us our first taste of Judaism in what turned out to be a marathon teach-in.

"For many of us, this experience proved life-changing. Shlomo awakened and expanded our souls in a way nobody had before, and turned us on to Judaism. For a significant number of us, the 'Shlomo Teach-In'—which unofficially launched 'The House of Love and Prayer'—was just the beginning of a journey back to our roots.

"Shlomo's genius was his spontaneity. Renting the top floor of the Shattuck Hotel for a 'Jewish Experience' had never been part of his plan. But when he saw our spiritual hunger, he immediately responded. Shlomo knew how to seize the moment. Consequently none of us were ever quite the same."

———

By dint of two very different and separate curious twists of fate, Charismatic Catholics ended up figuring prominently in the establishment and maintenance of Shlomo Carlebach's House of Love and Prayer. In 1966, when Shlomo first arrived in the Bay Area to play at the Berkeley Folk Festival, he confronted with anguish the sight of thousands of dazed, drugged, and dispirited teenagers and young adults wandering aimlessly through the streets of Haight-Ashbury. "Look at these kids . . . my heart is breaking," Aryae Coopersmith remembers Shlomo saying in anguish. "I'm sure that half of these kids are Jewish . . . They came here looking for something, and what are they getting—nothing! Aryehla, we have to do something. We have to give their hungry *neshomos* (souls) the spiritual sustenance they're looking for. I've come to a decision. We have to establish some kind of spiritual center, right here in Haight-Ashbury where we can reach them, a place where when you walk in, somebody loves you, and when you walk out, somebody misses you! You're in charge, Aryehla. Go find a house!"

Aryae recalls looking at Shlomo in panic and disbelief. "Shlomo," he countered, "it's a great idea, very necessary. But I don't have any money." "Don't worry," Shlomo responded cheerfully, "something will come up."

A few days later, Aryae was pouring his heart out to John Seaman, a Charismatic Catholic, who was one of several devout Christians drawn to Shlomo. "Shlomo Carlebach is unreal," he grumbled. "He believes in miracles! Somehow he's decided that I'm going to be able to pull it all together and help him establish an outreach center, when there's not a penny in the till. Did you ever meet such an optimist?" "Wait a second," said John slowly. "This is a really important project. It could change people's lives. It could rescue kids, even save them. I'll tell you what . . . I'll give you my entire life savings!" "That is incredible!" Aryae said. "How much do you have?" "Three hundred and fifty dollars." Although Aryae's heart sank when he heard the sum, he was by then enough of a disciple of Shlomo's to cherish John's magnanimous heart and sincere, if naive, intentions. He showered his thanks upon John. "Three hundred fifty dollars! Wow, that's great!"

The next day, Aryae was wandering through the streets of Haight-Ashbury when he came upon a small, dingy real estate office. Impulsively, he walked in and asked, "I know this is a thoroughly unrealistic request, but I'm looking to rent a very large house in this neighborhood, very cheap."

The real estate agent looked at Aryae. "What a curious coincidence!" she muttered. "I just got off the phone with a lawyer who is having difficulties with a deceased client's estate—a large, but I must warn you, neglected, Victorian mansion. Until the legal difficulties are disentangled, he wants to rent it. You're in luck. It just got on the market literally this minute!"

"So how much is the rent?" asked Aryae, heart palpitating.

"It's a bargain," answered the agent. "Three hundred dollars a month.

"Oh, but I must tell you one thing," added the agent. "I require a fifty dollar security deposit. . . ."

"You've got a deal," Aryae exclaimed.

Subsequently, Shlomo's outreach center, which he named "The House of Love and Prayer" (he frequently explained that if he would have called it something like "Temple Isaiah" no one would have come) was an instant success, and thousands of disenfranchised Jews passed through it during its ten-year span. Its continued existence, however, was often precarious, for financial and other reasons, and the center was frequently in danger of being closed. This is where Charismatic Catholics came to Shlomo's rescue once again.

The lawyer/executor of the building soon regretted his decision to let Shlomo rent. Neighbors constantly complained to him about the late hours the occupants of the House of Love and Prayer kept, the noise, the crowds that congregated on the sidewalk, the bizarre-looking people flitting in and out. Finally, the landlord couldn't take it anymore, and one day Shlomo stood outside the House of Love and Prayer looking

at the eviction notice in his hand. As it so happens, the House
of Love and Prayer was located not far from a convent, and as
it also happens, the nuns adored Shlomo. They perceived him
as a great spiritual master who was saving kids' lives, and
they had only the highest praise for him.

As Shlomo stood outside the House of Love and Prayer
sadly examining the eviction notice, one of the nuns walked
by. She approached him in a rush of concern and asked him
why he looked so solemn. Shlomo handed the eviction notice
to the nun. "He has some nerve!" she fumed. "I'm going over
to give him a piece of my mind right now!" "You know him?"
Shlomo asked. "Do I know your landlord?! He's a member of
my church! Don't you worry about this, Reb Shlomo; the
matter's as good as taken care of."

A few hours later, a trembling landlord stood before
Shlomo, stammering apologies and tearing up the eviction
notice. Shlomo knocked at the convent door to thank the nun.
"Tell me," he asked her after proffering his appreciation.
"What exactly did you tell him that moved him so pro-
foundly?"

"Oh . . . it was very simple really!" replied the nun
with a beatific smile. "I told the landlord that if he ever brings
grief to Rabbi Shlomo Carlebach . . . he's going to burn in
hell!"

After that, the landlord never bothered Shlomo again.

––––––––

"As a long-term resident of Shlomo Carlebach's House of
Love and Prayer in the '60s, it was natural for me to
turn to Shlomo for help in composing the text of my wedding
invitation. I should have known!

"Shlomo beamed happily at my request and assured me
he would take care of everything. 'Don't worry, it'll be the
holiest wedding invitation in the world!' he told me in a jovial
voice.

"A few days later, he entered the house bearing a box of

wedding invitations, completely finished. Proudly, he handed me one.

"With a just a little chagrin I noted the wording of the text. It read: 'The whole world is invited to the wedding of Ne'eman Rosen and Malka Gorman.'

"The invitations were distributed all over Haight-Ashbury and, consequently, many people whom I didn't even know showed up to celebrate! Despite my initial reservations about Shlomo's wisdom in inviting 'the whole world' to my wedding, it turned out to be a joyous affair!"

———

"Shlomo never criticized, chastened, or reprimanded us. During all the months I lived in the House of Love and Prayer, I cannot recall a single time I heard him vent anger or disapproval. He taught exclusively by example. Only one time do I remember him saying something bordering on mild reproach, and then it was directed at me.

"I was standing on the second floor balcony of the House of Love and Prayer one day surreptitiously smoking some grass, when I saw Shlomo walking up the steps towards the front entrance. Just at the moment that I saw him, he sighted me, and our eyes locked. In a second, his glance had absorbed everything. It was useless to try to conceal the cigarette. He gazed up at me, hanging over the railing, and said a little sadly, 'Yisroel, if it would make you learn Torah better, I'd encourage it. But as it is, you end up falling asleep in class, so what's the point?'

"I stubbed out the cigarette, and never smoked marijuana again."

———

"He called us the 'holy hippalach.' It was Shlomo's term of endearment, his affectionate nickname for those of us living in the House of Love and Prayer in San Francisco in

1968, spiritual seekers, new to *yiddishkeit*, and ardently devoted to him. We were such loyal *hasidim* of Reb Shlomo's in
fact, that wherever he went in California, we would follow.

"So when he called us one day from New York and told
us he would be doing a *Shabbaton* (Sabbath happening) that
weekend at a Reform Temple in Los Angeles, we did what we
always did: we got ourselves ready to drive down the coast
and meet Shlomo at the L.A. airport. Although just being with
Shlomo always proved an adventure, we could never have
envisioned exactly what lay in store for us that particular
Shabbos!

"Two of us had little 'hippie' cars—a tiny VW Bug and
something similar—into which we packed ourselves, pregnant mothers, babies, strollers, guitars, drums, tambourines,
etc. and headed down the coast. Late Friday afternoon we met
him on time at the airport and tried valiantly to rush him into
the car, but with Shlomo, it wasn't such a simple thing. First,
he busied himself with greeting just about everybody in the
airport, and then he started making phone calls to people all
over the world. We were very anxious about getting to the
Temple before sunset and kept on frantically tapping our
wristwatches while he spoke animatedly on the phone. 'Just
one more call!' he kept on pleading, as we looked with
growing consternation at the airport clock. Finally, we managed to hustle him into the VW Bug, and get onto the freeway.
Collectively, we heaved a huge sigh of relief!

"We were making excellent time, and our nervousness
about getting to the Temple before *Shabbos* had just about
dissipated, when traffic came to a complete halt. A truck had
overturned, spilling a thick white powder on the freeway, and
the police had blocked off the entire area. We looked at each
other in panic as the sun began to sink lower and lower in the
sky. What we were going to do next? Finally, Shlomo announced, '*Chevra*, I'm so sorry, but it's almost *Shabbos*; we're
going to have to get out of the car and walk the rest of the
way.' We pulled over to the side of the road, emptied our
pockets (carrying is forbidden on *Shabbos*), put on several
layers of clothing, locked the cars, did something clever about
the car keys, and started walking. We didn't know where we

were, how to get to the Temple, or how long a walk we were in for. But we did have faith—both in God and in Shlomo—so we figured everything would turn out OK.

"For several minutes, we walked along the highway until we came to an exit sign that read 'Sepulveda Boulevard.' Somebody in the group excitedly shouted that the name sounded familiar—he was quite certain that the Temple was located on this avenue—so with a raucous cheer, we exited. See, we told each other happily, it wasn't so bad after all. Only about fifteen minutes of walking and we're almost there, already. Our optimism turned out to be very short-lived. We soon discovered that our excitement had been premature, to say the least.

"We had been walking along Sepulveda Boulevard for almost an hour. The Temple was nowhere in sight, and the few passersby we encountered could offer us no assistance. We were not dispirited, however. Even as we walked, Shlomo was lightheartedly 'doing *Shabbos*' with us, telling us hasidic stories, teaching Torah, singing *zmiros* (*Shabbos* songs). We were still walking when a car pulled up alongside our little group, and the female driver started gesticulating wildly. The woman inside turned out to be the secretary from the Reform Temple who was sent by the frantic congregation to search for us. She started yelling: 'Shlomo, we've been worried sick! Everybody is waiting for you! Come on, get into my car!' Shlomo replied softly, 'Darling, I appreciate your offer so much, but I'm so sorry, as bad as it is, I can't get into the car with you. I have to walk.' 'But Shlomo,' the secretary protested, 'It's *27 miles* to the Temple!'

"Our hearts sank. The pregnant women and mothers with babies were struggling. There were those among us who had never kept *Shabbos* before, and truthfully, we wouldn't have minded if Shlomo had managed to find a *heter* (dispensation) that would get us off the streets and into the car! But Shlomo was strictly halachic (adhered strictly to Jewish Law), and nothing was more sacred to him than the *Shabbos*, so our hopes were dashed when we heard him say to the secretary instead: 'Darling, please do me the greatest favor in the world. Please tell the members of your congregation that humble me and the holy *hippalach* have to walk to the Temple, and we're walking as fast as we can. Please don't lose heart. Maybe if they feel up to it, everyone can stay and do something and wait until we get there.'

"So we continued walking, Shlomo calmly and cheerfully doing *Shabbos* with us, still telling hasidic stories, still teaching Torah, still singing songs. We tried to concentrate and ignore the cold night air, the ominously overhung cloudy sky, the wailing babies, our hunger and thirst. It was about 10:00 at night, and we seemed to have made little headway. Every once in a while the Temple sent another car to check on our progress and see how we were doing. At about midnight, our fears about the weather were confirmed when the skies opened. No mere drizzle or mild rainfall, mind you, but a downpour, a torrential storm, and there we were—caught right in the thick of it, defenseless and soaked to the bone. We groaned, but from Shlomo we never heard one word of complaint, not a single sigh. '*Chevra*, have I ever told you the story of Yossele the Miser?' he turned to us, his face shining, thoroughly unperturbed.

"At about 1:30 in the morning, the rain was still coming down hard, when another car pulled up alongside us, one that we hadn't seen before. To our surprise, the man inside turned out to be a famous L.A. personality, the talk show host the 'Night Owl,' from a local radio station, who had somehow heard about our *Shabbos* walk. He was so intrigued that he had jumped into his car and driven to Sepulveda Boulevard to see for himself!

" 'Hey, what are you doing?' he shouted at Shlomo in a not unfriendly manner as he rolled down his car window and drove alongside us. 'Why are you walking in this downpour? Why can't you drive? How long have you been walking? What is this all about?' Shlomo began to patiently and eloquently explain about the beauty and sanctity of *Shabbos*, and how we couldn't violate it. The talk show host—impressed, perhaps moved by Shlomo's explanation—asked Shlomo many questions, engaged in an animated dialogue with him for several minutes, thanked him, and left. We had no idea that all this time a tape recorder had been hidden—and secretly running—in his lap.

"At about two in the morning, when Sepulveda Boulevard is usually quite deserted, and we ourselves hadn't encountered any traffic for some time, we suddenly saw three cars trailing us. They pulled up alongside us, and the people inside excitedly asked Shlomo, 'Are you Rabbi Carlebach?' 'Yes, darling,' Shlomo replied without missing a beat, 'and who are you?'

"These people had been listening to The Night Owl who, after his encounter with Shlomo, returned to the station and broadcast the entire discussion. He had been so overwhelmed by Shlomo's spiritually uplifting words that he decided to air his entire soliloquy on *Shabbos*. The people in the cars told us that they too had been equally moved by Shlomo's talk. In fact, their imagination had been so captured by The Night Owl's dramatic description of our *mesiras nefesh* (sacrifice for Jewish principles and laws) that they had come to join us as a gesture of brotherhood!

"We were touched by their action, particularly since it was still raining very heavily, and Sepulveda Boulebard had been virtually transformed into a surging river. We thanked our new friends for their display of fellowship, but urged them to return home, where they would be safe and dry. They refused. Undaunted by the rushing waters now swelling Sepulveda Boulevard, they insisted on accompanying us the rest of the way. And they were not alone.

"One by one by one, the cars began to pull up, as we watched in wonder. People who had been listening to The Night Owl's broadcast—alternately intrigued, inspired, and charmed by the story of our *Shabbos* march—trailed us down Sepulveda Boulevard with their cars, then parked them and joined our ranks. First there were a dozen, then two dozen, then three. Soon there was more than 200 people walking with us in this veritable parade for *Shabbos*! We didn't know who was Jewish and who was not, but did it matter? The strong sense of unity and harmony surged as powerfully throughout our ranks that night as the waters swirling around us. We clasped hands with our brothers who had come with such love to escort us safely to the Temple, hugged them close and wished them a joyous '*Gut Shabbos*' (Good Sabbath)!

"And all this time . . . as we were wading through the flooded Boulevard, Shlomo continued serenely to tell stories, teach Torah, sing songs, and everyone was singing with him. The energy was high, the spirit great, and we were all feeling happy. Finally, at 4:30 in the morning, all 200 of us got to the Temple, and to our shock and delight, the place was packed! Members of the congregation had been waiting for us all night, so they were ready for us when we came in: they had towels, dry clothes, even hot chocolate. At about 5:00 in the morning, Shlomo started *davening* (praying) *Kabbolas Shabbos* (the Friday night service), and—despite everything we had endured—conducted a full *davening*, told more stories, taught more Torah, and we eventually got to *Kiddush* at 8:00. At about 8:30 Saturday morning, we finally sat down to our Friday night meal.

"For as long as I live, I will never forget that *Shabbos* walk with Shlomo Carlebach. Everyone who did that walk was transformed. We were a bunch of kids who didn't know anything about *Shabbos* until we took that walk, and this is how he taught us. After witnessing Shlomo Carlebach keeping *Shabbos* with such passion, devotion, and fervor . . . how could you not keep *Shabbos* after that?"

———

The House of Love and Prayer was different things to different people; for some it was the only synagogue they had ever entered, for others it was a yeshiva where they were introduced to Torah for the first time, and for others still it was a crash pad where they could obtain free room and board. But the House of Love and Prayer was also a home where teenage runaways of all faiths could find sanctuary.

A girl named Chrissie* from somewhere in the South was

———

*Denotes a pseudonym. Several of those who contributed their staying at the House of Love and Prayer. Nobody ever quite knew how she had found her way to the House; she was clearly not Jewish but received as warm a welcome as anybody else. She was in a lot of pain, as lost as could be. She had a father about whom she told such horrible stories "it was enough to make you shake." Even though Chrissie frequently characterized her father as a "terrifying" man, it was not until she had stayed at the House for several months that she revealed the truth about him: He was a Grand Dragon in the KKK or an Imperial Wizard. She often told Shlomo "If my father discovered that I've found refuge with a group of Jews, oh man, I don't know what he would do."

One day, Chrissie was on the phone talking to her mother (with whom Shlomo had urged her to maintain contact), when her mother said: "Chrissie, I have to tell you something. Your father hired a detective to track you down and a couple of hours ago discovered where you've been living. Dad's on his way right now to the House of Love and Prayer to bring you back home." Chrissie got off the phone fast. "Quick! We're in trouble!"

Overhearing her screams, Shlomo came running from his room. "What's happening? What's going on?" he asked. "Shlomo, my father's coming to get me! He should be here any minute, and Shlomo, really, you don't understand how frightening my father can be." Shlomo replied wryly: "Chrissie, darling, we get the picture."

Shlomo and the *chevra* didn't know what to do. Just as they started trying to figure out a game plan, there was a knock at the door. "*Oy Gevalt!*" shouted Shlomo and everyone, totally terrified by the specter of a KKK monster, ran for cover. Some hid in closets, others in the shower, and some actually clambered out of the high back windows. In an instant almost everyone had vanished except for Shlomo and Chrissie.

Meanwhile the knocking had become louder and more

<hr />

experiences to this book asked that their names be changed to preserve their anonymity.

persistent. Reluctantly, Shlomo rose to open the door for Chrissie's father, a beefy-looking man with a ruddy complexion and mean eyes. As Shlomo opened the door, those eyes traveled the length and breadth of Shlomo's body, absorbing with great astonishment and growing fury the details of Shlomo's *yarmulke*, beard, and *tzitzit*. Shlomo extended his hand, but the man coldly ignored it, and demanded, "Where's my daughter? Where's Chrissie?"

Shlomo didn't directly answer his question, but told him in a tone of wonderment instead, "Do you know how long I've been waiting to meet you?" Taken aback, the man looked at Shlomo with mingled surprise and suspicion and replied in a hard voice, "Oh yeah, why?" "Because your daughter says the most unbelievable things about you!" An expression of bewilderment, hurt, and confusion flitted across his face. "She does? What does she say exactly?" Shlomo answered, "Your daughter loves you so much, it's incredible how much she loves you." Chrissie's father started to blink, but retained his tough, skeptical stance, saying sarcastically, "Yeah, sure. Sure she loves me. That's why she ran away from home, she loves me so much!" "Listen to me. Maybe it's a little hard for her to express it, but brother, her love for you is so deep, so deep! You must believe it and you must accept it."

Suddenly, the hardened KKK monster started to cry. When Chrissie saw the tears streaming down her father's face, she emerged from her hiding place to greet him, and they embraced.

Father and daughter spent several hours talking in the living room of the House of Love and Prayer, laughing, hugging, and crying together. When Chrissie's father finally left, having agreed to let her continue at the House, he told Shlomo in parting, "You're the only Rabbi I give my permission to spend time with Chrissie. I don't want any of the other Rabbis near my daughter."

Several weeks after the rapprochement with her father, Chrissie went back and didn't keep in touch. So the *chevra* never learned what happened to the Grand Dragon after his fateful meeting with Shlomo. But there was really no question in anybody's mind, that he left the encounter with "The Rabbi of Love" a changed man.

————

"Looking at me today, it's hard to imagine I was once a free-spirited hippie living in a dome in the woods of Northern California," laughs Sarah Frankel.* It's true. Coiffed in a *sheitel* (wig), she's wearing the high-necked, long-sleeved modest garb of the ultra-Orthodox woman, and is carrying under her arm several books of a religious nature: a *Tnach* (Bible), a *Tehillim* (Book of Psalms), and a Siddur (prayerbook). "It's probably even more difficult to believe," she chuckles, "that I was actually once a Unitarian!"

Her conversion she credits completely to Shlomo Carlebach's influence. "Not that he ever went out looking for potential converts," she remarks, "if anything it was the other way around. We went looking for him!"

Although Shlomo Carlebach's House of Love and Prayer had been established as an outreach center for alienated Jews, it drew spiritual seekers of all faiths. "In fact, there was an entire contingent of Charismatic Catholics who followed him around faithfully like the most *fahrbrenta* (impassioned) *hasidim*," she smiles fondly. "And many of these kids, like myself, invariably underwent halachic (Orthodox Jewish Law) conversions to Judaism, and are today strictly observant Jews.

"We felt a void, an emptiness, that our respective religions were not filling. Shlomo Carlebach was the most 100% authentic spiritual person we had ever met, and the Judaism he presented to us was the kind of spirituality we had been seeking. It was the same for all of us. When we met him, we instantly knew, 'Yes! This is what I've been looking for all my life!'"

But what Sarah remembers most vividly from her House of Love and Prayer years is her wedding day. "Of course you can understand that a '60s hippie would not opt for a conventional wedding at a staid and sedate wedding hall," she smiles. "Some of my friends had been married at Golden

Gate Park, others had desired a simple street wedding, while still others had selected a ceremony in the Muir Woods. As for me, I was really original; I chose a secluded mountaintop.

"Shlomo was naturally designated to officiate, and I harbored no illusions about him being on time. Still, as all of us assembled under the hot sun fidgeted with impatience, I began to worry about his exceptionally long delay. For him to be one hour late was quite typical. Two hours late was already a little unusual. But three hours late was downright abnormal. And he was, at this point, three hours late.

"My range of emotions had changed and shifted as we waited. First I had fretted, then I had become infuriated, and finally, I had grown terribly alarmed. Where was Shlomo?

"As we drew together and discussed our distress about Shlomo's non-appearance, someone gently pointed out that perhaps we had made a terrible mistake. We were all very young—in our teens and twenties mostly—so climbing the mountaintop had not been a formidable feat. Some of us had walked up, while others had used mountain bikes. One or two creative souls had even come on horseback. But in our enthusiasm about a mountaintop wedding, we had not even considered the plight of poor Shlomo. We had forgotten that he wasn't a youngster anymore. His spirit was so energetic and vital, we had overlooked the fact that he was middle-aged and might experience difficulty in getting to the wedding site. How had we expected Shlomo to get to the top of a mountain that had no accessible car roads?

"Suddenly, we heard an engine and Shlomo came into view. There he was, perched on the back of a red motorbike, tightly clutching the driver's back, waving happily, black eyes popping in mischievous glee. '*Chevra*, I'm so sorry I'm late,' he offered his apologies, 'but I had a little problem getting transportation.'

"We laughed, and as the ceremony began to get underway, I reflected on just how emblematic this scene truly was. The 'can do!' spirit that had gotten Shlomo up the mountain to my wedding was the same spirit that infused the House of Love and Prayer. It was the same spirit that animated all of Shlomo's extraordinary achievements. The word 'obstacle' simply had no place in Shlomo Carlebach's vocabulary."

2

Everyone Is Precious

"Tears flow up. When you see someone's tears flowing from their eyes, they are not going down. . . . Gevalt, are they going up to heaven! Gevalt, are they going up! When somebody is crying, God gives you the greatest, deepest privilege . . . to kiss away their tears!"

"What is it to really have a covenant with God? A lot of people have a covenant with God and they are God drunk. They are completely with God, but they are not world drunk. They don't see the people anymore, especially if the people are pagans, according to their theory. A person who has a true covenant with God has to be completely aware of every little pagan in the world. If Abraham would not have welcomed the three angels who were disguised as pagans, he would never have had Isaac and there would never be a Messiah, and the whole world most probably would be destroyed one way or another!"

—Rabbi Shlomo Carlebach

Shlomo Carlebach was delivering a noon-time lecture to Jewish members of Manhattan's Diamond Dealers' Club, when a truculent man suddenly interrupted and challenged him belligerently. "Shlomo!" he demanded, "We love your music, and your *hasidishe meisalach* (hasidic tales) are also very nice, but there's one thing about you that bothers some of us and which we just can't understand: Why are you always so busy with low-lifes and *meshugoyim* (crazies)?"

Shlomo stroked his beard reflectively and, looking around the room, said, "You know, I'm sure that all of you here today are among the greatest specialists and top authorities in the world when it comes to jewelry. Is that true?" Members of the audience bobbed their heads in quick agreement. "And," Shlomo continued, "many of you are also probably big experts in diamonds, right?" "Oh yes, we're BIG experts!" the diamond dealers concurred. "So tell me," Shlomo asked them, "Did you ever accidentally throw out a million dollar diamond in the garbage can?" Everyone in the room burst out laughing. "Are you crazy?" shouted a man. "A million dollar diamond in the rough? In a second we would know what we're holding in our hands! We're experts!"

Shlomo paused for a moment, surveyed the men thoughtfully, and then said in a quiet voice, "You know, my sweetest friends, I'll let you in on a secret; I'm also an expert on diamonds. I walk the streets of the world every day and all I see are the most precious diamonds walking past me. Some of them you may have to pick up from the gutter and clean a bit, polish a little. But once you do, my friends, oh how they shine! *Mamesh* (really) like the purest, bluest, most perfect gems you'll ever uncover during your own distinguished careers.

"So, my sweetest friends," Shlomo concluded, "please try to remember this because it's *mamesh* the most important thing you have to know in life. Everyone . . . everyone . . . is a diamond in the rough."

"Very few people were aware of this particular dimension of Shlomo Carlebach's work," reflects Rabbi Tzvi Mandel, spiritual leader of Brooklyn's Khal Bnei Israel, "but he routinely visited inmates—both Jewish and non-Jewish—in prisons all over the world. Wherever he happened to be, he tried to visit local prisoners, whether they were confined in a huge state penitentiary or humble village jail. Occasionally, he would encounter a Jew or two, but more often than not he wouldn't.

"Who has compassion upon prison inmates? There are squadrons of well-wishers visiting the sick and lonely in hospitals, in nursing homes, in senior citizen centers. But when was the last time you heard about Good Samaritans organizing to visit prison inmates? They are among the most reviled, abandoned, and forlorn people in the world. But Shlomo Carlebach didn't forget them, and he had compassion.

"About two years ago, I had the privilege of accompanying Shlomo to a prison in upstate New York. This time he had actually been invited by the Jewish chaplain, who asked that he perform a Chanukah concert for the Jewish inmates there. There weren't many there, not even a minyan (quorum needed for prayer services), only about eight. There was no payment involved, but Shlomo accepted the invitation without a moment's hesitation. It was a shlep; three hours each way. 'No problem!' said Shlomo cheerfully.

"The concert was a huge success, and Shlomo made the event into a real Chanukah celebration, but that was only the beginning. When the Chanukah *chagiga* (party) was over, Shlomo turned to the chaplain, and said, 'Please . . . I would like to visit with the rest of the inmates here. Could you get permission?'

"Shlomo went into every cell, where he hugged, kissed, and talked with each inmate. Then he went into the dining room, into the recreation room, into the kitchen, into every possible nook and cranny of the prison where he was permitted to go, not satisfied until he had ferreted out every prisoner, making certain that no one had been overlooked. Finally, he was ready to leave, and we were walking down the hall when a big, black, burly inmate with a scarred, pitted face started running after us. 'Rabbi, Rabbi,' he shouted. 'Please wait.' We stopped immediately and Shlomo turned to beam at him. 'Yes, my holy friend?' he inquired sweetly. The man began to shift in embarrassment, almost as if he regretted his impulsive act, and then, finally gathering courage, blurted out, 'I just loved that hug you gave me before! Would you mind giving me another one?' Shlomo gave him the most radiant smile in the world, and then tenderly enfolded him in his arms. They stood clasped together for a long time.

"Finally, the inmate broke away and heaved the deepest sigh in the world. 'Oh Rabbi,' he said. 'No one, no one, ever hugged me like that before.' And then tears began to stream down his face.

" 'You know, Rabbi,' he sobbed in remorse, 'If only someone would have hugged me like that ten years ago, I surely wouldn't be here in this prison today.' "

———

"In April 1964, when I was ten years old, I suddenly became stricken with a mysterious disorder of the autoimmune system. The illness was very insidious. First, I felt a stiffness of the joints, then my knees swelled up, and finally I couldn't walk anymore. *Erev Pesach*, I had great difficulty breathing, and was hospitalized. I ended up in the hospital for more than seven weeks, and when I was eventually discharged—in only slighter better condition than when I had first entered—my parents were told that in all probability, I would never walk again.

"My classmates at Prospect Park Day School were very distraught over my condition and couldn't do enough for me. Bedridden for months, I had a constant flow of calls, visits, cards, and gifts. During recess one day my friends decided to do something special for me; they would chip in and buy me a great gift—a Shlomo Carlebach record!

"At that time I was very into Shlomo's music. My classmates knew I owned his first two records and was eagerly looking forward to the third album, which had just been released. But when they tried the local Hebrew book-stores where his records were usually sold, they were told that the third album wasn't in stock. A persistent bunch, they turned to Mrs. Braverman, our music teacher, to help them track down the record. When Mrs. Braverman's explorations of local stores also proved fruitless, she picked up the phone and called Shlomo at his home in New York.

"'Listen, Shlomo,' she said, 'Maybe you can tell me which stores in Brooklyn are carrying your newest album? I can't find it anywhere, and I need the record desperately.'

"His interest was immediately piqued. 'Why do you need my album so desperately?' he inquired sweetly. When she told him about my condition, he instantly said: 'Listen, forget about looking for the record in local stores. I'm coming to bring it to her myself!'

"Shlomo Carlebach showed up at my home a few days later, guitar in one hand, record album in the other. He stayed for several hours, giving me my own private concert, telling me stories, teaching me Torah, and in every possible way trying to cheer me up. Finally, he turned to me and said in an emphatic voice, 'Malkala, let me tell you something. You are going to walk again, I promise you! And when you do, I want you to call me, and I will come to wherever you are at that time to watch how you're walking. And it doesn't matter how far away you'll be at the time, even a foreign city if you should so happen to be in one. Just know I will be there when you start to walk. Because it's not only going to be the most special moment in your life; it's also going to be the most special in mine.'

"In August, I tremblingly took my first few steps. I was in a bungalow colony in the Catskills, which at that time (this was before the new highway—Route 17—was built) took about four hours to reach from New York. I called Shlomo Carlebach and he came the next day. His arrival created a sensation in the colony, and I became a celebrity! He watched me walk, beaming happiness, radiating love, as if I were his very own child. Then he took out his guitar and once again gave me my own personal concert. In September I returned to school, with all the symptoms—save for a slight ache in the knees—completely gone.

"In the summer of 1994, a few months before his death,

my twenty-year-old daughter was working at a summer camp for retarded Jewish children, where Shlomo was scheduled to give a concert. She approached him tentatively. 'About thirty years ago,' she said, 'you came to Brooklyn to visit a little girl who was very sick and couldn't walk. Do you by any chance remember?'

"'*Mamesh* such a *gevalt* to meet her daughter!' Shlomo bubbled, his face lighting up. 'To know that she's well, is married, and has such beautiful children like you . . . what a blessing! I'm so happy to meet you! Of course, I remember your mother. I want to know everything about her!'

"My daughter wasn't sure if Shlomo really remembered or if he was just being polite, until he asked, almost as an afterthought, 'So tell me . . . does she still have the record album I brought her that day?'"

———

In 1984 I was a Rabbi in upstate New York, where I served as founder/director of the "Torah Center of Buffalo," a *kiruv* (Orthodox outreach) organization. The community was a little stodgy, so to get their "juices going," I decided to organize a Lag B'Omer concert featuring the well-known Jewish folk singer, Moshe Yess. The day before the concert, I received a call from Mr. Yess. He had broken his foot, was in terrible pain, and would not be able to get to Buffalo. I was sorely disappointed and also in a quandary. Flyers had been distributed, ads had been printed, and there was no way to notify people that the concert had been canceled. For the Jews living in the outlying areas and surrounding rural communities, Buffalo was an important Jewish touchstone, and many would be traveling from great distances to attend the concert. There was no way I could cancel the concert. I just had to quickly replace Mr. Yess.

But whom could I get on such short notice? Lag B'Omer was an important date in the Jewish calendar; surely all the major Jewish entertainers would be booked. I conferred with several people on my Board, and they all suggested that I try

Shlomo Carlebach. "Shlomo Carlebach!" I exclaimed in disbelief. "Someone of his stature would have been booked long
ago." "Listen," they urged, "it doesn't hurt to try. You never
know."

Before contacting Shlomo's manager in New York, I first
called my Rebbe, Rav Shainberg in Israel, for permission to
use Shlomo. My organization was ultra-Orthodox, and there
were those in the strictly religious camp who objected to
Shlomo's hugging of women at concerts. I called Rav Shainberg,
described my dilemma, and posed my question, "So should I
use Shlomo Carlebach?" "*Nu, nu,* Shlomo Carlebach . . .
he's very good, why not?" he answered. I had to keep from
laughing. I had turned to Rav Shainberg for a halachic
opinion, and he was giving me musical advice instead! When
I clarified the issue at hand, he said, "Carlebach . . . I know
him just a little bit . . . but he has tremendous ability to be
mekarev (to reach out to) people, tremendous *siyata dishmaya*
(bearing God's imprint). Certainly you can use Shlomo. But
before the concert begins, just respectfully request that he
refrain from his usual warm displays of affection!"

Now that I had permission, I called New York. Shlomo's
secretary told me that Shlomo was out-of-town, but she
would try to reach him and leave a message. Exactly ten
minutes later the phone rang, and I heard a jovial voice
whoop, "Holy Reb Haber, is that you?" (I had never met
Shlomo before). I outlined my dilemma to him and there was
silence on the other end. Then he exclaimed, "This is *mamesh*
an unbelievable *nes* (miracle) because Lag B'Omer is the
holiest day of the year."

Shlomo explained that he was in Nashville to do a Lag
B'Omer concert himself. "But," he half-laughed, half-cried,
"the Rabbi and the *chazan* (cantor) had a huge *machloikas*
(argument) over which one of them would introduce me, and
as a result the whole concert has been canceled. So your call
is *mamesh hashkocha protis* (divine providence)."

We were both jubilant about the synchronicity and excitedly discussed the concert. Then Shlomo rather shyly asked,
"And what about *parnosa* (payment)?" "Well," I said nervously, "I'm embarrassed to offer someone of your stature this

amount, but my organization had earmarked $500 for Moshe Yess." He was quiet for a moment, and then he gave a little *krechs* (sigh). "Oy!" he said, "My dear friend, I usually get thousands for a concert!" "I know," I said sheepishly, "but that's what was earmarked." He was quiet again. "Look," I said impulsively, "I'm really desperate to have you. I'm willing to forego any profits I make on this event. How about we strike an agreement that whatever comes in the door— minus expenses—is yours?" "Done!" he agreed.

I quickly set to work to spread the word. I distributed new flyers, placed announcements on the local radio station, made phone calls. I didn't have to do much to galvanize attendance; tremendous excitement surged through the community about Shlomo's imminent appearance, and the next day my makeshift concert hall (the shul's dungeon-like basement) was packed with wall-to-wall people. The hall was so makeshift in fact that I didn't even have a stage or podium, so Shlomo goodnaturedly stood on a table and, beaming, told the crowded room, "Mamesh *chevra*, it's so sweet being here. And I want to tell you the best things in life are the things that aren't planned!"

Shlomo was incredible—as always—and I know that dozens of people who were in the audience that night became turned on to Judaism, and are today observant Jews. The concert was a great success, and $2,700 in profits came in that night. A deal was a deal, so when the concert was over, I handed Shlomo the $2,700 in a wad of cash. At that point we were standing outside the shul, and when I gave him the roll of money, he enveloped me in a huge hug, gave me a kiss, and a hearty *shakoach* (thanks). "Oh, thank you, thank you Reb Haber!" he said gratefully. "You don't know how much I need this; I'm a little broke right now!" he laughed.

Just then, a young Lubavitcher fellow—who had been waiting patiently to talk to Shlomo—approached him and asked him for a *brocha* (blessing) for *shalom bayis* (peace in the marriage, a happy marriage). The young man was a complete stranger to Shlomo, but immediately elicited his concern. "A *brocha* for *shalom bayis!*" Shlomo exclaimed with distress. "My sweetest friend, what's going on? What's happening in your life *nebech* (such a pity) that you need such a brocha?"

"Well," exclaimed the Lubavitcher, "when we first got married a couple of years ago, neither of us was religious. I had an excellent job in my field, drew a very good salary, and felt secure in my position. My marriage was terrific and overall everything was great. About a year ago, my wife and I both decided to become *baalei teshuva* (literally, returnees, religious Jews) and that's when the trouble started. Since I became *shomer shabbos* (sabbath observant), I've lost one job after another. Maybe it's easier in New York City to be an Orthodox Jewish professional, but here in Buffalo, it's practically impossible. I just lost my latest job, and the effect on my marriage has been disastrous. I'm practically penniless, and I don't know what I'm going to do. This is the reason I asked you for a *brocha* for *sholom bayis*."

And then, without blinking an eye, Shlomo Carlebach dug into his pocket, took out the entire wad of $2,700, and handed it over to the Lubavitcher with a hug and a kiss.

Rather impolitely my mouth gaped open as I stared at this scene in utter astonishment. If I had not been there myself, I never would have believed it.

And I said to myself, "Hugging women or no hugging women . . . I don't care what anybody says, this man is a tzaddik!"

"Last year I drove Shlomo Carlebach to a concert engagement in Wilkes-Barre, Pennsylvania. After several minutes of conversation he asked if I would mind if he studied the Talmud for a while in silence. It was clear from his apologetic manner that he was fearful of offending me and appearing discourteous. Knowing how hectic his life was and how rare the opportunity for private study must be, I assured him that I didn't mind at all, and he should please go ahead. He opened the *Gemara* with an enraptured look and was quickly immersed in its study, intent on the words and oblivious of our surroundings. He seemed to be transported to a different world, a different dimension. However, each time we pulled up to one of the dozens of toll booths we passed that day, he would snap out of his reverie, close the *Gemara*, look up at the toll booth attendant, smile broadly, wave a greeting, and exchange a few warm words of friendship. No matter how ill-tempered or brusque the toll booth attendants appeared at the start, by the time Reb Shlomo had finished waving, smiling, and joking, they were transformed. After we passed each toll booth, Reb Shlomo would return to his *Gemara*, closing it again as we approached the next toll booth station. Despite his complete immersion in the text, he didn't miss a single station or attendant. Reb Shlomo's light touched and blessed them all."

———

Ten years ago, Chaya Adler, a new congregant of the Synagogue, met Shlomo Carlebach near a subway station on the Upper West Side. After a few moments of animated discussion, Shlomo said to her with a mischievous twinkle in his eye, "Holy Sister Chay, I'm on my way to meet a hasidic man who works in the diamond district. If you're not busy and have the time, I would be so honored if you would please accompany me." Chaya looked at Shlomo in shock and surprise. "Reb Shlomo," she stammered, "I would love to come along, but I don't want to offend the hasidic men in the diamond district. As you can see, I'm not dressed properly. I don't think my skirt is long enough!" "Don't worry, Sister Chay," Shlomo tried to soothe her, "You have such a holy Jewish face no one will even notice your skirt!"

Certain she would encounter a sea of hostility if she ventured into the hasidic enclave, Chaya valiantly tried to extricate herself from the expedition. But curiously, the more she explained to Shlomo why she couldn't accompany him, the more insistent he became that she do. Before long, Shlomo allayed Chaya's fears, and she joined him on the IRT downtown. As soon as Shlomo hit 47th Street, he was encircled by throngs of hasidic admirers. Awkwardly, Chaya tried to stand unobtrusively on the side, but each time she made an effort to slip away unnoticed, Shlomo deliberately drew her back to his side and announced to the men, "Everybody should meet my sweetest friend, holy sister Chay. Do you know that she is an outstanding scholar and learns *Hasidus* (hasidic thought) brilliantly?" Each time Shlomo made this and similar announcements to the men, Chaya thought she would die of embarrassment. She was sure that the men would regard her with scorn and derision, and greet Shlomo's statement with a patronizing sneer. Instead, to her amazement, they were respectful, friendly, curious, and open. They politely inquired as to which *seforim* (holy books) she was studying, and were intrigued to learn that she was currently immersed in the esoteric teachings of the *Ishbitzer Rebbe*. Up and down 47th Street, the interactions were unexpectedly the same: positive and upbeat. Having braced herself for trouble, Chaya was not only relieved but pleasantly surprised. Returning to the Upper West Side in a bemused and contemplative state, Chaya suddenly had an epiphany.

"It was only upon my return home that I realized that Shlomo—who never wasted an opportunity to perform an act of loving-kindness or impart a moral message—had deliberately choreographed the entire encounter. When he saw me near the subway, he seized the occasion to combine his visit to the diamond district with the opportunity to deliver an important teaching. The teaching—directed both at me and the hasidim we met—was quite clearly the importance of letting go of conventional stereotypes. On that fateful day, both they and I learned a valuable lesson: to suspend judgment and look beyond dress and appearance for the divine spark that resides in each soul.

"From that day forward, I began to look at hasidim as individuals, not stereotypes. I am equally certain that their own perception of modern Jewish women had altered perceptibly as a result of our exchange and would never quite be the same again."

"I was an artist living in Haight-Ashbury in the '60s when a friend dragged me—kicking and screaming—to a Shlomo Carlebach concert in the area. I came from an assimilated Jewish home and was more of an atheist than a believer. I had little interest in Jewish music or hasidic tales, but my friend was so insistent that I accompany him that I finally caved in and went.

"At the concert, which was extremely crowded, one aisle of seats was pointedly empty. A grossly deformed man, so grotesquely handicapped that it was impossible to look at him, sat miserably alone in this aisle, sadly shunned by everyone, including myself.

"Shlomo Carlebach was singing up front, when suddenly, apparently for the first time, he noticed the hideously disfigured individual, sitting alone. He immediately stopped singing, put down his guitar, and made his way to the back. When he reached the man, he embraced him warmly, and exclaimed loudly, 'My sweetest friend, you are so beautiful!' Frozen with shock, the crowd remained quiet for a long moment, and then spontaneously burst into song. Silent tears trickled down the face of the man, whose monstrous features suddenly, miraculously, seemed to take on more human, more normal proportions. Obviously, he hadn't been hugged for a very long time.

"I was so moved by this single act of great compassion, that I thought long and hard about my current hedonistic lifestyle and what being authentically religious must do for the soul. Consequently, I packed up my bags, moved to Jerusalem, enrolled in a yeshiva, and am today a respected *Maggid Shiur* (Teacher of Advanced Talmud) in Israel."

Many years ago, while on tour in Copenhagen, Shlomo had the occasion to walk by the seashore, where he saw a group of rowdy teenagers on the beach taunting a young, frantic-looking girl. To his horror and consternation, he saw her wade out into the ocean, and he knew with absolute certainty that she was trying to commit suicide. Shlomo immediately took off his shoes and dived into the sea to rescue her. Swimming behind her, he begged her to turn back, but she screamed wildly that she didn't want to live anymore. In desperation (still swimming behind her), he shouted, "What about me? You're not only going to kill yourself, but you're going to kill me as well. Please . . . if you go out any further, I'll never make it back, I won't have the strength to swim back." When she heard those words, the young girl turned towards him, and allowed him to pull her out. For hours later, he lay exhausted on the beach, unable to move, his strength totally sapped.

It was only after a terrible tragedy struck my family that I became aware of the existence of the Carlebach Shul in Manhattan. My 18-year-old son had just been killed in a car accident, and I was devastated. I came from a secular Jewish background and never had a need for religion, but suddenly, for the first time in my life, felt a yearning for some spiritual sustenance. Not familiar with the organized Jewish community, I didn't know where to go. Someone told me that if I was looking for religious comfort, the person to seek out was Rabbi Shlomo Carlebach.

Shlomo befriended me, comforted me, and took me under his wing. I began to attend all of his gatherings and classes. One night, I impulsively showed up at the synagogue, not knowing that a Shlomo concert had been scheduled and was about to begin. I wanted desperately to attend, but didn't have a penny in my pocket. I was on welfare at the time and destitute. I thought about sneaking in, but someone was aggressively guarding the door to the entrance, collecting the $10 admission fee in a very determined fashion. I considered throwing myself at the cashier's mercy, begging him to waive the admission fee, but somehow felt discouraged about the prospects of this particular person awarding me a freebie. I really wanted to stay; I needed to be uplifted that night. So I began to wave and motion and beckon to Shlomo, whom I had caught sight of from a distance, and finally managed to summon him to my side.

"Can you sneak me in?" I asked urgently, explaining my situation to him. "Hmmm . . ." he looked at me thoughtfully. "Why don't you come upstairs with me."

His home was a spartan suite of rooms one flight above the synagogue. I was sure that there was some kind of secret back entrance to the synagogue leading from his living quarters, through which he was planning on sneaking me in. However, to my surprise, when we ascended to his apartment, he stopped at a closet, opened the door, and began hunting frantically for something inside. After much hoisting, heaving, hurling, and tossing things aside, he finally found the object he was looking for and emerged triumphant from the closet, clutching a well-worn pouch with many zippered compartments.

Then Shlomo proceeded to zip open each compartment, only to find it empty. Finally, he opened the last compartment and jubilantly pulled out a $10 bill, which he handed to me. "There!" he said with great satisfaction. "Now you can go buy a ticket!"

I returned downstairs to the synagogue, approached the person collecting the concert monies, gave him my $10 bill, and entered the hall, my dignity intact.

In 1973 Shlomo embarked on a comprehensive tour of Israel's military hospitals, where he visited the soldiers who had been wounded during the Yom Kippur War. Hospital personnel escorted him into every room, where he spoke at length to the injured and dying. During one such tour, he noticed the staff deliberately bypassing a certain room. Stopping, he asked the staff why they had skipped the previous room, and dismissively they said, "Forget about him—he's a goner, he's in a coma, he's going to die any moment!" "How can you pass any soldier by?" asked Shlomo, insisting that he see him. Reluctantly, the staff led him into the room of a soldier who had been incinerated inside his tank, extensively scarred and disfigured. Shlomo reached for the man's hand, and began speaking softly to him. Suddenly, to the hospital staff's shock and amazement, tears started rolling down the soldier's cheeks, trickling in rivulets down his face. They realized for the first time that although the man had lost his ability to speak, he was very much alive, and had been misdiagnosed and left for dead. After Shlomo's visit and the soldier's amazing response, doctors began a much more vigorous and aggressive protocol of treatment. After several months of rehabilitation, the soldier recovered.

———

"Thirty-four years ago, when I was a first grade student at Prospect Park Day School, Shlomo Carlebach was invited to perform for the student body at a special assembly. We were thrilled and thought of nothing but the upcoming performance. On the actual day of the concert I woke up with a fever, and my mother had to keep me home from school. I was disappointed and climbed into bed, crying. Several hours later, the doorbell rang, and when my mother opened the door, she stared in shock at the celebrated figure of Reb Shlomo Carlebach smiling broadly, guitar in hand. 'I hear there's a sick little boy inside who missed the concert today,' he beamed. 'I didn't want him to feel left out, so I came to give him a private concert of his own. You don't mind, do you?' Astonished, my mother stepped aside and Shlomo Carlebach gave me the concert of a lifetime."

———

In the early '80s, Shlomo was invited to give a concert at the Women's Prison in Ramlah, Israel, a maximum security detention center that houses both Jewish and Arab women prisoners. When he entered the auditorium with his entourage, he realized to his great distress that only Jewish prisoners were present. He approached the concert organizer and asked, "Where are the Arab women?" Scowling, the organizer looked at him in surprise, and asked, "Are you crazy? Why would they want to come to your concert, and why would you want them here?" Shlomo said, "I want them here. It's important that they be here." The organizer shrugged, "You want them here? Go get them yourself!" Flanked by guards, Shlomo went into each and every prison cell, and personally invited the Arab prisoners to join him at the concert. At first, they shook their heads no, but finally succumbed to his soft, insistent pleas and reluctantly filed their way to the concert hall where they sat in silence. Shlomo gently asked an Arab woman—a terrorist who had blown up a supermarket—to translate his stories about the Ishbitzer Rebbe into Arabic so that the women would understand, and slowly, very slowly, their faces relaxed into smiles. At the end of the concert, Shlomo had the Jewish prisoners, the Arab prisoners, and the prison guards singing and dancing together in a circle. For a shining, brief moment, it looked like the Messiah had finally arrived!

———

"In the States he was most frequently called 'The Singing Rabbi.' In Israel he was known as Harebbe Harakid, 'The Dancing Rabbi.' But in South Africa, Shlomo Carlebach was affectionately referred to as 'Master Jesus.'

"Here's how it happened," recounts Dr. Joshua Ritchie, a frequent member of Shlomo's entourage, who traveled with him extensively. "The Jews of South Africa adored Shlomo, and whenever he came to their country, couldn't do enough for him. They always put him up in a luxurious hotel, which in the days of apartheid typically boasted a huge black staff. There were black maids, bellboys, doormen, and maintenance men. Since labor was so cheap in those days, the fancy hotel was practically teeming with black labor!

"Well, as soon as Shlomo entered the portals of this opulent palace, he began doing his thing. First, he hugged and kissed the astonished black doorman, then he hugged and kissed the thunderstruck black bellboy, and finally he hugged and kissed the dumbfounded black elevator man. Everyone in the lobby was standing open-mouthed, watching the incongruous sight of a white man hugging black staff, calling them 'my most precious brothers' in apartheid South Africa! Some people watched stonily, others chuckled, while still others observed the scene with a tear in their eye. But no one who observed Shlomo Carlebach's love remained unaffected.

"Finally, one black employee whispered to a second, 'My lord, who is that holy white man with the skullcap and beard?' The second one shrugged, and in awe, answered, 'It can only be Master Jesus, can it not?' 'Master Jesus . . . it's Master Jesus!' one black staff member whispered to another until the lobby was filled with silent hallelujahs and fervent amens.

"The name stuck and spread. Whenever he was in South Africa, Shlomo would occasionally steal a few hours from his Jewish commitments to play for black groups for free, to express his solidarity with their plight. When he couldn't get transportation from the white neighborhoods to the black ones, he would walk to his destination, sometimes for miles. And, as he would pass through the black community, waving, smiling broadly, hugging and kissing its impoverished residents, little black children would point excitedly at him and shriek happily, 'Mamma, come quick! Master Jesus just walked by!' "

3

Master of the Moment

"People walk around sad because they don't know what to do with their future. You have this minute right now. What are you doing with it? The difference between sadness and joy is very simple. Sadness always tells you: 'Oy vey! What are you going to do in ten minutes? What will you do ten years from now?' If you are really filled with joy for one minute, then you will know what to do the next minute also. What is God giving you? He is giving you this minute. He hasn't given tomorrow. Of course, I don't know what to do tomorrow, because I didn't receive it yet. Sadness is very much concerned with what I don't have, and I really don't have tomorrow yet. The truth is, I am always standing before nothingness, because I am nonexistent yet for the next minute. I'm not here yet. Time isn't there. The world isn't there. The world is here . . . right now!"

—Rabbi Shlomo Carlebach

In the late '60s and early '70s, Shlomo amassed a huge following at the University of Oregon in Eugene, which was at that time a hotbed of radical ferment and activity. Everyone in Eugene loved him, and his concerts there drew standing-room-only crowds.

He was in the middle of performing at just such a concert, when a group of radicals burst into the room and angrily advanced towards the stage. "Hey!" one of them shouted accusingly at Shlomo, "You've siphoned off our people! Don't you know there's a mass rally for the Sandinistas taking place right now?"

Shlomo looked at him apologetically. "I'm so sorry, my friend, but this concert was scheduled a long time ago. If I had known there was a conflict, you can be sure, I would have changed it."

The radical was not placated. "Well, don't you think," he challenged Shlomo, "that a rally for the Sandinistas is more important than a concert?"

Shlomo paused. "You know," he said to the radical, "you're absolutely right. *Chevra*," he turned to the audience, "I have no problem with postponing this concert for a couple of hours. Let's show our solidarity by joining our holy friends at the rally, and then when it's over, we'll return to the auditorium and continue."

Shlomo promptly left the stage for the rally site, several hundred people in tow. Gratified that they had Shlomo Carlebach in their midst, the radicals invited him to speak. He delivered an impromptu, impassioned address that turned out to be the most fiery and eloquent speech of all those delivered that day, and he received a standing ovation.

When the rally was over, Shlomo returned to the concert hall, his fans trudging faithfully behind, many of the rally participants now also following, and immediately picked up where he had left off!

———

"Everyone in the Jewish world is familiar with the fine work of Hineni (an international Jewish outreach organization)," says Rebetzin Esther Jungreis, founder and president. "Very few people, however, know that it was really Shlomo Carlebach who was responsible for its birth.

"In 1972 I was invited to address the National Convention of the Young Israel Intercollegiates, which was being held over Labor Day Weekend at the Pine View Hotel in the Catskills. My topic was assimilation and what I viewed as the current spiritual holocaust of Jews in America. 'So what are you doing about it?' I challenged the hundreds of Young Israel delegates attending my talk. 'If I had an organization such as yours, with energy, financial resources, and membership, there's no limit to what I would do!' At that point, a young woman in the audience raised her hand, and threw the ball back into my court. 'Well what exactly would you have us do?' she wanted to know.

"My mind raced. I had often despaired about the way Madison Square Garden was at that time being used by Israel Bonds for lavish galas featuring Hollywood entertainment. But what did all these galas achieve, I had wondered time after time. Nothing spiritual, nothing meaningful, nothing that would really have an enduring effect on the Jewish people for generations to come. So when the young woman asked me what I would recommend her organization do to combat assimilation, I impulsively answered, 'How about a rally for *neshomas* (souls) at Madison Square Garden, a mass spiritual gathering where you teach people what it means to be a Jew!' A silence fell over the room as everyone pondered my idea. 'Sort of like what Billy Graham does?' someone suggested. 'Yes,' I answered excitedly. 'A Jewish answer to Billy Graham!' At the conclusion of my talk, everyone left the room discussing my idea which was viewed as exciting, dramatic, and thoroughly unrealistic!

"*Motzei Shabbos* (Saturday night, when the Sabbath is over), Shlomo Carlebach came up to the Pine View from Manhattan to give a concert, and someone must have told him about my idea. Because after singing a couple of songs, he suddenly started strumming his guitar, making up a new *niggun* (melody) with the words: 'The *Heilege* (Holy) Rebetzin is going to go to Madison Square Garden and change the Jewish world . . .' 'Shlomo!' I rushed over to him, embarrassed. 'Please stop that immediately!' Shlomo, however, seemed not to have heard my pleas, because once again he picked up his guitar and insistently strummed 'The *Heilege* Rebetzin is going to go Madison Square Garden and change the Jewish world . . .' 'Shlomo please!' I begged him again. 'You're making fun of me!' '*Chas v'sholom* (God forbid),' he said with the greatest sincerity. 'I am not teasing you. You *will* do it!'

"That night I invited Shlomo to my son's bar mitzvah, which was being held the following day, and he warmly accepted. At the bar mitzvah, we asked him to honor us with a few songs, and, to our guests' delight, he performed an impromptu concert. I was in the middle of congratulating myself for having thought of such a wonderful idea, when, to my mortification, I heard him once again singing the *niggun* from the night before 'The *Heilege* Rebetzin is going to go to Madison Square Garden and change the Jewish world . . .' He then told the guests, who were unaware of what had transpired over the weekend at the Pine View Hotel, about my idea, endorsing it heartily. People were staring at me as he talked—some with raised eyebrows, others with approving glances—and I thought I would die of shame! When he finally left the stage, I was much relieved. Thank God that's over, I thought. Little did I know.

"Toward the end of the evening, when dessert had been served and people were slowly beginning to gather their things and look expectantly at the door, I saw Shlomo, unsolicited this time, striding up to the stage. Seizing the microphone he exhorted the crowd, 'Listen to me, my sweetest friends, let me tell you something very deep, so please please open your hearts. If we don't do this now, it'll never get done! After the bar mitzvah, everybody should go directly to the Rebetzin's house and start planning the Madison Square Garden event immediately.'

"I was horrified. I looked at my husband and whispered nervously, 'Do you think anyone will take Shlomo seriously?' 'Nah, don't be silly,' he answered.

"We returned home from the bar mitzvah, happy but exhausted. Gratefully, I threw off my shoes and sank into the couch. Suddenly, the doorbell rang. My husband and I exchanged startled looks. Who could it be? I opened the door and was stunned to discover one of the bar mitzvah guests standing on the threshold. 'Hi!' she said cheerfully, 'I've come to help plan the Garden event!' I gulped. How could I tell her that Madison Square Garden was only a pipe dream, a fantasy, a figment of an overactive and yearning imagination? I didn't know what I would say to Shlomo the next time we met, but surely I would come close to wringing his neck! I couldn't believe he had done this to me.

"I ushered her into my home as I struggled to tell her the truth. I didn't have the time however, because the doorbell rang again. And again. And again. The bell in fact didn't stop ringing all night and my house was soon overflowing with people galvanized by Shlomo Carlebach's bar mitzvah behest!

"At that time, I had no money, no organization, no membership, no nothing, just an idea that had popped into my head. But what could I do? Everyone who came to my house that night was so excited and sincere, I had no choice. I was literally *forced* by their presence to concretize my dream.

"That night Hineni was born. Barbara Janov, the woman who was to become my Executive Director for the next 25 years, was among those who came that night, and the following week she and I—with great trepidation—signed a contract with Madison Square Garden.

"As many people still remember to this day, the Hineni Rally at the Garden was an unparalleled success. We packed the Garden with standing-room-only crowds, captured the media's attention, and were carried on every major television and radio station in New York. But more important than the publicity, was the tangible effect we had on human lives. We turned thousands of alienated Jews on to Judaism, and began a worldwide movement of return.

"Today, Hineni is an international outreach organization responsible for returning thousands of Jews to their heritage. We have a national television program that airs on dozens of stations throughout the United States, a Hineni Heritage Center in New York that features ongoing classes in Judaism, a Hineni newsletter, and the deep satisfaction of knowing we have changed lives.

"And who really is responsible for all this? Why Shlomo Carlebach of course!"

———

"Oy, was it a mistake to ask Brother Pinny* to drive!" Yaakov Braude clasps his forehead in rueful recollection. "We were on our way to a gig in the Catskills—Shlomo, myself, and a couple of other guys who played with him—and Brother Pinny had generously offered us the use of his car. He was the sweetest *neshama* in the world, and was going to drive us back and forth from Manhattan to South Fallsburg for free, but we had totally forgotten what an absentminded genius he was. When the car suddenly conked out on the West Side Highway in Upper Manhattan, he turned to us with a dazed and flustered look, and said rather sheepishly, 'Uh oh. I think we're out of gas.'

"We were ready to murder him, but Shlomo patted his shoulder reassuringly and said something gracious and consoling like 'My sweetest brother, when your thoughts are so heavenly it's hard to think of earthly matters like gas!' Brother Pinny, who had sunk into a state of abject mortification, was immediately cheered by Shlomo's comforting words, but the rest of us remained distraught. The concert was scheduled to begin in two hours, and we were stuck on a shoulder of the West Side Highway. What were we going to do? 'Surely a tow truck or a police car will come by shortly,' someone suggested. 'They're always cruising down the Highway. Let's wait in the car and help will come soon.'

"It didn't. After close to forty minutes, help had still not arrived, and a lively discussion about our options was now underway. 'Listen, Shlomo,' one person advised, 'first things first. Let's leave the car, walk to the nearest exit, get to a phone, and cancel the concert. Then we'll find a gas station, bring gas back to the car, and head back home. It's that simple!' Shlomo shook his head. '*Chevra*, please understand

that people are waiting for me; I cannot disappoint them . . .'
'But Shlomo,' somebody else objected, 'you're doing this
concert for *free* for a small insignificant bungalow colony.'
Shlomo gave him a reproving look. 'My sweetest friend,' he
said quietly, 'nobody is insignificant. It doesn't matter whether
I'm scheduled to perform at Town Hall for $10,000 or a
bungalow colony for free. A commitment is a commitment.
Let's go get some gas!'

"We reached the closest exit and turned in. We found
ourselves in one of the roughest neighborhoods in Manhattan,
and all of us, with the exception of Shlomo, were scared. The
streets were littered with debris, the buildings were bombed-
out hollow craters, and the characters lining the doorways
looked wicked. Some of us trained our glances downward so
our eyes wouldn't have to meet theirs. Shlomo, however, was
unruffled by our surroundings and didn't seem to notice that
we were in hostile territory. In fact, even as we walked down
the streets, he cheerfully greeted and made ebullient peace
signs to throngs of drunks and drug addicts. To our amazement, many of them immediately lit up and made peace signs
back in return. Several smiled, others waved, and one or two
even tipped their hats in acknowledgement. Our terror subsided. With Shlomo at the helm, there was nothing to fear.

"We finally found a gas station, bought gas, heaved a
sigh of relief, and made our way back to the West Side
Highway. We had been gone for a little less than an hour, but
upon our return found the car in a very different condition
than when we had left.

"As our eyes silently surveyed the car, we gasped at the
violence that had been wreaked during our absence. The windows and windshields had been punched in and were now
only shards of glass. All the tires had been slashed. Now
what? Shlomo turned to us soberly and said, '*Chevra*, we're
running very late and the people are *nebech* waiting.' And
with that, he stepped out onto the West Side Highway, raised
his arm and yelled 'TAXI!'

"If we hadn't been so traumatized, surely we would have
laughed. There wasn't exactly a taxi stand on the Highway;
how did Shlomo expect to find an empty taxi cruising down

the West Side? But in about five minutes, an empty taxi obligingly pulled up to the shoulder, and waved us inside. 'Bless you, holy brother,' Shlomo murmured, 'could you do us the biggest favor in the world and please take us to South Fallsburg'? The cab driver blinked. 'South Fallsburg, as in South Fallsburg the Catskill Mountains?' he asked. 'Right,' said Shlomo. 'Mister, do you realize that such a trip will cost you a few hundred dollars?' he asked. 'No problem!' Shlomo replied.

When we finally arrived at the bungalow colony, the charge was $260. 'Shlomo,' urged one of the *chevra*, 'at least let the bungalow colony pick up the bill!' 'Shh!' he admonished. 'Don't tell a soul how we got here!'

"When the person in charge of the concert saw us come into the casino, she rushed over. 'Shlomo, we were so worried. How was your trip?'

" 'Perfect,' he beamed and, pulling out his guitar, quickly ascended the stage."

It was during intermission at one of his concerts in San Diego in 1967 that Shlomo Carlebach first learned of the death of his beloved father, Rabbi Naftali Carlebach. I happened to be standing next to him when he received the call from New York. He blanched suddenly, and squeezed my hand so hard, he almost crushed the bone. "I'll explain the situation to the audience and cancel the rest of the concert," I said to him, turning to ascend the steps to the stage. "No!" Shlomo's voice summoned me back to his side. "Many of these holy brothers and sisters have traveled very far to hear me. For some of them, it's their first taste of *yiddishkeit* (Judaism), maybe the only encounter they'll ever have with Torah. Their *neshomos* are thirsting for a word that will change their lives; their need to sing joyously is greater than my need to cry. I will cry later. For now I'm continuing the concert."

Shlomo headed for the stage, then turned back and said urgently, "Promise me you won't tell anyone about my father's death. I don't want anyone to know until the concert's over. I don't want to spoil their joy."

No one in the audience ever suspected that anything was amiss. The second half of the concert was as joyous and exultant as the first. When Shlomo finished, I accompanied him to his hotel room. As soon as the door closed behind us, the tears that he had put on hold during the concert were unleashed and he began to cry. He didn't stop the entire night. Towards dawn, I heard him humming an unfamiliar melody. He had just composed *Mocho Dimoh* (Erase the Tears), one of his most exquisite and searing songs of all time, a Carlebach classic that endures to this day."

Many years ago, Shlomo happened to be staying in a small village in England, a predominantly Catholic town where not a single Jew was known to reside. Thus he was surprised one evening to receive a telephone call from a local dignitary by the name of Lady Astor, who seemed to be familiar with his music and had gone to great lengths to track him down.

"Oh, I'm so glad to have found you," she gurgled. "This must be fated—I was so pleased to learn about your presence in our town.

"You see," she explained, "I'm involved in a civic organization that's sponsoring a fundraising concert this week featuring music from different cultures and religions, and I would like the Jewish religion to be represented as well. I've heard of you from many people, and I wanted to know if you would be interested in participating."

"Thank you so much for this great privilege you're bestowing upon me," Shlomo answered. "Tell me, when is the concert taking place?" "Friday night." Shlomo paused. "When Friday night?" he asked.

"Well, the concert starts promptly at 7:00." "Lady Astor," Shlomo said, "I am so honored and appreciative that you called me, and I will be glad to participate in the concert, but you should be aware of one thing: I am an Orthodox Jew, and I observe the Sabbath. I will be happy to perform, as long as you promise me that I'll be the first to go on and that I'm out by 8:00 sharp. Also, would you please be able to arrange for a car to take me back to the hotel?" Lady Astor promised to accommodate all of Shlomo's requests.

Because the village was a small, isolated one far from any large cities, Shlomo was astonished on his arrival at the concert hall to note the size of the crowd: at least 4,000 people, and from what he could tell, not a single one was Jewish! "Lady Astor," he asked in surprise, "where have all these people come from?" "Oh, this is a big event in our part of England," she replied. "People have traveled from great distances to attend. Anyway, you're up! I've placed you first on the program, as I promised, and we're ready to begin."

Shlomo opened with one of his classics, *Borchi Nafshi.* "I want you to know," he told the audience of what he thought was 4,000 'holy *goyalach*' (non-Jews) "what it means to be a *Yid* (Jew). A Jew is always thankful, a Jew always says 'Thank you God for everything. There's so much to be thankful for!'" The audience responded warmly to Shlomo, and he continued performing until a few minutes before 8:00. "Listen, my sweetest friends," Shlomo said, "it was wonderful being here with you and I'm very sorry that I have to leave, but soon it will be sundown, and I observe the Sabbath. So, in honor of the holy *Shabbos*, my last song tonight will be from the Friday night prayer service and is called *Lecha Dodi* (one of Shlomo's most famous songs)."

Shlomo turned to the audience ruefully: "How I wish I had more time to tell you about *Shabbos*," he passionately exclaimed. "Why don't you precious friends do me a favor. After the concert is over, come join me, come help me celebrate the Sabbath. Everyone is invited!" Shlomo then bid the audience a final farewell and left for the hotel.

Shlomo was getting ready for *Shabbos* when he heard loud banging. Soaking wet, he ran out of the shower to answer the door, where a security guard stood framed. "Are you Rabbi Shlomo Carlebach?" he asked. "We have a problem. There are some people here to see you." "That's okay,"

Shlomo answered, a bit puzzled, "please just send them right up." "You don't understand, " said the security guard, "there are *hundreds* of people outside! They took all the rooms in the hotel, but we don't know what to do with them, and they're all here to see you." "Oh, these are my holy friends from the concert," said Shlomo, "I invited them! Don't worry, my friend, I know what to do." Shlomo took his satchel out of the closet, and, pulling out some *challahs* (braided Sabbath bread), *bilkalach* (little rolls), and several bottles of grape juice, turned to the security guard and said, "Listen, do you have a big room in the hotel?" "Sure," answered the security guard, "We have a ballroom that we use for wedding receptions and dinners."

"Excellent," said Shlomo excitedly, "so can I rent the ballroom for the weekend?" "I think it's available," said the guard, "but I'll have to double-check with the manager." "Can you do me the greatest favor in the world?" Shlomo asked. "If the ballroom is available, could you please set up some tables, put the grape juice and rolls on the tables, invite the people in, and tell them I'll be down soon?"

The security guard agreed, and Shlomo started dressing hurriedly, when he heard another knock on the door. This time, there were three teenage boys standing at the threshold, one of whom looked wan and forlorn. "Rabbi Carlebach, could I speak to you for a moment?" he asked in a despondent voice. Shlomo warmly ushered the three into the room, and the boy began: "My name is Mayer Ben Simone,* and I am a Jew." Shlomo stared at him in shock and said: "A Jew! How can you be a Jew? There aren't any Jews living in this village." The boy answered, "You're right. There aren't any Jews living here. I'm originally from Spain. I'm fifteen years old, and my father passed away when I was very young. Life was very difficult without him. We were very poor and I didn't get along with my mother. I ran away from home and ended up in England. These are my buddies. I happened to be at the concert tonight and heard you perform. I just had to meet you in person. I didn't know Judaism was so beautiful, and I wanted to thank you for everything I learned from you tonight."

Shlomo looked at the young boy with tears in his eyes, and said: "Holy brother, welcome back! I've missed you so much. I've waited my whole life to meet you." Enfolding Mayer in a warm embrace, Shlomo asked, "Look, Mayer, would you like to spend Shabbos with me?" The boy brightened, and for the first time since they had met, flashed Shlomo a happy smile. With his arm draped around Mayer's shoulder, Shlomo went down to the ballroom and discovered a crowd of several hundred 'holy goyalach.'

With Mayer at his side all night, Shlomo "did *Shabbos*" with the hundreds of townspeople until 5:00 in the morning. He had just fallen asleep, when he was awakened by persistent knocking. This time a distinguished-looking man stood framed in the doorway, who said, "*Shabbat Shalom!* My name is Rabbi Saks,* and I am a Reform Rabbi from a town about 80 miles away from here. I happened to be at your concert last night and I was so overwhelmed, I had to drive back this morning to meet you." Shlomo ushered Rabbi Saks into his room, and as they started talking, Shlomo was impressed by the Rabbi's sweetness and sincerity. Suddenly, Shlomo was seized by a wild impulse and, apropos of nothing, asked him, "Rabbi Saks, do you believe that every Jewish child should be well-versed in his heritage?" "Absolutely," Rabbi Saks nodded earnestly. "And would you agree with me that someone who is the future Messiah—who is going to lead the Jewish people—especially needs a Jewish education?" "For sure!" Rabbi Saks replied with conviction.

Shlomo looked into Rabbi Saks' eyes and said slowly, "Last night I met a young Jewish boy who is *mamesh* a *gevalt!* Such a sweet *neshama,* and so brilliant, I think he has the potential to be the Messiah. So let me ask you a question. I know you're a Rabbi and I'm sure you do an unbelievable job as a teacher with your people. Would you be able to commit yourself to educating this young Messiah?" Rabbi Saks began to shift uneasily in his seat and darted Shlomo a nervous look. "Whoa, wait a minute," he stopped Shlomo. "I have a family, a job, all kinds of obligations. I don't know, this is a big commitment . . . how could I do what you are asking of me?" "You know," answered Shlomo, "I have people in Israel who are ready to dedicate every minute of their lives to nurturing the souls of young boys like this potential Messiah. So tell me: how would you and your congregation like to be known as the ones responsible for finding the Messiah and bringing him to the land of Israel?" Rabbi Saks looked at Shlomo with a twinkle in his eye and asked, "Rabbi! What do you need?" Shlomo grinned back: "A ticket to Israel for the boy." "Say nothing more. I'll have a ticket for you first thing tomorrow morning!"

Sunday morning, Shlomo received a call from the hotel switchboard telling him that there were two first class tickets waiting for him at the front desk. (Shlomo didn't need a ticket, he already had one). When, later that day, Mayer Ben Simone returned for a final meeting, Shlomo handed him the ticket. He explained what he had in mind for him, and Mayer agreed to study at the *Baal Teshuva* yeshiva, where Shlomo had already arranged for him to go.

Today, Mayer Ben Simone, a religious Jew, is one of the most pious, respected, and well-known scribes in Israel. He hasn't been proclaimed as the Messiah yet, but who knows? He may still reveal himself to be the Messiah one day soon. And even if that day never does come, Mayer Ben Simone will have lived his life as if he carried within him the potential to be the ultimate redeemer, consecrating his life to the holy, like all the other thousands of Messiahs living in Israel today who had the privilege to meet Rabbi Shlomo Carlebach!

4

Keeper of the Flame

"We have 613 mitzvot (commandments), 613 laws. I don't like the word 'laws' because they are not laws. The word law reminds you of police, some straight character sitting there telling you what to do. Very bad translation. 'Mitzvah' means that God gave us 613 ways to come close to Him. The ways are divided into two parts, 248 ways of reaching God by doing certain things, and 365 ways of reaching Him by not doing certain things. If there is a red light and I don't go, nothing happens, right? I just don't cross the street. However, if God's red light flashed and I stop when I have a chance to do wrong, then something happens inside me. Something happened to me; I walked a few steps higher."

—RABBI SHLOMO CARLEBACH

"In the '40s, Shlomo Carlebach was probably the most cele-brated young Torah scholar studying at the Talmudical Academy of Lakewood, New Jersey," reminisces Rabbi Zal-man Schachter-Shalomi, who knew Shlomo from childhood. "Shlomo was in fact the darling of the great Torah Sage, Rabbi

Aharon Kotler, who had pronounced him an *ilui* (Torah prodigy). Rabbi Kotler had frequently shared with other Torah sages his conviction that Shlomo was destined to be the next *Godol Hador* (Torah Giant of his generation) in America. He carefully nurtured Shlomo's genius, tried to orchestrate its growth, and watched him flower with pride. Shlomo occupied an enviable and exalted position in Lakewood, one that few others could ever hope to attain. Thus, it came as a shock to everyone at the yeshiva, including Rabbi Kotler himself, when Shlomo made the decision to leave the rarefied atmosphere of Lakewood for what was considered to be then—in terms of erudition—an inferior choice: the Lubavitcher Yeshiva in Crown Heights.

"When I met Shlomo in front of the Lubavitcher Yeshiva one day soon after he had transferred there, I posed the question that everyone had been asking. 'Shlomo!' I said. 'You had the opportunity of a lifetime in Lakewood. Your prospects were brilliant! You were taken in under the personal wing of Reb Aharon Kotler, who adored you and treated you like a son. You left Harvard . . . you left Princeton . . . for City College. Why?'

"Shlomo looked at me with burning eyes. 'Don't you see,' he cried out, *'os de velt ees choruv gevoren* (the Jewish world has just been destroyed in the Holocaust)? *Leider, leider* (how horrible, how tragic) there are no Jewish teachers left and the religious leaders are all dead. The shepherds of our people are gone and there is no one to guide us. Someone has to take their place!

" 'Lakewood grooms scholars, but Lubavitch grooms outreach workers. At Lakewood, I would have had the privilege of expanding my soul, but only mine. Hopefully, here at Lubavitch, I'll learn how to expand the souls of thousands.

" 'You ask me why I left Lakewood, Zalman. The answer is heartbreaking but simple. I left Lakewood because of The Six Million!' "

"Igrew up in a Conservative Jewish home where religious practices were rarely observed. My understanding and knowledge of Judaism was minimal. In 1980, when I turned 15, my grandfather, who was more traditional than his children, grew alarmed about my lack of interest in Judaism, and decided a trip to Israel would remedy my indifference. He offered me an all-expense-paid trip on a summer tour organized by USY (United Synagogue Youth—a Conservative affiliate), which I eagerly accepted. What all-American teenage boy would turn down a free trip to another country half-way across the world?

"Our first day there, we were taken on a tour of Jerusalem's religious sites. Included in our itinerary was a stop at Mea Shearim (Jerusalem's ultra-religious quarter) where we walked along its narrow, twisted, cobblestone streets. I happened to be innocently wearing my Walkman, unaware that in this neighborhood it was taboo.

"As we wandered down Mea Shearim Street, a door from a local *cheder* (little boys' yeshiva) burst open, and hundreds of kids started pouring out, dismissed for the day. Most of them pointedly ignored us, but a couple threw interested looks in my direction. One inquisitive little boy with dancing mischievous eyes, detached himself from the group, boldly approached me, and pointing to the Walkman asked in broken English, 'What's that on your head?' I started to explain, but the language barrier was too great, so I said impulsively, 'You know what? Instead of telling you, let me show you!' I pulled off my Walkman and put it on his head. He was entranced. Just then, the door of the *cheder* opened again, and a stern-looking older man walked out. When he saw the Walkman on the little boy's head, his face turned purple with rage. He ran over to the kid, pulled the Walkman off his head, and violently hurled it onto the cobblestone street where it smashed into smithereens. Then he rushed me, twisting my left ear so hard I yelped in pain, waving his arms and screaming '*Shegetz! Gay Avek!* (You non-believer, get out of here!)'

"I was stunned. I had no idea what I had done wrong, why a warm spontaneous encounter had suddenly turned

into such a terrible act of violence. I was filled with anger and
infinite sadness. As I boarded the bus, I thought to myself,
rather bitterly, 'So . . . this is what religious Judaism is all
about . . . hate, anger, fanaticism, intolerance . . . I despise
it! I don't want to have anything to do with it ever again!'

"The rest of the day, I refused to go off the bus to explore
other religious sites. I adamantly shook my head each time
the tour leader tried to coax me off the bus, and sat with my
arms stubbornly crossed until he sighed and gave up. As the
day progressed, my rage at the injustice done me accelerated;
I brooded about the scene continuously.

"Finally, toward the end of the day, the tour leader stood
up in the bus and made the following announcement: 'Boys,
we have one last religious stop to make. But I have to tell you,
this place is unlike any other religious place we've stopped at
all day, and the Rabbi of this place is unlike any other Rabbi
you've met here in Jerusalem or any other place on this earth!
I know some of you are bored and some are turned-off—but
I promise you this place is a treat!'

"My friends looked at me hopefully. 'Gonna come in,
Ozair?' 'Nah,' I scowled. 'Anyplace that's religious, not for
me. No way Jose.' Then the bus rolled into Moshav Modiin
(Shlomo Carlebach's settlement located halfway between
Jerusalem and Tel Aviv).

"As soon as the bus driver honked his horn, hordes of
yarmulked men wearing long beards, *peyos* (sidelocks), and
tzitzit (religious undergarments with four strands of strings)
hanging out of their shirts, came streaming out of buildings,
bearing guitars and other musical instruments, singing *have-
niu shlomo alechem* (a song of welcome). As soon as the kids
descended from the bus, they were hugged, kissed, and
pulled into frenzied dancing circles. I was hypnotized by this
passionate display—the men looked like the Mea Shearim
Rabbis but they sure didn't act like them—but still remained
stubbornly fixed in my bus seat. 'Come on, Ozair!' shouted
my friends from outside, 'this is great stuff!' but I shook my
head no. Then Shlomo Carlebach emerged from a building,
and I will never forget the first time I saw his face. Instantly
I knew that this was the unusual Rabbi the tour leader had

spoken of. His face was bright, shiny, radiant. His huge eyes were everywhere and took in everybody, including me. He noticed immediately that I was sitting sullen and alone on the bus, and swiftly veered toward my direction. He boarded the bus and walked right up to me, giving me such a warm embrace that I felt suffused with light. It was impossible to say no to him. He drew me off the bus and I joined the dancers. For hours, Shlomo sang, told stories, and taught Torah. He told us: 'Do you realize how beautiful it is that you're Jewish? Do you know that by coming to Israel, you're living the dreams of your grandparents?' We felt moved by his words, spiritually touched. So we listened, we sang along, we danced, we inhaled all the warmth of Shlomo and his *chevra* (people). And I said to myself, with a deep, contented sigh, 'So . . . this is what religious Judaism is all about . . . love, joy, acceptance, tolerance . . . This is for me! This is what I've been searching for all my life!' And that night I took my first step back to the heritage of my forefathers.

"Today I am an Orthodox Jew. Coincidentally, I am married to the daughter of Yankele Shemes, one of the original cofounders of Moshav Modiin. So you see, Shlomo Carlebach not only drew me back to Judaism, he drew me to my *bashert* (destined soul mate) as well.

"All of us boys were delighted with the encounter at Moshav Modiin, which we assumed had been a singular performance arranged strictly for the benefit of our tour. But later we learned from the tour operator that this was not the case at all. All summer long, dozens of buses containing Reform and Conservative Jewish teenagers, continuously rolled into the grounds of Moshav Modiin, where they were accorded the same joyous welcome we had received. Sometimes, more than two dozen buses a day would arrive at the Moshav, and each time, Shlomo and the *chevra* would tirelessly run out into the hot summer day, again and again, to greet them, dance with them, and love them.

"No one ever took any surveys or ran any polls to determine how many alienated teenagers became intensely Jewish as a result of their encounters at Shlomo's Moshav. Few people were even aware of Shlomo's outreach efforts

there; they were certainly never publicized. But I can personally testify to their success, because if any such studies had
been conducted, I would have been one of the vital statistics!"

––––––

H is thumb was arched hopefully in the vague general
direction of Chicago, but his eyes were clouded with
pessimism and defeat. The young hitchhiker standing on the
dusty road that hot summer day in 1984 had not only lost
faith in his chances of catching a ride, he had lost faith in life
itself.

From across the other side of the road, a man in a battered
Chevy with kind eyes and a gentle smile, waved warmly. "I'd
gladly give you a ride," he yelled, "but it kinda looks like I'm
going in the wrong direction!" "Where ya headed?" asked the
hitchhiker. "Boulder, Colorado," the driver answered with a
wide grin, "to a New Age Conference. Wanna come?" "Why
not?" the young man shrugged. "At this point, I'm so
exhausted from standing in the sun, I'll accept any offer that
comes my way!"

At the New Age Retreat, the hitchhiker walked aimlessly,
feeling lost and alone, when he heard the familiar strains of a
Jewish melody. He blinked and wondered if his anguish was
causing him to hallucinate. He had picked up a little Hebrew
from his bar mitzvah lessons six years ago, and he could have
sworn that it was Hebrew he had been hearing. But . . .
Hebrew at a New Age Conference in Boulder? Impossible!

"Hey!" he grabbed a man's shoulder. "Do you know . . .
are there any Jews at this retreat?" The man laughed. "First
time at a New Age Center, huh?" he chuckled. "Are there any
Jews here? You gotta be kidding. The place is crawling with
Jews! I'm a Jew myself," he offered, "any particular reason
you wanted to know?"

"Well, I could have sworn I heard a Jewish melody a
minute ago, and something about hearing it made me feel so
happy. I guess I'm imagining things?"

"No," the man answered. "You didn't hear wrong; you

heard right. Somebody is singing Jewish songs right now . . . somebody I think you should meet."

He was led to a grassy knoll where Shlomo Carlebach stood playing his guitar. As he listened to Shlomo sing, teach Torah, and tell hasidic stories, he knew his trip to Boulder had been foreordained.

He spent the entire week at Shlomo's side, basking in his light, spiritually uplifted, in love again with life. But many of his most rapturous moments were pierced by self-doubt and gloom as he wondered where he would go when the New Age Conference was over. He needn't have worried, however; Shlomo had already taken his fate into his hands.

On the last day of the conference, Shlomo called him over to his side and handed him a plane ticket to Israel. "The next stop," he murmured softly. "The final destination."

Overcome by gratitude and relief, the hitchhiker turned to embrace Shlomo with tears in his eyes.

Shlomo kissed him tenderly on the cheek and said: "Sometimes my sweetest friend, God's plan isn't immediately apparent. Because you didn't hitch a ride to Boulder . . . you hitched a ride to *Yerushalayim!*"

———

In the 1970s, I was living in Gainesville, Florida, dabbling in Eastern religions, definitely on a spiritual path, but far removed from my Jewish heritage. For many years, I had explored spirituality with a number of masters from various traditions, but in 1975 something started nudging at me. "There has to be something like this in Judaism," a little voice started whispering inside of me, getting louder with each passing day. I began to feel guilt-ridden and tormented. Maybe I hadn't given Judaism enough of a chance? I didn't know where to turn. Suddenly, I remembered Rabbi Shlomo Carlebach.

I had seen him fleetingly on an airplane once. He had been recognized by fans who begged him for an impromptu concert and obliging them, took out his guitar. As he softly played his beautiful melodies, hordes of curious passengers

were drawn to his side, myself included. He had also spoken
about hasidism and told a few Torahs. In a way, he had
reminded me a lot of the different gurus I had encountered
during my travels. I had been too shy to approach him then,
and now I was sorry I hadn't. But because something about
him had impressed me, I decided to write to him in New York.
I poured out my yearning to be reconnected to *yiddishkeit*.
Could he give me any advice?

Exactly two days after I mailed the letter, at 8:00 in the
morning, my phone rang. "Good morning, Faygela (I had
signed my name as Faye), this is Shlomo Carlebach."

At first I thought it was a goof, because how could a letter
from Florida get to New York in two days? I was so skeptical,
in fact, that Shlomo had to spend a few minutes assuring me
that it really was him on the phone! After I was finally
convinced, he said: "Listen, my most beautiful friend: It just
so happens that I'm going to be in Miami tonight. Can you get
there?"

I hopped onto a motorcycle and drove all the way to
Miami. The ride was rigorous, and my back ached. As I drove,
I realized I didn't know anyone in Miami, and had no place to
spend the night. I also had no money. What was I going to do?

By the time I reached Miami, I was a wreck. I could no
longer think about my spiritual quest; all I longed for was a
chiropractor and a bed! I entered the concert hall where
Shlomo was scheduled to perform, ascended the stage wearily, and introduced myself to him. There was a person
flanking him on each side, a man and a woman. The first
thing he did was turn to the woman on his right and say,
"Chanala, can Faygela stay with you tonight? She probably
has no place." Chana smiled at me and nodded yes. Then
Shlomo turned to the man on his left, and said "This is brother
Tom. He's the personal cook of the Guru Maharaji, and also
his number one bodyworker. *Nebech*, you must have had such
a hard trip on your motorcycle, maybe you would like him to
work on your back a little bit?"

I stayed with Shlomo for a week, and found that he was
saying the exact same things as all the swamis I knew, but he
was saying it from a Jewish context. Slowly, but surely, he

brought me back to *yiddishkeit*, but it was a gradual process. At first, I juggled Shlomo with the other masters, continuing to study with them even as I studied with Shlomo. But eventually, my involvement with all of them fell away, because through Shlomo I had finally found my way back home.

In the late '60s, Shlomo Carlebach participated in a tour of Jewish Prague, led by a tour guide who turned out to be a doctrinaire Communist. To the despair of the participants, the tour guide mocked each Jewish site he showed them, denigrating their holiness. At the Jewish cemetery, he scoffed at the participants' scramble to leave *kvitlach* (notes of supplication) at the gravesites. At the various synagogues he mocked their belief in the efficacy of prayer. As the guide spewed out a continuous stream of anti-semitic invective and atheistic philosophy, Shlomo valiantly tried to counter his venom with loving, gentle statements, but to little avail. At the "Altnoy Shul," Shlomo could withstand the man's deprecatory remarks no longer. "Imagine!" howled the guide in laughter as he waved his hand at the Altnoy Shul. "Fools actually believe that the so-called Golem's bones are supposedly buried in the attic. There are so many idiots in this world; people are actually afraid to go up to the attic; they think something terrible will happen to them. Stupid Jews tell a story that during World War II, Nazi soldiers went up to this attic and never came back! Ha, ha, how funny!" His patience finally gone, Shlomo quietly stepped up to the tour guide, and asked, "Could you please take us up to the attic?" Taken aback, the man asked "What's that?" Shlomo repeated, "Since you think the legend is such a joke, I want you to please take us up to the attic so that you can prove to us yourself what a lie this legend is." The man looked uncomfortable, and muttered, "No, I can't do that; it's not on the program." "Are you perhaps afraid that the legend is indeed true?" asked Shlomo. "Of course not!" replied the man. "Everybody knows it's lies and garbage." "So, in that case, please take us up to the attic; it will just be a few extra minutes. Think of what an opportunity this is for you." "No, I can't do it!" replied the tour guide in discomfiture. "We'll be behind schedule." "Look," said Shlomo pulling out his checkbook. "I'll give you $200 (in the '60s quite a princely sum) to take us up to the attic now. Surely you can use the money?" Angrily, the man shook his fist at Shlomo, and, wide-eyed with fear, grabbed his coat, looked over his shoulder, and fled.

––––––

On a cold wintry day three years ago, when New Yorkers were experiencing one of the most frigid winters in recent history and barely a soul was seen venturing outside, Shlomo Carlebach received a frantic "SOS" phone call from one of his *hasidim*. "Shlomo!" the man cried in distress, "I'm at my wits' end; I don't know what to do; I desperately need your help." "My sweetest friend," Shlomo murmured, "tell me, what's going on?" "I have a good friend—a young Jewish kid—who's in a very bad state. He's run away from his family and he's suicidal. He's given up on Judaism and is about to join a bizarre cult somewhere in the West. I've tried to talk him out of it, but he won't listen to me or to anybody else for that matter. Nobody seems to be able to get through to him, nobody at all. He's already gotten his plane ticket, and he's scheduled to leave tomorrow. You are my last resort. Can you try to help him?" "Give me his phone number and I'll set up an appointment to meet him at once," Shlomo responded.

Although the temperature readings were in the single digits that day and meteorologists had warned that the windchill factor made it seem like minus ten, Shlomo didn't hesitate in proceeding with his plan. He immediately phoned the young boy and said, "My name is Shlomo Carlebach. I'd love to meet you; can we get together today?" There was a long pause. Finally, the boy asked in a flat voice: "Why do you want to meet me?" "Because I care about you," Shlomo answered, "and your friend told me you're going through a tough time right now; I'd like to help." There was another long pause, and then the boy said, "Listen, thanks for your concern, but I don't have the time, I have things to do, places to go; I can't come to the Upper West Side today. I live in the Village, and it's just too far for me to travel, especially in this weather." Shlomo exclaimed, "Oh, my sweetest friend, you misunderstood me. I never expected you to travel to me; it is my intention to come to you. In fact, it would be my honor and privilege. So where do you live?" The young boy became hysterical. "No, absolutely not!" he shouted, "I don't want you in my apartment." "That's okay," Shlomo answered calmly, "I'll meet you at a street corner." The young boy was quiet for a moment and then began to regale Shlomo with a litany of reasons why he couldn't meet him. After listening respectfully to his catalog of excuses, Shlomo finally said in a forceful voice that would brook no dissent, "Listen, I'm going to meet you on the corner of West 4th and 6th Avenue at precisely 2:00 in the afternoon and I want you to be there." The boy sounded agitated. "Nah, it's not a good idea . . . I don't know . . . I don't think I can make it . . . I don't think I want to come." Shlomo listened carefully, and then said in a gentle tone, "My dear friend, listen to me. I am an old man, not exactly in the best of health. It is absolutely freezing outside; it's bitter. I hear in fact that it's the coldest day of the year. But I promise you I'm going to be at West 4th and 6th Avenue at precisely 2:00, and I give you my word I'm not going to budge from that street corner until you show up. Have some mercy on me; I beg you please!" The boy muttered something unintelligible under his breath and angrily slammed down the phone.

Unsure of whether the boy would show or not, Shlomo nonetheless donned his overcoat, braved the elements, and headed for the IRT Downtown.

On the corner of West 4th and 6th, Shlomo waited patiently for close to an hour when he suddenly felt a tap on his shoulder. "Okay, you win, I'm here," he heard a young voice say grudgingly. "Oh my sweetest friend, you've made me so happy!" Shlomo gave the boy a big hug. "Let's go into a cafe where we can talk." As they headed for the nearest shop, Shlomo asked, "So what made you come?" "Listen," the boy answered, "I couldn't exactly let an old man not in the best of health stand out in the freezing cold, could I?" For just a fraction of a second, a mischievous twinkle flitted in and out of Shlomo's eyes, then vanished quickly as turned towards the boy.

They spoke for hours, and the boy was persuaded to abandon his plans for joining the cult. Shlomo convinced him to enroll in a *baal teshuva yeshiva* (yeshiva for returnees to Judaism or the newly religious) instead, where he is currently ensconced, studying Torah to this very day.

———

I once went through a serious religious crisis, at which time I considered dropping out of the Orthodox Jewish world in which I had been raised and lived. Because I knew Shlomo Carlebach to be an extremely liberal and tolerant Rabbi, I decided to take my spiritual conflicts to him. In retrospect, I realized that probably on an unconscious level, I was hoping he would give me his blessing to renounce my roots.

He listened intently while I poured out my heart, stroking his beard thoughtfully, rolling his eyes into the back of his head as he frequently did when he was concentrating hard. Finally finished, I gazed at him expectantly, hoping to hear the words that would magically release me from my family, my society, my heritage.

"My sweetest friend," he said gently. "Let me tell you something that happened to me in *Yerushalayim* last week, OK? I was strolling down a street in *Mea Shearim* (the most religious section of that city) when I saw *mamesh* a most unusual and striking sight. A beautiful *chussidel* (little hasid) walked by with *peyos* flowing down to the middle of his back! This I had never seen before in my life and I was dumbstruck by his appearance. It was *mamesh* a *gevalt*, right? So I stared at him in shock as he passed, and stood on the corner trying to figure out who he was and what the purpose of such long *peyos* could possibly be. Finally, unable to contain my curiosity, I ran after him, just as he was about to turn the corner and disappear.

"'Excuse me, my holy friend, could I talk with you a minute?' I panted as I caught up with him. He nodded yes. 'Please forgive me, I don't mean to pry, and I'm not *chas v'sholom* (God forbid) making fun of you, but could you please tell me why you wear your *peyos* down to the middle of your back?'

"'It's very simple, really,' he replied. 'If *I* wear *peyos* down to the middle of my back, I can expect that my children will probably wear them down to their shoulders. And if my children wear their *peyos* down to their shoulders, then I can expect that probably *their* children will wear them down to their chins. And if *their* children wear *peyos* down to their chins, then I can expect that, hopefully, *their* children will wear them to their earlobes, as actually prescribed by Law!'"

Shlomo finished the story and gave me a meaningful look. "You have four holy *kinderlach* (little children), right?" "Right," I responded. "That's all I have to say," he concluded, pulling a *Gemora* toward him, in which he was soon immersed.

I went home and thought about the story Shlomo had told. My children were asleep in their beds and I gazed at them tenderly. Thoughts of leaving Orthodox life had vanished. I also approached my husband that night and told him that from now on, I would like to grow our little boys' *peyos* just a little bit longer!

———

"In 1989, feeling disenfranchised by Torah Judaism, I went to explore alternative lifestyles at Omega—a New Age Meditation retreat in upstate New York. I welcomed the opportunity to shed my identity and experiment with other options. I felt free and unencumbered. I arrived at the retreat, and was directed to go to a room to await 'orientation.' Imagine my shock and surprise upon entering the room, and seeing . . . of all people . . . Reb Shlomo Carlebach! 'Sh-Shlomo,' I stammered in discomfiture. 'Wh-what are you doing here?'

"He looked at me tenderly and sweetly smiled. 'Someone has to collect lost Jewish souls,' he said lovingly.

"So what happened?

"Rather than meditating all weekend with the Guru, I ended up studying Torah instead with Shlomo, and returned to Brooklyn a renewed Jew!"

On a flight from Tel Aviv to New York, Shlomo Carlebach was seated next to a famous American rabbi, renowned for his erudition. They were engaged in animated discussion when the captain's voice came over the loudspeaker, announcing the plane's approach to Paris, where a brief stopover was scheduled.

"Well, Rabbi," Shlomo said, turning to his neighbor with an extended hand and a departing smile, "it was a great honor to sit next to you and talk with you, and I wish you a good year!" "Wait a second," the Rabbi asked in confusion, "you're not going to New York? You're getting off in Paris?"

"Yes," Shlomo smiled as he scrambled to collect his scattered belongings, "I'm getting off in Paris to catch a flight to Bombay."

"Bombay!" the Rabbi snorted. "*Azalicha meshugas vos du tost!* (The craziness that you perpetrate!) For what good reason are you going to Bombay, please tell me! To get inspiration from some Indian masters maybe? Oy Shlomo," the Rabbi shook his head mournfully. "If only you had stayed in Lakewood Yeshiva where you could have become a scholar and done the Jewish people some good!"

Shlomo waited for the Rabbi's outburst to subside and then turned to him and said with a patient smile: "My dear friend, do you know there are 3,000 Israelis living in Bombay today—Israelis who went to India on holiday and never returned home? And do you know that there are thousands of young American Jews wandering the streets of Bombay in search of enlightenment? And do you know that there are no Jewish resources for these people in India—absolutely none at all? They have been utterly forgotten and forsaken by their Jewish brethren, and their *yiddishe neshomos* (Jewish souls) are dying. Somebody has to save them."

"I try to go to Bombay as often as I can—at my own expense—to bring *yiddishkeit* to these *neshomos*. Such sweet *neshomos*, looking so valiantly for God, just *nebech* looking in the wrong places! My humble mission is to show them that the spirituality that they're seeking in Eastern religions they can find in Judaism also. All these people need is just one taste of *Shabbos*, but who in India is going to give them this taste? So I go. I give a couple of concerts, put together a *Shabbaton*, and hopefully I can help at least some of them find their way back.

"So that, my friend, is the reason I'm off to India. And now, you tell me," Shlomo turned to the scholar, "when you return to New York, where exactly will you be going?"

———

"I met Shlomo Carlebach the summer before he died, at Sullivan's Department Store in Liberty, N.Y., and he invited me to accompany him into the coffeeshop where he ordered a soda to go. After being told his charge was $.50, he handed the cashier $2.00, and told her to keep the change. Thinking that Shlomo, in his childlike naivete and trusting simplicity didn't know the mechanics of tip-giving, and concerned about his constant penniless state, I whispered, 'Shlomo, when you order to go, you don't give a tip, and certainly you don't give a $1.50 tip for a $.50 soda.' He smiled patiently and lovingly at me and said: 'Holy sister, Yitta, I know, I know. But I'm trying to make up for *unzer tierla yiddalach* (our sweet Jews) who don't give tips, and consequently make a *chilul hashem* (defame God's name).'

"Even in the most mundane and prosaic of situations, Shlomo Carlebach felt the burden of *klal Yisroel* (responsibility toward his people) and the need to sanctify God's name."

———

Sometimes a chance encounter, a piece of dialogue, or even a word or two can turn your life around. For poet Rodger Kamenetz, author of *The Jew in the Lotus* and Professor of English at Louisiana State University, it was one line uttered by Shlomo Carlebach.

"In 1970 I was a college student at Yale, dating a woman who was the daughter of a rabbi. I myself came from a Reform Jewish background and didn't have particular interest in religion. However, in an effort to please the current love of my life, I found myself sitting in the Hillel House with her one evening, awaiting the arrival of the 'Singing Rabbi' who was scheduled to perform a concert that night.

"I had never set foot in the Hillel building before, and mainly I was annoyed because 'The Singing Rabbi' was over two hours late!

"When he finally did arrive, I thought 'At last he's going to start the concert already,' but instead he began walking around the room, going up to each person, saying hello, giving him a hug, and looking into his eyes. He made a connection with each person there, including myself, and transformed the group from an annoyed audience to a close circle of friends. All the tension that had built up in me throughout the evening dissolved. Shlomo began singing and I really started enjoying myself. Then he said something that jolted me.

" 'My sweetest friends,' Shlomo proclaimed fiercely, 'the whole world is waiting for Jews to be Jews!'

"As simple as this declaration sounds, it hit me hard, it was so powerful. On a logical level, it didn't really make much sense. What do you mean, the whole world is waiting for Jews to be Jews? If anything, the whole world is waiting to kill us! But the statement wasn't delivered to the head; it was addressed to the heart. And on an intuitive level, it seemed so completely and overwhelmingly true: Each group has a singular and distinctive contribution to make to the world. If it does not develop and cultivate its own particular uniqueness, the whole world will suffer as a result.

"I never forgot Shlomo's words, although I didn't really

understand them until much later, when they became pivotal in my spiritual quest. I felt that the path we are born to is the path each one of us is meant to take. All this I gleaned from Shlomo Carlebach's one-line statement, articulated with such deceptive simplicity at Yale. Deceptive . . . because it was really so deep!

"For years, I thought about that concert at Yale. It had proven to be such an important catalyst in my life. I remembered how we had all been waiting for Shlomo for such a long time, but his own message was about waiting, too. A message I have never forgotten."

"I went from being a rock and roll star and recording artist to a *chazan* and a Jewish performer as a result of Shlomo Carlebach's influence," reflects Michael Elias, an L.A. musician. "In fact, it was Shlomo who inspired me to turn religious in the first place.

"So there I was, a 'returnee' to Judaism and newly *shomer Shabbat* (sabbath observant) when . . . wouldn't you know it . . . I'm offered the principal lead in a Broadway musical. What a quandary. I was still struggling a little with my religious commitment, I wasn't 1000% yet, and all my life I had dreamed of a Broadway career. And this was no small part either; it was the starring role!

"I asked the producer if there was any chance of my taking off Friday nights and Saturdays, but he said that would be impossible. If I would accept the role, it would be with the complete understanding that I was going to violate *Shabbos*. I didn't know what to do.

"Luckily, Shlomo was in town the same weekend I received the offer, so I went to him for advice. He was doing a *Melave Malka* at somebody's home and was in middle of saying Torah, when he saw me enter. 'Hey, it's holy brother Michael!' he shouted exuberantly. He turned to the crowd, 'Does everybody here know the greatest singer in the whole world? Michael,' he shouted, 'have you changed the world yet with your gift?'

"I waited for Shlomo to conclude his talk, and when there was a window of opportunity, drew him aside and described my dilemma. 'Oy!' Shlomo sighed, a deep heartfelt compassionate sigh. 'Michael, *nebech*, I feel so bad for you, *mamesh* my heart is breaking for you. This is truly a great *nisoyun* (trial by fire). What a test! What a test!' He sighed again in commiseration and then fell silent.

" 'So, Shlomo, what should I do?' I pressed, wanting his advice. 'What should you do?' he repeated. 'Michael, what you should do is . . . follow your heart!' And then he gave me a hug and kiss and moved away.

"I turned down the offer and embraced Orthodoxy more fervently than before. How fortunate for me that it was Shlomo Carlebach whom I had approached and not somebody else."

"I come from a hasidic home in Mea Shearim, but its flavor was not for me. In my teens, I left *yiddishkeit* altogether, and was not on a spiritual path for some time. I did not 'drop out' casually or easily. My decision to leave caused me unbearable pain and suffering, both psychologically and spiritually.

"To renounce everything I knew and loved—my heritage, my society, and my family—put me in agony. Yet I wanted my life to be authentic, and although hasidic life is very beautiful, it was not the right life for me.

"Then I met Rabbi Shlomo Carlebach. He must have sensed my torment, because almost as soon as we met, he said, 'Holy sister, Miriam, *mamesh* it's a *gevalt* to meet you. I've been waiting my whole life to meet you. Can I call you tonight?' I looked at this famous personage, whom I had just met for the first time, skeptically, 'Do you really have time?' 'Oh, all the time in the world!' he reassured me.

"Two o'clock in the morning, the phone rang. It was him. I unburdened myself to him, reciting all my theological doubts, questions, and problems with *yiddishkeit*, yet also speaking at the same time of my great love for Torah and yearning to be reconnected. When we finished talking, I noticed light coming into my room. Bewildered, I looked at the clock on my desk and saw with a start that it was 6:30 in the morning. During our long discussion, I had been unaware of time passing. I was shocked to realize that Shlomo Carlebach had just spent four and a half hours with me on the phone. But this first marathon session was only the beginning of a long series of similar calls from Shlomo that would stretch across the span of many years and bring me back to my heritage.

"Today, I am an Orthodox Jew. There is no question in my mind that were it not for my *Heilege Rebbe*, my return to my roots would never have taken place."

———

A few weeks after Shlomo Carlebach died, a friend and I were sitting in a cafe in the Village, poring over newspaper articles about Shlomo that we had individually collected and were now trading. The obituaries were spread out on the table before us, and we were studying them intently. Engrossed in our scrutiny, we were startled out of our respective reveries by a curious voice that asked, "Hey, whatcha guys doing?"

We looked up in surprise at a tall, husky biker-type emblazoned with tattoos and wearing rings in both his ear and nose. "Uh . . . it's not anything you would be interested in," I answered hurriedly, a little intimidated. "It's just some obituaries about a rabbi who died recently." I was sure he would turn away in boredom or wrinkle his nose in distaste, but his curiosity was piqued rather than deflated. "Oh, really?" he said with a genial smile. "Now just which rabbi is that?" "Oh, I'm sure you never heard of him," I replied quickly. "His name was Rabbi Shlomo Carlebach and . . ." "Shlomo Carlebach!" he interrupted excitedly. "I knew him. He sent me to Israel once."

My friend and I were avid collectors of Shlomo stories, so we eagerly waved the biker into an adjoining seat and waited for his tale to unfold.

"I know I don't look it," said the biker, "but I'm Jewish. I was walking in the Village once, when I bumped into Shlomo Carlebach, and we got into a lengthy conversation. He seemed genuinely concerned to learn that I was alone in the world, and saddened to discover that I knew virtually nothing about Judaism. He promptly announced his intention to 'adopt me' and immediately proceeded to take me under his wing. I spent the next two weeks in Shlomo's company all day and practically all night, too. It was a wonderful experience, one that I'll treasure for the rest of my life.

"Anyway, about two weeks later, he told me gently that he had to go to Israel the next day but would keep in touch. He began speaking tenderly about his love for the country, when his eyes took on a special shine, and he turned to me and asked, 'Have *you* ever had the privilege of traveling to the Holy Land?' When I told him that I had never been to Israel, he exclaimed passionately, 'Oh, but you must! Jewish history is engraved on every stone, contained in every crevice. The very air is fragrant with holiness, and God is everywhere. It would be *mamesh* a *gevalt* for your *tiera neshoma* (sweet soul) to be there.' Mid-sentence he paused, surveyed me for an instant and asked, 'So how would you like to go?' I blinked. 'What do you mean? You know I can't afford it.' 'No, I mean I'll send you; I'll pay for everything.' I looked at him in disbelief. 'You'll buy my ticket for me? You know me exactly two weeks. You've got to be kidding.' 'No, my friend, I'm very serious.'

"A couple of days later I found myself enroute to Israel, compliments of Shlomo Carlebach. Shlomo set me up with a *Baal Teshuvah* yeshiva, where I studied for six months and got free room and board. As you can see, I didn't exactly become religious, but I am certainly more knowledgeable and attached to my heritage today than I ever was before. And who knows? Maybe one day that little spark that Shlomo nurtured in me will burst into flame!

"But what I also want to tell you guys is this: When I got

to the yeshiva, I discovered that I was not the only one sent there via the good offices of Rabbi Shlomo Carlebach. Many of my classmates told me they owed their return to Judaism to Shlomo. Not only had Shlomo inspired them, but he had personally paid for their plane tickets as well. Many of them told me 'I wouldn't be here today if it weren't for Shlomo Carlebach!'

"So move over guys and let me look at those obituaries with you. Although I ask you, could any of them possibly do Shlomo Carlebach justice?"

One month after Shlomo Carlebach's death, Edna Braude of Brooklyn, New York, was sitting in a waiting room at Kennedy Airport lamenting the fact that she had just missed her plane to Israel, when a sophisticated-looking woman in a chic pants suit approached her and asked, "Mind if I join you? I also just missed the flight and I desperately need someone to talk to." Because Edna was wearing the traditional high-necked, long-sleeved modest dress and *sheitel* (wig) of the hasidic woman, she was surprised that the woman had approached her, but quickly murmured her assent. The woman's eyes were red-rimmed and swollen; it was obvious that she had been crying. Sitting down next to Edna, the woman asked without preamble, "Did you ever hear of a man named Shlomo Carlebach?" Taken aback, Edna replied that not only had she known him well, her son had played keyboard at his concerts. "I'm devastated by his death," the woman sobbed. "I'm utterly lost without him!" And the woman began to tell Edna the following story:

"Many years ago, my oldest daughter was ensnared by a dangerous, fanatic cult, and my efforts to rescue her were unsuccessful. I even hired several cult deprogrammers, but they all failed to extricate her from the cult. I was desperate. One day someone suggested that I try Rabbi Shlomo Carlebach. I had never heard of him before, but when I called him and described my situation, he immediately made an appointment to see me. He was the kindest, sweetest man I ever met. He comforted me, reassured me, and gave me his word that he would save my daughter. I never knew what techniques he used; he never shared these with me. All I can tell you is that several weeks later he did what dozens of well-meaning and skilled people before him could not do: he delivered my daughter back home to me, safe and sound. Shlomo Carlebach not only rescued my daughter from the cult, today she is a participating Jew who has returned to her roots and embraced her heritage."

"This is a beautiful story," Edna Braude exclaimed as the woman concluded her tale. "But please excuse me, Shlomo died over a month ago, why are you crying so violently now?" "You don't understand," the woman sobbed. "My oldest daughter is fine, but now my *younger* daughter has become ensnared by the *same* cult. I called Shlomo Carlebach with the expectation that he would help me once again, only to hear a recorded message that he's dead. That's why I'm so hysterical. With Shlomo Carlebach dead, who's going to rescue my younger daughter now?"

"There are many dedicated Jewish outreach professionals today who do important work," reflects Rabbi Zalman Schachter-Shalomi, father of the Jewish Renewal Movement. "Yet none of them have ever gone to the places that Shlomo Carlebach did to find—and bring back—Jews. *Mitzvah tanks* (the outreach vans of the Lubavitch movement) may roll down Fifth Avenue, but they don't roll into the ashrams, New Age centers and yoga retreats, which Shlomo Carlebach perennially haunted in his perpetual search for lost Jews.

"Once, on just such a mission, I had the privilege to accompany him to "Yogaville"—the ashram of Swami Satchidananda in Pomfret, Connecticut. Shlomo began doing his usual things—singing songs, playing guitar, teaching Torah, telling tales—and slowly but surely, all the ashram *yiddalach* started coming out of the woodwork, singing with him, dancing with him, listening to him with rapt attention. One by one, the ashram *yiddalach* began forsaking the corner of the room where the Swami had been holding court, and made their way to the sea of mesmerized admirers now encircling Shlomo, galvanized by his light.

"Suddenly the Swami, who had been practically all but abandoned by his followers and was beginning to feel a little neglected, stood up, strolled towards Shlomo's direction, and took him aside.

" 'Shlomo,' he asked a little petulantly. 'Are you trying to take my people away from me?'

" 'No Swami,' Shlomo responded politely but firmly, 'I'm just trying to invite them to come back home!' "

"In the 1940s, my father was a student of Reb Moshe Feinstein (one of the most celebrated post-Holocaust Torah giants and spiritual leaders of American Orthodox Jewry, until his death several years ago), whose renowned yeshiva, Mesivta Tiferes Jerusalem, was located in New York's Lower East Side.

"One day, my father had an appointment with Reb Moshe, and was sitting in the reception area awaiting his turn, when he saw him leave his study to escort to the front door a distinguished, saintly looking man, with a long, flowing beard. When final farewells had been said and the man had departed, Reb Moshe waved my father into his room. My father was extremely curious about the identity of the man who had preceded him, and, almost as if he were reading his thoughts, Reb Moshe said to him, 'You know who that man was? That was Reb Aharon Kotler (an equally famous Torah Sage, who founded the renowned Lakewood Yeshiva for Torah scholars), who came on a visit. And do you know what he just told me? He told me that he has such a rare, brilliant, and extraordinary young man learning in his yeshiva right now, that he is convinced that one day this disciple will light up the world with his Torah! Reb Aharon also told me that this student absorbs Torah learning in a unique way that he has never witnessed before, and that in all his years as *Rosh Yeshiva* he has never encountered such a mind.

"'Now understand,' Reb Moshe told my father, 'Reb Aharon has learned with the greatest Torah scholars in the world. Yet he says that this one student is different from anybody else. He was practically jumping up and down in excitement as he described this student to me.

"'And do you know what he said this student's name is? He said his name is . . . Shlomo Carlebach.

"'By any chance, have you ever heard of him?'"

5

The Holy Beggar of West End Avenue

"I often mention Holy Beggars, but people ask me who mamesh really is a Holy Beggar? Open your hearts my most beautiful friends. A Holy Beggar is someone who is begging you to allow him to give!"

"If your ears are not open to the crying of the poor, then your ears are deaf, and you will not hear God calling either."

—RABBI SHLOMO CARLEBACH

After giving a concert in Dubrovnik, Yugoslavia, in 1978, Shlomo Carlebach went for a long walk in a local park to clear his head. Hearing sobs, he followed the sound to its source: a forlorn young man leaning against a tree, wailing in an almost inhuman manner. Rushing to his side, Shlomo asked in distress, "Holy brother, why are you crying your heart out like this?" The young man, a non-Jew, answered that his parents were very poor, he was the hope of the family, and he had just won a scholarship to a prestigious medical school in Paris. "That's so joyous, holy brother," Shlomo answered, "so why are you crying?" The young man answered that he didn't have the money for the plane fare to Paris, and had been unsuccessful in his attempts to secure a loan. "How much is the plane fare?" Shlomo asked. "One hundred fifty dollars." Shlomo fumbled for a moment in his pockets, and pulling out all of his cash, counted out the sum mentioned by the man and gave it to him. The young man looked at Shlomo in disbelief. "You don't even know me. How do you know I'll ever pay you back?" he demanded. "It's not a loan," Shlomo answered quietly, "it's a gift." "No, no!" screamed the man, "I want to pay you back!" "Okay," Shlomo mollified the young man, giving him a slip of paper. "Here's my name and address, but repay me only when you truly can." Ten years later, an envelope postmarked Dubrovnik arrived at the Carlebach Synagogue, containing a check for $150 and a short note. "Because of your great kindness, I am today a successful physician in Dubrovnik with a thriving practice. I owe everything to you and will never forget you for the rest of my life."

"I was walking down Broadway one Friday night when an African-American panhandler approached me for money. In the tradition of my *Rebbe*, I apologized to him and explained that I observe the Sabbath, and therefore didn't have any cash on me. 'That's okay!' he said genially, 'I respect your religion!' Seeming hungry for human contact, he continued talking to me. 'So are you going to Temple tonight?' he asked. I assured him that I was, and that in fact I was on my way right now to my synagogue located at 79th Street. His eyes lit up. 'Oh, I know your rabbi,' he said enthusiastically. 'Rabbi Shlomo Carlebach—the Rabbi of Love!

"'Do you know,' he turned to me, eyes filled with wonder, 'that every single time he meets me, he brings me over to his apartment and gives me food, money, and clothing? I never met a man like him.

"'I've wanted to repay him in different ways thousands of times, but he won't let me. Rabbi, I've said to him over and over again, at least let me work for free as a maintenance man in your synagogue; let me give something back to you.

"'But he always refuses. "Holy brother," he always tells me, I want to do you a favor for the sake of a favor!"

"'So, I'm very happy to hear Shlomo Carlebach is your rabbi. Can there be a greater man around? When you get to Temple tonight, please be sure to send my regards, and tell him that James wishes him *Good Shabbos!*'"

"I was in the Carlebach shul one *Motzai Shabbos*, right after *havdalah* (the ceremony that marks the official end of the Sabbath), when a bedraggled-looking street person walked in, headed straight for Shlomo, and said pleadingly, 'Rabbi, can you give me something?' Since the Sabbath had just ended, Shlomo didn't have any money on him. A lesser man would probably have said 'Sorry, nothing on me tonight,' but of course let's remember we're talking Shlomo Carlebach here.

"So first Shlomo apologized profusely to the man, explaining that he didn't have any cash on him but would look for some in his apartment above the synagogue. 'Please forgive me, holy brother, for making you wait; I'll try to be as fast as possible.' Then Shlomo asked me to accompany him upstairs. At this point, Shlomo was not well—he suffered from heart problems and his feet were horribly swollen—and climbing the stairs proved to be an ordeal. But I didn't hear a word of complaint or self-pity from him; his sole concern was that his slow ascent was keeping the man *nebech* waiting.

"When we got upstairs Shlomo invited me into his room while he went to his closet to search for money. I was a bit shy about entering the inner sanctum of the holy Rabbi, but he insisted I come in. Shlomo then went over to a hook where his everyday pants were hanging, and began hunting through all his pockets, until he found a wad of dollars. Without counting it, he pulled out the entire bunch, handed it to me and said, 'Please give this to the holy man downstairs, and tell him I'm very sorry that it's such a small amount. Please tell him to come back tomorrow and I'll have some more for him.' Shlomo gave me everything there was in his pocket, and there was nothing left."

———

"I was startled out of a heavy sleep late one night by the insistent ringing of the telephone. Groggily, I glanced at the alarm clock on my bedside and saw with consternation that it was 3:00 in the morning. Who could be calling me at such an ungodly hour, I thought with dismay; it must be an emergency. I picked up the receiver and heard Shlomo Carlebach's jovial voice. 'Holy brother Zalman, I'm so sorry to wake you, but could you please loan me $2,000 right away?' I knew that Shlomo was only busy with *zarchei hatzibur* (needs of the community) so I asked him what the money was for. 'This man on the Upper West Side, *nebech* he just died, and his children live in Israel. They are both very poor, and they don't have the money for plane fare to New York for the father's funeral. I promised I would help them, but the truth is I'm a little broke myself and my travel agent doesn't trust me anymore. Could you please loan me the money and I'll return it to you in a few weeks?' I readily agreed, and a few weeks later he repaid the loan as he promised.

"This was just one of a series of late night calls I began receiving from Shlomo on a regular basis. What filled me with admiration was that these frantic phone calls were always about somebody else's problem. Not once did any of these late night appeals have anything whatsoever to do with Shlomo Carlebach himself."

———

"Ioften spent *Shabbosim* in Manhattan, *davening* (praying) in Shlomo's shul, and when I couldn't get a hotel room, would stay in his apartment above the synagogue. Early *Shabbos* morning, about 2:00 in the morning, the doorbell rang and I woke up with a start. Alarmed, I ran out to the corridor where I found Shlomo unconcerned. He opened the door, and there, standing on the threshold, were five scruffy-looking black men. They stared at him entreatingly. 'Excuse us, Rabbi, but we're so hungry!' 'Welcome, holy brothers!' Shlomo immediately ushered them in. 'It's my honor and privilege to share my Sabbath meal with you.' Shlomo started pulling out food from the refrigerator, covering the table with whatever he could find. The men sat down, devoured the food while Shlomo spoke to them gently, and then left. It was clear from both their manner and Shlomo's own, that this was a ritual that had been repeated many times before."

"Every time I *davened* at a certain *shtiebel* (small, informal synagogue) in Boro Park, one particular *yungerman* (young man) would always start *tchepping* (teasing) me about 'The Hippie Rabbi,'" recalls Rabbi Itzik Aiesenstadt of Jerusalem. "I had been Shlomo's *Gabbai* (personal assistant) for many years, and my affiliation with him was well known. Although this excited great admiration in many circles, it elicited less enthusiasm in others. Unfortunately, there were those who misunderstood Shlomo's unconventional ways and didn't appreciate the great work he was doing all over the world. This young man belonged to the second camp and never failed to seize the opportunity to remind me of his position. As a former Talmud scholar, I'm well-versed in the intricacies of intellectual discourse, so vociferous arguments don't faze me. In fact, not only did I always anticipate a good heated debate with this young man the minute I stepped into the *shtiebel*, I had actually come to enjoy it.

"So one day, I walked into the *shtiebel*, saw the young

man, and braced myself for attack. This time, however, none came, and I was perplexed as well as disappointed! Perhaps he hadn't caught sight of me as I opened the door, I wondered, as I circled closer to where he was sitting. He noticed me and smiled. I smiled back and waited expectantly. No attack. Instead, he politely inquired after my health, my family, my life in Israel. But no sneering mention—as was typical, indeed even customary—of Shlomo Carlebach's latest escapades. I was in a feisty mood, looking forward to our traditional verbal match, but for some strange reason none seemed to be forthcoming. We continued to talk pleasantly about every topic under the sun except for Shlomo, and I was downright mystified. Our heated debates about Shlomo had spanned close to a decade, and they represented an important dynamic of our relationship. Why the sudden silence now? Finally, I couldn't take it anymore, and I shouted at him, 'So what's the matter with you? Why aren't you *tchepping* me about Shlomo? Are you trying to torment me?'

"He looked at me sheepishly. 'Tell you the truth,' he said, 'I've had a complete change of heart about Shlomo Carlebach. I wanted to tell you how wrong I was all these years, but it's hard for a person to confront and even harder to confess that they've made a terrible mistake.'

" 'So what made you change your mind?' I asked curiously.

" 'I'll tell you what happened,' he answered. 'A friend of mine—a real *mitnagid* (opponent) of Shlomo's—was very down on his luck. He had been laid off from his job for months, had used up his unemployment benefits, had borrowed money from every *Gemach* (Jewish Free Loan Society) in town, and didn't have a penny to his name. At home, he had six small children and a pregnant wife.

" 'One day, he became so depressed that his friends grew alarmed and tried to think of ways to get him out of the house and uplift his spirits. So what recreational outlets are available to a real *frum* (extremely religious) guy? Movies are out, theatres are out, nightclubs are out. There aren't too many options, right? But it just so happened that there was a Shlomo Carlebach concert scheduled for that night somewhere in Brooklyn, and his friends forced him to go. They felt that Shlomo's music would have a therapeutic effect.

"'As soon as Shlomo walked into the auditorium, my friend realized he was no mere entertainer, but an extraordinary man. Even though he was late, Shlomo didn't march up to the stage and start performing right away. Instead, he walked around the room, greeting, hugging, and kissing everyone, making each person feel significant. When he reached my friend—who had never met him before but was at this point vulnerable to any show of warmth—and embraced him, my friend burst into tears. Shlomo looked at him with concern. "My sweetest friend," he inquired gently, "What's going on?" "Oh, Shlomo," my friend whispered back, "My *matzav* (financial situation) is so bad that I don't even have enough money to make *Shabbos* this week!" "Listen, my holy brother," he said softly, "*mamesh* my heart is breaking for you! I have to go on stage now because I'm two hours late already and people are angry, but please come to me during intermission and I'll try to help you."

"'Sure enough, my friend approached Shlomo during intermission, and Shlomo shepherded him into a small private nook backstage away from public scrutiny. He pulled out a check from his pocket, and said; "Someone gave this to me earlier today, and I want you to have it." Shlomo endorsed the check and then handed it to my friend with an apology, "I'm sorry it's not *mamesh* a major sum, but I hope it will help you out temporarily." My friend was in a state of shock. He had just met Shlomo for the first time an hour ago, and already he's trying to assist him! He accepted the check with embarrassment but gratitude, certain that the amount was for twenty-five, fifty, maybe a hundred dollars. It wasn't until he returned home and opened the envelope, that he discovered that the check was for $3,000!

"'And that is why, Reb Itzik, *blineder* (God willing), I will never *tcheppa* you about Shlomo Carlebach again. Nu, so what do you say to my story?' he ended, somewhat miffed at my seeming lack of surprise.

"'Frankly, my friend, this is not an unusual story about Shlomo,' I responded smugly. 'In fact, these episodes happen all the time. Even as you were relating your story, I was reminded of the time I accompanied Shlomo to a huge concert in Chicago, for which he was paid $10,000. I knew he needed the money desperately. He was broke at the time and had counted on getting paid right away. Well . . . wouldn't you know it! Right after the concert ended, a stranger approached Shlomo and told him about this poor widow who was in need of a serious operation, but had neither medical insurance nor money to pay the surgeon. On the spot, Shlomo pulled out the check for $10,000 that he had just received from the concert manager, and handed it over to the friend of the sick woman. So the man left with the check, and Shlomo left penniless.'

"After I recounted my story to the *yungerman*, we were silent for a moment as we considered the character of Shlomo Carlebach. Then we both exclaimed in unison, 'What a tzaddik!' shook hands, and exited the shul."

———

"I was walking down Broadway and 80th Street one day, when I noticed in the distance an unruly throng of street people congregated on the corner of 79th. They seemed to be excitedly clamoring for something from a man poised in the middle of their group. I wondered what was going on and moved closer for a better look. It was then that I realized that the man in the center of this vortex was none other than Shlomo Carlebach, who was distributing $10 bills to each of the homeless men, together with a smile, a hug, and a kiss.

"There must have been close to two dozen men assembled there at that time. Because I had often heard about Shlomo's celebrated generosity towards the homeless, but had never witnessed it myself, I stood transfixed by the scene taking place several feet away from me.

"When Shlomo had depleted his supply of bills, one man was left who had not received his share of the bounty. The man looked imploringly at Shlomo and cried out in a beseeching voice, 'Please, Rabbi, don't forget about me, man!' Shlomo had probably thought all of the men had been taken care of, because his face assumed a distressed look when he realized that one had been omitted. He began checking all his pockets, fishing tremendous amounts of paraphernalia out of them—keys, cards, torn scraps of paper—but no money. Suddenly, he spied me observing him from afar and his expression cleared in vast relief. 'Holy Brother Mendel!' he yelled jubilantly, waving me towards him. '*Mamesh*, it's a *gevalt* to see you. You came just in time. Can I borrow $10, please?' "

He was about six feet two, white as a sheet, and had stringy blond hair cascading down to his shoulders. His rumpled, torn, and dirty clothes emitted a dank and sour odor. Yet only moments before, seemingly oblivious to the offensive smell, Shlomo Carlebach had led the young man proudly to my side, his arm draped warmly around his shoulder, exclaiming cheerfully, "Sister Anne will gladly help you!" Surreptitiously, Shlomo whispered into my ear, "Please give him as much food as he wants to eat."

It was a special shul (synagogue) dinner, and I had been sitting at a table with my companions when Shlomo approached me. I sprang to my feet, ran into the kitchen and heaped generous amounts of food onto a plate. In a matter of minutes, the young man had devoured the meal, so I went back into the kitchen for seconds. This too was consumed rapidly, so I went back again for more. Finally, when he appeared satiated, I looked at his blond hair and blue eyes and blurted out rather impolitely, "Are you Jewish?"

"No Ma'am," he replied courteously. "I'm a Christian from Texas!"

"So, how'd you end up at our shul dinner?" I asked.

His eyes lifted heavenward. "I was sitting on a bench in Central Park late this afternoon, when your Rabbi walked by. I had never met or seen him before, but he took one look at me, turned around and walked right up to me. With the kindest eyes and sweetest smile, he asked ever so gently, 'Brother, do you need a meal?' I started to cry and gratefully told him yes, I desperately did. He gave me the name and address of your synagogue, and told me to come right over. He said there was good food and plenty of it. That's how I came to be here tonight.

"I really don't know what I would have done if your Rabbi hadn't come by," the blond Texan said slowly. "I'll tell you honestly, this is the first meal I've eaten in three days. When he walked right up to me and asked 'Brother, do you need a meal?' I said to myself, this here man is surely an angel from God."

———

"I was at Shlomo's shul one *Shabbos*," recalls Joey Greenblatt, "and was partaking of the Friday night communal meal when Shlomo got up to address the crowd. '*Chevra!*' he said. 'I have to tell you about an incident that happened to me yesterday. It troubles me so much I simply can't forget it.

"'This is what happened: I was walking along the Upper West Side yesterday, when I saw *nebech nebech* a young fellow whose legs were both amputated, sitting in a wheelchair, wearing tattered clothing, begging for handouts. Everybody knows that on Broadway it's quite common to meet many unfortunate souls, but this man struck me as especially broken and my heart went out to him. I approached him, gave him all the money I had, and started talking to him, "How are you, brother? What's your name?" He gave me a strange look and didn't answer. "So where do you live?" I continued. "Why? What business is it of yours?" he asked suspiciously. So I said, "Why don't you come over to my place? I live right here on 79th Street." Again, he gave me a wary look and said, "What do you mean?" "I'd like to take care of you, you can stay with me; I have a temple over there and an apartment, too." The man looked at me mistrustfully and said, "No, I gotta go!" and started pushing the wheelchair away from me.

"'*Chevra*,' Shlomo sighed, 'You don't know how hard I tried. I ran after him pleading, "You don't understand, I'm going to take care of you. I'm going to love you like you can't imagine!" He kept rolling the wheelchair away from me, and I *mamesh* pursued him down Broadway, until finally, I couldn't catch my breath anymore and I gave up.

" *'Chevra!'* Shlomo looked at us with anguish. 'This is the most painful part of the story: the young fellow couldn't believe that I was sincere! Why do you think I am telling you what happened? To give over to you, what a terrible, tragic world we live in that this man must have been so hurt, so misled, so abused in his lifetime, that he could no longer trust. He couldn't accept the fact that I really wanted to help him.

" 'And you know something, *chevra*? *Gevalt, gevalt* would I have loved this guy. I would have taken him in, and given him so much, he doesn't even know what he missed out on . . . he doesn't even begin to understand.'

"But the real story," reflects Joey, "is that Shlomo didn't stop telling this story! He told it Friday night, he got up and told it a second time *Shabbos* morning, and then he told it *Shalosh Seudos* (the third and final Sabbath meal) again. Then he told it the next *Shabbos* and again the next. For three weeks he didn't stop *hocking* (hammering away) with this *meisa* (story) until it was coming out of our ears already! We started wondering how long is he going to continue to talk about this?

" 'He didn't believe me . . . he didn't think I was really going to help . . .' Shlomo would mutter over and over again to whomever would lend an ear. And it bothered him so much . . . that for some tragic souls love is only a phantom, that for some broken spirits love no longer exists.

"It was incomprehensible for a man like Shlomo Carlebach to grasp that *nebech* there are some people in this world who dwell in such dark places so devoid of love, that when it finally comes their way, they don't even know that it's for real . . ."

A mong the bereft who gathered wordlessly near the Carlebach Synagogue the night before Reb Shlomo's funeral to mourn quietly together, was a contingent of homeless men and women whom he had befriended over the years. As congregant after congregant rose inside the shul to deliver a moving tribute or share a poignant memory, members of the homeless delegation nearby were also stirred to honor Reb Shlomo with eulogies of their own.

"I was on Rabbi Carlebach's 'payroll,'" one man proclaimed. "Every Thursday night, I came to Rabbi Carlebach's home for a weekly stipend. The amount always varied because he gave the money in a very unusual way. He would close his eyes, dig deep into his pockets, and with his eyes still closed, hand me everything he had found. He blessed me, and then I left. His eyes were still closed, because he didn't want to know how much he had given me. Sometimes there wasn't much—only a couple of singles—sometimes there were a few fives, a couple of tens, but sometimes there were hundreds."

Another man murmured that he too was on Shlomo's 'payroll.' "Actually, we had cut a deal. The Rabbi tried hard to help me get clean; he promised me that every week that I would stay off drugs and booze, he would totally support me. And he kept his word. Nobody ever cared that much about me."

"It wasn't his money that kept me going," a third added. "It was his music. Every so often he would show up on Broadway with his guitar, sit down with us on the benches or even on the grass and start playing his songs for us. He gave me back a feeling I hadn't had for a long time; he made me feel like a man!"

A fourth man recalled Shlomo's frequent visits to the makeshift homes (cardboard boxes) of the street people in Riverside Park. "He always came to check up on us, see how we were doing, kid around with us, give us some money. He made us feel that someone out there really cared about us. It didn't matter whether we were Jewish or not. He was our Rabbi."

———

"During the first days after Shlomo Carlebach's death, clusters of homeless people from Broadway and Riverside Park congregated in front of his synagogue, weeping. Members of the shul, crying inside, were astonished at the depth of feeling the street people had for Shlomo, and wanted to assure them that they would not be forgotten. One day, a man was dispatched by the *chevra* to deliver such an announcement to the throng outside, but unfortunately— perhaps because he felt awkward and was rushed or perhaps because he was not articulate to begin with—his rendition of the message proved rather inelegant. 'Don't worry,' he said hurriedly to the people. 'You don't have to cry . . . we'll give you money.'

" 'Is that what you think?' one woman in tatters pulled herself up indignantly. 'That we're crying because of the money?'

" 'We're not crying because of the money we're no longer going to get from the Rabbi,' yelled a ragged man. 'We're crying because now that Shlomo Carlebach's gone . . . who's going to come to us at 2:00 in the morning and sing to us and tell us stories and hold our hands?' "

———

"I was walking down Broadway the day after Shlomo Carlebach's funeral, when a black homeless man, spotting the yarmulke perched on my head, approached me mournfully. 'Brother, did you hear the news?' he asked sadly. 'Our Rabbi died a few days ago. What are we going to do without him?'

"Tears welled up in my eyes as I thought of how bereft the homeless of New York, to whom Shlomo Carlebach personally ministered, would now truly be. The man, seeing the tears in my eyes, touched my arm consolingly for a moment and said in commiseration, 'Strength, brother, strength! Somehow we'll have to find a way to get through this unbearable loss! We'll just have to go on! That's what he'd want, isn't it?' "

———

"The greatest story that can be told about Shlomo Carlebach," reflects Rabbi Dr. Abraham Twerski, the eminent hasidic psychiatrist from Pittsburgh, "is that a collection had to be taken up to pay for his funeral expenses. He died penniless. His entire life was in service of people; he gave all his money away."

6

The Holiness of Children

"Men talk about the holiness of God, but there is no peace. Men talk about the holiness of other men, but still there is no peace among them. Ah, but when the messianic time comes when men will talk about the holiness of children, then . . . then there will be peace!"

—Rabbi Shlomo Carlebach

Shlomo Carlebach always encouraged his congregants to bring to the synagogue their children, whom he honored (if it were possible) even more than adults. Toddlers and small babies were warmly welcomed. The synagogue was one of the first public facilities in the nation to install a diaper-changing station in its ladies' room, so integral and cherished was the presence of children to the Carlebach community. Nursing mothers were free to discreetly suckle their infants in the back of the synagogue, and toddlers to play quietly on the side. A delightful cacophony of infants' cries, gentle coos, and contented burps, together with the joyous shrieks and bois-terous yells of toddlers often filled the synagogue and wafted into the air. Shlomo was never irritated by the noise; to him it was the sweetest music. But what demonstrated more vividly than anything else the reverence Shlomo had for children was a ritual he repeated whenever they interrupted him at a concert or lecture.

The children adored Shlomo; they perceived him as a kind grandfatherly figure who indulged their slightest whim. They felt uninhibited about approaching him in the middle of a speech or song, even if he were performing for or speaking to thousands. Toddlers would habitually waddle up to Shlomo as he was talking or singing, and start tugging on his sleeve impatiently. Rather than be annoyed, Shlomo would instead smile warmly at the child, caress his cheek softly, and plant a kiss on his head. If he were sitting, Shlomo would place the child on his lap and stroke his hair. Sometimes, Shlomo would attempt to continue his talk or song with the child enfolded in his embrace, but sometimes he would break off in the middle of a sentence or refrain and just start talking with the child. Occasionally, Shlomo would look at the child with a certain wistfulness and tell the audience: "Do you know? One million children died in the Holocaust. They are so precious, so holy." Usually, the child, contented, would soon waddle away in search of its mother, but occasionally he would walk a few paces, make a U-turn and come right back for more. Shlomo would laugh good-naturedly, the audience would laugh with him, and he would ply the child with more endearments, until its mother would make an appearance and take him away.

There was never a time that Shlomo Carlebach didn't honor any child who approached him. Any child who interrupted him was paid the highest homage, and thousands of adults around the world today who were once those children can eloquently testify to this truth!

———

"My sister and I come from a dysfunctional family in Boro Park and were both placed for several years in Ohel's

Children Home when my parents were unable to take care of us. This was a terrible period in our lives, and one day, looking for a little solace, we went to Shlomo's shul on the Upper West Side. It was the first time we had ever met him, and we were overwhelmed. In his usual warm and friendly style, Shlomo greeted us at the door, asking our names and wanting to know everything about us. When we told him we were living at Ohel, his eyes became misty and sad, and he asked if there was anything he could do for us, anything we needed. We didn't take him very seriously, but we said that the one thing we both really wanted in the whole wide world was a pair of bikes. His eyes twinkled, and he gave us a big hug.

"The very next day, two bright, shiny, brand-new bikes were delivered to us at Ohel, compliments of Shlomo Carlebach."

———

Late one night, Seth Glass was driving home with his eight-year-old son, when the bright, unusually philosophically bent child suddenly asked, "Dad, are we alive and real, or are we only part of God's dream?" Jolted by the profundity of the question, Seth replied, "That's a great question! I don't really know the answer to that; let me go ask some Rabbis."

Seth approached several different Rabbis with his son's question, but none could come up with a satisfactory answer. Finally, in frustration he turned to Shlomo Carlebach.

"Wow, what a *gevaldig* (awesome) question!" Shlomo enthused, his eyes lighting up with excitement. "Let me think about it for a while, and I'll get back to you soon."

A few days later, Shlomo telephoned Seth and said, "In response to your son's question about whether we are alive and real or only part of God's dream, please tell him both are true. We are alive . . . in God's dream!"

In reflecting on this story, Seth Glass remarks, "Not only is the response important because it was quintessential Shlomo, but because it demonstrates vividly how seriously Shlomo took an eight-year-old's question."

———

"Several years ago," reminisces Devorah Davi, "I accompanied Shlomo to a concert in Northampton, Massachusetts, a rural community with a tiny Jewish population, so small in fact that it couldn't even support a synagogue. Instead, the Jewish farmers would meet in one another's homes for prayer services and classes. Few people knew of the existence of this miniscule Jewish farming enclave, with the exception, of course, of Shlomo Carlebach. It wasn't clear whether he had found them, or they had found him, but at any rate, they had found each other, and it was a *shidduch* (match) made in heaven. Shlomo brought a taste of *yiddishkeit* to a place where there was virtually none.

"One time Shlomo was performing before a packed house, crowded with both adults and small children. Although all the children were quite noisy, one little boy was getting particularly out of hand, and his father became incensed at his behavior. He reprimanded the toddler, who must have been all of two, and then spanked him. 'Bad boy!' he shouted at him. 'Bad, bad boy!' The little boy began to wail. At this point, Shlomo, who was up front performing but had heard the commotion in the back, put down his guitar right in the middle of a song.

"'Excuse me sir,' Shlomo addressed the father from across the room. 'Instead of screaming at your child, why don't you get down on the floor with him. Hold him, play with him, kiss him. Because this child is quite clearly calling out for your love. There's no such thing as a bad child!

"'Let me tell you something, my holy friend,' Shlomo added softly. 'I know you've come here because you're searching for something more in your life, something spiritual. But listen very deep. You're missing out on the whole point of spirituality if you think it's separate from your children. Spirituality isn't separate from your children; it *is* your children.'

"The man, duly chastened, sat down on the floor, put the child in his lap and enfolded him within his arms. For the remainder of the concert, the child was blissful and still.

"For many years," reflects Devorah, "I had heard the story that Shlomo had been fired from his first job as a Rebbe (teacher) in a yeshiva, because he had asked the parents to be sure to talk to their children at least fifteen minutes a day. Infuriated at his so-called intrusiveness and presumption, they had him dismissed. I had always been impressed by this story, but I hadn't been there when the incident had occurred. However, when this particular scene in Northampton took place before my eyes, it was truly a vivid demonstration of just how precious children were to Rabbi Shlomo Carlebach."

7

You Never Know!

"The more real a thing is the less you can see it. After you reach the level where you see all those things which are not to be seen, then you open your eyes and everything is clear to you, and it feels like you saw it all the time. To love someone is the deepest thing in the world, but you can't prove it. You can't put your finger on it, but it's the most real thing in the world. God is the most, utmost real thing in the world, and you can't see Him, but after you don't see Him, you see Him. Then you can see Him everywhere, in every flower, in every cloud, in every little stone, in every candle. When we say the Shema, God is One, we close our eyes, because first we don't see God, we're blind, we just believe, but then we open our eyes and it is so clear, He's always there."

"Everybody likes God to do miracles, but the big question is, are you a miracle? If you are living on the level of miracles, if you trust in God on the level of a miracle, then miracles happen to you. If you are not living your life on that level, then miracles don't happen to you."

—RABBI SHLOMO CARLEBACH

In the 1970s, Shlomo Carlebach embarked on the first of many pilgrimages to the former Soviet Union to reach out to and inspire a disenfranchised Russian Jewry. Since the early days of Communism, three million Jews had effectively been deprived of all forms and structures of religious expression and practice, and had been physically isolated from their brethren worldwide. With the publication of Elie Wiesel's landmark *Jews of Silence* and the establishment of the Student Struggle for Soviet Jewry (SSSJ), the attention of international Jewry had finally become riveted on the plight of their Soviet brothers, and a massive global outcry was raised on their behalf. When the first fissure in the walls blockading them appeared and travel restrictions were subsequently eased, Shlomo Carlebach was among the earliest Jewish leaders to travel to Russia, seeking contact with this beleaguered group.

On his first visit, Shlomo smuggled in siddurim (prayer books), *machzorim* (holiday prayer books), Jewish tapes, Hebrew books, yarmulkes (skullcaps), tefillin (phylacteries) and other religious paraphernalia. The Russian Jewish activists with whom he met accepted them gratefully, and within a few short days, all the religious materials he had brought along with him were gone. On his last day in Moscow, Shlomo was packing and preparing to depart for the airport, when he heard a timid knock on his hotel door. A young boy stood on the threshold and whispered urgently, "Please can I come in?" Inside the room, the boy turned to Shlomo and said, "I hear that you are distributing tefillin and yarmulkes. I came to get a set for myself." Shlomo looked at the boy mournfully and said very gently, "My holy child, I am so sorry, but I have given them all away. There is nothing left." Instantly, the boy threw himself on Shlomo's bed and began to cry wildly. "Holy brother!" Shlomo sat down next to the boy, putting his arm around him. "Why are you crying so hard?" "Next week is my bar mitzvah. I have been secretly studying Jewish texts with some other boys my age, and although my knowledge is limited, I know enough to know that on one's bar mitzvah day, one is instructed to don tefillin for the first time. There's no place in Russia where one can obtain them, and I only heard today that you were distributing them. As soon as I heard about you, I rushed here immediately. I want so badly to fulfill this *mitzvah*. You were my only hope. I can't bear the disappointment!" And the young boy began to cry again. Thoughtfully, Shlomo looked at the boy, turned to his suitcase, and took out his own personal pair of tefillin and handed them to him.

"My holy father, blessed be his memory," said Shlomo, "gave me this pair of tefillin when I was bar mitzvahed. They have very deep, sentimental value for me. I'm not attached to my possessions, and in fact own very little in my life. From the tefillin, however, one of my last links to my deceased father, I thought I would never part. But if it means so much to you to have tefillin for your bar mitzvah, then I will gladly give you mine." The young boy, unaware in his naivety of the enormity of Shlomo's sacrifice, took the tefillin happily and murmured his thanks. As he was about to leave, he turned towards Shlomo once again and in a plaintive tone asked, "But what about a yarmulke? Shouldn't I wear a yarmulke at least on my bar mitzvah day?" "My holy child, I am so sorry, but I gave away all the yarmulkes too." As the boy's eyes began to well up with tears, Shlomo hastily took off his own yarmulke and handed it to him. "It would be my privilege and honor if you would please take mine." The boy took the yarmulke, kissed Shlomo's hand, and left.

Shlomo Carlebach had never walked anywhere in the world without a yarmulke, but on the day he departed from his first visit to Russia, he left bareheaded. Later that morning, on a connecting flight to Israel, he saw a group of Jewish men *davening* (praying) in the aisles, and he asked one if he could borrow his tefillin when he was finished using them. "Listen, Shlomo," said the man with a derisive laugh. "I think that before you worry about tefillin, you should first concern yourself with the yarmulke that's missing from your head!" "Oh, my holy brother," said Shlomo gently to the man. "If only you knew the story behind the missing tefillin and if only you knew the story behind the missing yarmulke. If only you knew. . . ."

———

"When Shlomo walked into Jerusalem's Ramada Renaissance Hotel with two 'ladies of the night,' one hooked into each arm, and punched the elevator to take him to his room, everyone in the lobby stared, shaking their heads in righteous indignation. Trailing behind him by a few feet, I saw and heard it all. 'What decadence!' one woman trumpeted to her neighbor. 'It's disgusting, absolutely nauseating!' I heard another proclaim in a loud stage whisper. No one chose to consider other possibilities. No one questioned whether Shlomo might actually be engaged in some holy mission. Which in fact he was.

"I had been with him and the two women all night, so I knew the truth. They were indeed 'ladies of the night,' but Shlomo was trying to rescue them, not use them. One was a former *Bais Yaakov* girl from Boro Park, who had run away from home and was now making her living plying the streets of the Old City; the other came from an assimilated Jewish home in California and was living with her non-Jewish pimp. Both were on drugs and had a life expectancy that could be measured in months. Somehow, miraculously, they had stumbled into Shlomo's life that night. I say 'miraculously' because both girls desperately needed a miracle, and Shlomo was that miracle.

"He had taken them under his wing all night, treating them with love, compassion, and respect. He had broken some important ground with them, but it was clear to him that much work still had to be done. Because he was leaving for Europe the next day, he didn't have much time. So he took them into his room for an all-night orgy . . . of Torah learning and hasidic story-telling! When they left Shlomo's room the next morning in tears, he escorted them to a *baal teshuva yeshiva*, where they were promptly enrolled (at his expense). Shlomo then headed for the airport, satisfied that his mission had been fulfilled.

"Today these women are pious, law-abiding ultra-Orthodox Jews who wear high-necked, long-sleeved dresses and *sheitels*. They live in Jerusalem, are married, and have about half-a-dozen children each. This is very happy news. The sad news is that many people find it hard to see beyond the surface and are too quick to judge. If they could only adopt Shlomo's 'You never know' teaching and make it operational in their own lives, the world would be on a different spiritual plane and certainly a much better place in which to live."

―――――

"A young woman in Boston named Sara,* who had been an avid follower of Shlomo's for many years, became stricken with cancer. Although she had battled the disease valiantly, her condition became progressively worse, until her physician said there was no longer any point in continuing medical treatment. He told her gently that she didn't have much time left.

"Sara had returned to her Jewish roots as a result of Shlomo Carlebach's influence, and loved him like a father. She desperately wanted to see him one last time before she died. Under ordinary circumstances, Shlomo would have traveled to her home in Boston, but for some compelling reason that I no longer remember, he had to remain in New York. Consequently, the two arranged to meet at New York's Pennsylvania Station, to which Sara would travel from Boston via Amtrak. The plan was for Sara to spend several hours with Shlomo in the station—she was too feeble for anything more strenuous—and then immediately return home.

"At this point, Sara was bald and weighed under 100 pounds. Shlomo met her at the station with his guitar, and they retired to a private corner where he played and sang for her. She began to cry on his shoulder, and it was then that the Rabbi of a major Orthodox Synagogue—where Shlomo was scheduled to perform the following week—passed by.

"The Rabbi threw a hostile, contemptuous look in Shlomo's direction and stalked by wordlessly. Undeterred by the Rabbi's animosity, Shlomo called him over to his side, genially introduced Sara to him, and tried to engage him in polite conversation. The Rabbi was cool to Shlomo's efforts, responded tonelessly, and swiftly departed. Shlomo knew what was coming.

"The next day, Shlomo's manager received a call from the Orthodox Synagogue where that Rabbi served as spiritual leader. The Rabbi, his secretary reported, had found Shlomo's 'cuddling with a girl at Pennsylvania Station to be absolutely disgusting behavior' and the concert was herewith canceled. Two days later, Sara died.

"'What does the Rabbi know'? Shlomo said without bitterness, shrugging his shoulders, when told of the cancellation. 'To this Rabbi, I'm unholy. We think we see the truth, we think we know the truth, but what do any of us . . . any of us . . . really, really ever know?'"

———

"Shlomo was always very big on blessings," reminisces Carol Rose of Winnipeg, who knew Shlomo from the '60s on. "Whenever I was in his company, he would shower profusely a multitude of blessings on anyone who crossed his path, and ask for their benedictions in return. Often, during concerts or *shiurim* (classes), he would intersperse his remarks with blessings such as 'So I want to bless you and bless me back that we should all see the coming of the Messiah in our lifetimes' or 'I want to bless you and bless myself we should live very long lives' and so on and so forth.

"Once I was in the company of some friends—a childless couple who were Carlebach hasidim—when Shlomo came to visit. They had been married for many years and their childlessness caused them much pain. They had sought the counsel of infertility specialists the world over and had undergone many painful and expensive procedures, but nothing had worked. For various reasons, they had been equally unsuccessful in their bid to adopt. Everyone's heart ached for them.

"'Carol!' Shlomo commanded me almost as soon as he had entered the room. 'Bless Mayer* and Devora* they should with God's help have a child by next year!' Because this was typical of Shlomo, I was not fazed by his request and happily proffered my friends a heartfelt *brocha*. Then Shlomo went around the room and asked everyone present to bestow their own individual blessings upon the couple. Several hours later, when we escorted Shlomo to the airport, he stopped complete strangers in the terminal—whom he chose at random—and also asked them to bless Mayer and Devora 'who so much, so much are longing for a child!' The strangers were startled, to say the least, by the unusual request, but all of them good-naturedly complied. Shlomo even approached one man who definitely looked a little tipsy, and another woman who was quite clearly living out of shopping bags! Shlomo's perspective was that you should gather as many blessings as you can, because as everyone in the world is equally precious, so too are their *brochas*. Most of us are not on a high enough level anyhow to really see the holy people who dwell among us, Shlomo used to say. The 'Baal Shem Tov' stories that he loved to tell vividly demonstrated this point. In these tales, it was often the simple water carrier and not the saintly Rabbi who carried the most clout with the Lord and effected miracles. 'You never know!' Shlomo constantly adjured. 'You never know whose blessings really count.'

"Anyway, after Shlomo had accumulated an impressive number of *brochas* for the childless couple from a motley group of well-wishers up and down the airport, he turned to Mayer and Devora and said: 'Now when you get home, I want you to immediately go to your bank and open up an account for your child!' Mayer and Devora blinked, taken aback by the outlandish behest. 'This is a bad joke, right?' Mayer asked. 'No,' Shlomo insisted, 'I'm serious. Open up an account today for the child you plan to have nine months from now. This way, you'll be able to force God's hand. You'll be able to say to God, Listen, *Ribono Shel Olam*, how can you disappoint us, how can you hurt us like this, by not giving us a child? We already have a bank account prepared.'

"Mayer and Devora looked skeptical, but Shlomo said he wouldn't board the plane until they gave him their promise. Finally, tremulously, they gave him their word that they would open up an account that day. At the gate, he turned to wave to them one final time, smiled broadly, and gave them what positively appeared to be a conspiratorial wink.

"Shlomo died a few months later. Meyer and Devora

never did conceive, but they were finally able, after years of fruitless attempts, to successfully adopt an adorable baby boy. They brought him home almost nine months to the day that they had opened the bank account. And, in loving, grateful memory, they named him . . . Shlomo!"

———

The first time I met Shlomo Carlebach, I was in my teens and very religious. The second time I encountered him, at a bar mitzvah weekend at the Jackson Hotel in Atlantic Beach, I was in my twenties and no longer observant. The change seemed to sadden him to no end.

I explained to him that I had undergone a grueling *get* (Jewish divorce) process for years, had been an *agunah* (woman "chained" to her recalcitrant spouse) for an extended period of time, and was feeling bitter. I also complained that the *get* proceedings had left me practically destitute, and as a single mother, I was having a hard time putting bread on the table. As I poured out my heart to him, Shlomo shook his head in gentle commiseration, punctuating my remarks with his empathetic *nebechs* and *oy veys*. Finally, when I finished, his eyes seemed to roll into the back of his head in that unusual way he had when he was concentrating, and then he turned to me with a tender smile, "Jeannette, you have such a special *neshoma*, do me the biggest favor in the world. All I ask is that every Friday night, you do one thing. Light *Shabbos* candles. And I give you my word, whenever you light *Shabbos* candles, I promise you that you will definitely have *parnosa* (income) that week. Will you do it?"

What did I have to lose? I thought. Lighting *Shabbos* candles was no big deal. And anyway, Shlomo seemed so earnest and sincere, how could I refuse? So I agreed to light *Shabbos* candles, and he in turn gave me his blessing for *parnosa. Motzei shabbos,* we parted ways, and I never saw him again.

But that singular encounter—more than two decades ago—left its fateful mark. Because I freelance as a consulting editor, my income, rather than being fixed and secure, is relatively unsteady. As a result, my finances are frequently precarious. But despite this haphazard existence, Shlomo's blessing, throughout the years, has always prevailed.

I don't know how to explain this, but I promise it is true. Whenever I remember to light *Shabbos* candles, that week money pours in. And whenever I forget, that week the mail brings no checks, and I have a hard time making ends meet.

This pattern has happened consistently for twenty years, without fail, ever since I first gave Shlomo Carlebach my promise, and he gave me his.

"In 1973 I encountered Shlomo Carlebach for the first time at a rally for Israel on the steps of City Hall. Although other speakers spoke in a calm, controlled manner about the looming crisis confronting the Jewish State and the encroaching prospects of war, Shlomo was wild. His eyes blazed, his hand trembled, his whole body shook as he *mamesh* screamed about our responsibility to our holy brothers and sisters whose lives were on the line. What a nut, I thought, dismissing his fervor. Who could possibly care so much? This man's an outright *meshugenah* (crazy)! When the rally ended, I was sure I would never see him again.

"In 1975 a friend began raving to me about the classes he was taking at New York's (now defunct) Energy Center, with an unusual Rabbi named Shlomo Carlebach. 'Oh him,' I said dismissively. 'I saw him once at a rally. I'm shocked that you go for him. He's a nut.' 'No, you're wrong,' my friend countered. 'He's the holiest man I've ever met. Come with me just once and see if you don't change your mind.' Because my soul was hungering for something more in my life, and I happened to respect my friend's opinions of people, I decided to go. What did I have to lose?

"At the Energy Center, my soul started flying. Although I had a *yeshiva* background, I had never experienced Judaism being presented the way Shlomo did. The concepts he explained were deeper, more beautiful, and more spiritual than anything I had ever known before. His teachings and songs also contained a rare joyousness that was very appealing. But most of all, I was awed by the man himself. He seemed to be, as my friend had so accurately described, the holiest man I had ever met. I went home elated to know that such a man even existed, but soon the cynic inside of me emerged. 'Ah, he's probably a phony,' a skeptical voice whispered loudly. 'All this love business,' the voice scoffed, 'let's see what he's really like on his home turf.' So I decided to check him out by going unannounced one *Shabbos* to his shul on 79th Street.

"The first thing that struck me—overwhelmed me actually—was the fact that as I walked into the shul, I encountered Shlomo—not standing near the pulpit at the front of the synagogue—but sitting in the back, jumping up and greeting everyone who entered. And not just merely greeting, but hugging and kissing, too. The *davening* was exquisite and Shlomo's *divrei torah* (torah thoughts) inspiring, but still, I wasn't 100% convinced that I had truly found the real thing. Then, when the *davening* was over, he asked me to accompany him home. (At that time, he lived a short distance from the shul. Later he would move to the apartment on the second floor of the synagogue's building.)

"On the corner of 81st Street and West End Avenue, we stopped to talk, when an old, wizened man, totally bent and stooped over, and leaning on a cane, shuffled past us slowly. It looked like he was suffering from osteoporosis, and my heart went out to him. Shlomo was facing me, so his back was turned to the man, and he didn't see him. The man, however, had spied Shlomo, and must have known him from the neighborhood, because as he laboriously inched by, he shyly mumbled, 'Hello, Rabbi.' Shlomo whirled around, flashed the man a radiant smile full of love, gave him a warm embrace and shouted exuberantly, 'Hey holy brother, Holy Sabbath! I bless you that you should have a beautiful *Shabbos*.' Shlomo then turned back to talk to me, so he didn't see what happened next. I, however, was still facing the street, so I had the opportunity to behold a sight that I will never forget for as long as I live.

"After Shlomo warmly greeted and hugged the old man,

he stood frozen on the sidewalk for a moment, as if he were overcome by Shlomo's love. Then, he raised up his body, straightened his spine, and fully erect and upright now, began to walk down the street at a regular pace.

"I could not believe what I was witnessing. I was dumbfounded—staring in shock with my mouth open—as the man's briskly retreating figure turned the corner and vanished. How this was able to happen, I cannot begin to tell you. All I can say is that I observed it happen right before my eyes.

"Up until this point, I was a still a little suspicious about Shlomo's sincerity. Once this scene took place, however, all doubts vanished. I said to myself, is this a sign from God or what???

"So I threw my lot in with Shlomo Carlebach, and I haven't been the same since."

"In 1978 I served as band leader of the Kenny Ellis Orchestra, which played nightly at a popular kosher restaurant in Manhattan called 'La Difference.' Shlomo Carlebach was often the featured performer there, and I had the privilege of working with him on several different occasions. As uplifting as it was to be in the audience in *front* of him, playing *behind* him was also quite an experience! At that time, he still used to jump up and down as he sang, and all the loose change he had stuffed in his pockets for phone calls and *tzedakkah* (charity) jangled noisily as he jumped. Every time he jumped, the change jangled, and all of us in the band—who laughed heartily as we heard the clink and clatter of the coins—were also instantly reminded of the good deeds we saw him performing nightly. We always saw him goodnaturedly distributing *tzedakkah* to panhandlers who snuck into the restaurant, or sprinting between gigs to the public phone to call someone in distress. Thus playing behind Shlomo Carlebach not only made us laugh, it made us *learn* something as well.

"When the restaurant eventually closed, I moved to L.A. to attempt to pursue a career in show business. Ten years later,

I found myself teaching music and drama at Valley Beth
Sholom High School instead, my dreams unfulfilled. I was
single, lonely, and drifting. Although I found my teaching job
satisfying, a large part of me was still untapped. My talents
and potential were not being used properly, to say the least.

"One day I heard that Shlomo Carlebach was going to be
giving a concert at the school, and that he was coming in that
afternoon for a rehearsal. I was excited about seeing him
again, and wondered whether, well after a decade, he would
still remember me. I saw Shlomo strolling down the corridor
and was about to greet him when he preempted me by
shouting exuberantly, 'Brother Ken! It's *mamesh gevaldig* to see
you. You're the tops!' Then he put his arm around me and
said, 'You're a *chazan* now, right?'

"I was taken aback. From where had he gotten the
impression that I was a *chazan*? I hadn't ever considered a
career as a cantor; it was an idea that just had never occurred
to me, not even once. I responded, 'No, Shlomo, I'm not a
cantor.' Now, it was Shlomo's turn to look puzzled. Darting
a swift, intelligent, searching glance at me, he repeated in a
mild but insistent tone. 'Brother Ken, with your beautiful
voice, you're definitely a *chazan*!' I was beginning to feel
exasperated and almost yelled back at him, 'Shlomo, I am *not*,
I repeat *not* a *chazan*.' Shlomo patted my arm reassuringly, as
if to soothe me, and then said gently but with great conviction, 'Trust me, Brother Ken, you'll be a *chazan* within a year.'

"Several months later, I got a phone call from a Rabbi in
L.A. who was a total stranger to me. 'I'm looking for a *chazan*
for my synagogue,' he said. 'Someone highly recommended
you for the position, Mr. Ellis. I hear you boast talent, charisma,
and a magnificent voice—ingredients that certainly make for
a successful cantor. Could you please come down for an
audition?'

"Once again, I protested that I was *not* a *chazan*, but the
Rabbi persuaded me that there was no harm in trying out.
Needless to say, I got the job.

"As a result of getting this position, my whole life turned
around. At the synagogue where I was now cast as *chazan*, I
met the woman who eventually became my wife, and discov-

ered a community and network of friends. A vehicle for my talents had been finally found, and the added plus was the new spiritual dimension to which it led. Within the short span of a few months' time, everything changed for me.

"I promised myself that the next time I would see Shlomo, I would tell him everything that had transpired since our last meeting, but sadly, I never got the chance.

"I've often wondered about the role Shlomo played in my metamorphosis. Did he possess psychic powers, or had he himself arranged for me to get this job? Had he infused me with an optimistic spirit I previously lacked, which somehow changed my luck for the better? How *had* he turned out to be so uncannily prophetic?

"With Shlomo gone, I guess I'll never really know the truth. But one thing's for sure: if it had not been for that fateful encounter with him in the school corridor, I definitely would not be a *chazan* today."

———

Rivkah Haut's watchdog "Ginger" was an integral part of her family for over twelve years. A playful and devoted companion to Rivkah's little girls, an alert and conscientious guardian of the Haut household, Ginger had but one minor flaw: she hated men.

"It was the most amazing thing," Rivkah recalls. "Here was this sweet, gentle, loving playmate of my daughters, who became transformed into a rabid, vicious, foaming-at-the-mouth animal whenever she saw a man. The mysterious metamorphosis never failed to astound us. In the presence of men, Ginger grew unrecognizable. She would growl menacingly and move to attack. Even my own husband, after twelve years of living together, couldn't get within three feet of Ginger without fearing for his life. This scenario occurred all the time with men, without exception. The one and only time Ginger deviated from this behavior was when Shlomo Carlebach came to my home for a two-day visit.

"I was expecting Shlomo, but had forgotten to lock up

Ginger, as I normally did before a man entered the house. When Shlomo suddenly appeared in the kitchen (my daughter had responded to his knock, unaware that Ginger was loose), my heart sank. I was sure that Ginger would surface momentarily, and accord Shlomo the usual warm welcome she typically reserved for men.

"Sure enough, within a minute Ginger materialized in the kitchen, and stood stock still looking across the room at Shlomo. What happened next I will never forget; I was so startled by what occurred that I think a dish slipped out of my hand and crashed onto the floor.

"What happened was this: Ginger didn't snarl, snap, or bark. She didn't growl or arch her back, readying for attack. Instead, she bounded over to Shlomo eagerly, her tail wagging swiftly and enthusiastically, her throat emitting low, husky whimpers of delight. She acted as if she were warmly welcoming a long-lost friend, but Ginger and Shlomo had never crossed paths before. Shlomo bent down to pat Ginger, talking gently to her, and they developed an instant rapport, becoming fast friends. Indeed, during Shlomo's two-day stay at my home, Ginger stayed at his side constantly, rapturously devoted and completely in his thrall.

"In the twelve years Ginger lived with us, this situation never happened before and it didn't happen again. I'm not mystically inclined, but the experience with Shlomo and Ginger defied rational explanation. I can only suggest that there was something so singular and extraordinary emanating from Shlomo Carlebach that the dog, with its special animal sense, picked it up and responded to it immediately."

———

"In the 1960s Prospect Park Day School embarked upon ambitious and extensive outreach efforts to the nonreligious Brooklyn Jewish community. I was one of hundreds of children whose parents were convinced of the importance of a Jewish education and was consequently enrolled—with trepidation but hope—in the coeducational Orthodox yeshiva.

"One of the ways the principal attempted to open our hearts and kindle our spirits was by introducing us to the music and stories of Rabbi Shlomo Carlebach. Shlomo Carlebach was in fact a ubiquitous and major presence at Prospect Park Day School; he constantly performed at school assemblies, *chagigas* (parties) and other events. He made a real impression upon us, and helped infuse our lives with religious fervor.

"The first time I saw him, I was seven years old. He was performing at a special school assembly where one of the scheduled highlights—in addition to his own performance—was a raffle drawing for a religious prize. All of the students' names were placed on strips of paper in a huge barrel and Shlomo was assigned the honor of blindfoldedly fishing out the name of the winner.

"When his name was called to do the honors, Shlomo slowly walked towards the stage, but not before stopping to greet, hug, and kiss each child he encountered. As he approached the area in which I was sitting, I impulsively ran out of the aisle and intercepted him.

"I don't think there was a single child in the school present that day who coveted the religious prize more than I. Coming from a home where religious artifacts were a rarity, I literally ached for that prize. Emboldened by the intensity of my need, I shamelessly grabbed Shlomo Carlebach's sleeve and tugged hard. 'Please, please,' I implored him, as he lowered his head to kindly gaze down at me, 'please pick my name from the barrel. I want the prize sooo badly. It means so much to me . . . I beg you, please!'

"Probably overcome by the magnitude of my passion, Shlomo stood studying me for a long moment. Then, his eyes twinkling, his face creasing into a broad grin, he smiled at me impishly and solemnly declared: 'Don't worry: it's yours.'

"Then he ascended the stage, was duly blindfolded, plunged his hand into the barrel with hundreds of papers and promptly pulled out my name."

———

A s someone who was heavily involved in the music world, I had the opportunity to travel to Russia several years ago to participate in the Moscow Peace Festival—the biggest rock and roll concert in that country's history.

Although I come from an assimilated Jewish family (seven generations of Reform Jews) and was not actively involved in the Jewish community in any sense, some strange impulse led me to the local Jewish Federation before my departure. I told various department heads there that I was planning a trip to Russia, and asked if I could be of assistance to refuseniks in Moscow. Delightedly taking me up on my offer, they inundated me with shopping bags of religious paraphernalia, and instructed me to distribute them to various activists whose names appeared on a list.

In Moscow my schedule was extremely hectic, and I waited eagerly for a day off. When a break was finally scheduled, the President of Geffen Records asked me to join him and several others on the MTV tour of Moscow, but I declined, explaining that I had more important things to do. "Like what?" he challenged me. "Like deliver stuff to Jewish refuseniks," I answered airily, with a toss of my head. He stared at me in shock. "I didn't know you're Jewish," he said slowly, "You don't look Jewish . . . what's your Jewish name?"

He had me stymied. My parents were so thoroughly assimilated, that they had never considered giving me a Jewish name, which is quite the norm, even in the most peripheral of Jewish homes. "I-I don't have a Jewish name," I stuttered in awkward embarrassment. "Well, we can't have a nice Jewish girl from L.A. traipsing off to Jewish refuseniks without a Jewish name," he teased. "Why don't you choose one right now?"

My embarrassment grew more pronounced. "I don't know any Hebrew. I wouldn't know how to begin to choose a name!" "Okay," he winked conspiratorially, "Let me tell you something, I'm Jewish, too. So I'll do the honors and right here . . . on the spot . . . bequeath you with a nice Jewish name. You know what," he said playfully, "I'm going to call you *Hatikvah* (The Hope—which is the name of Israel's national anthem)." "Why *Hatikvah*?" I asked in interest. "Because that's the only Hebrew word I know!" he laughed.

From that moment on, I was no longer known as Jill, but

addressed in great hilarity by members of the company as "Hatikvah." Maybe it was because I was suddenly conferred with a Jewish name or maybe it was because of my poignant encounters with the refuseniks who were sacrificing so much for the sake of their religion, but something dormant in my soul began to stir. Maybe it was because for the first time in my life, I had defined myself as a Jew. Whatever it was, when I returned to L.A., I was not the same person who had left.

Over the course of the next several years, I slowly gravitated closer to my heritage, taking classes, participating in *shabbatonim* (sabbath encounter weekends) and gradually moving with a more committed Jewish crowd. And, of course, Shlomo Carlebach—whom I soon met, once I committed myself to traversing this spiritual path—ultimately proved a great spiritual influence.

During this time, I began to meet many people who would ply me with the oft-repeated question, "So . . . What's your Jewish name?" And always, I would answer with pride: "*Hatikvah*." Sensitive souls would look at me in bewilderment and dismay, but the more tactless would just laugh out loud. "There's no such Hebrew name as *Hatikvah*" (The Hope), they'd chortle. "Whoever gave you that name made a terrible mistake; the correct name is *Tikvah* (Hope); the extra *Ha* (The) is grammatically incorrect."

When I became engaged to my husband Michael a year ago, who also returned to Judaism primarily through Shlomo Carlebach, we agreed to ask him, as "our Rabbi," to officiate at the *tnoyim* (official engagement ceremony). I was told that during the ceremony my Hebrew name would be chanted out loud, and it was then that I tearfully told Michael that I had never been formally bestowed with a Hebrew name. "Don't worry," he reassured me, "I'll ask Shlomo to give you a name sometime during the ceremony itself."

A day before the *tnoyim*, Shlomo and I met to discuss the issue of the name. "You know, in Judaism, name-giving is taken very seriously," he said. "The name that is formally bestowed upon you is thought to confer a certain destiny. Do you have a particular name in mind?" he asked gently. "*Tikvah*," I instantly replied, deciding not to disclose the reasons for my choice or the embarrassing faux pas that had preceded it. Shlomo stroked his beard thoughtfully, and looked at me for a long time. "Hmm . . . let me mull this over," he suggested.

The next day, I met Shlomo at the door to the synagogue. "Listen, Jill," he said softly. "You gave me a name yesterday, but do you mind if I add something to it? Do you trust me?" "Of course I trust you, Shlomo," I replied, "You're my Rebbe."

"It is my great honor," Shlomo announced to the crowd during *laining* (reading of the Torah portion of the week) "to now formally give Jill a Jewish name. *Gevalt!* (It's awesome!) Can you even begin to imagine what it means to come from a Jewish family that doesn't think it's important to give their child a Jewish name? And how that daughter has now found her way back to her heritage? And do you know what a *gevalt* it is that she wants *mamesh* so badly her own Jewish name, and has waited so long for this day?

"When I think of Jill, I am reminded of the great possibilities of Jewish renewal for each and every one of us. There are tens of thousands of Jills in the United States today, whose souls are yearning, whose hearts are crying, and they don't even know *nebech* what it is they're hungering for. We have to reach these hungry *neshomos*. It's an awesome task, but when I look at Jill, I know it can happen, because it's happening every day . . . it happened with her.

"And that is why I am giving her the name *Ha-tikvah* . . . the Hope!"

"I had never shared with Shlomo—nor anyone else for that matter—the story of my original Hebrew name," recalls Jill. "I can only say, when I heard him formally announce my name as *Hatikvah*, instead of *Tikvah* as I had originally requested, I got goose bumps all over. When I confronted him after the ceremony and asked why he had given me this name as opposed to the other, his only response was a mysterious smile."

—————

"Everyone always thought Shlomo was talking to them personally when he gave a class or delivered a lecture," reflects Naomi Mark. "He had a remarkable way of approaching subject matter that seemed applicable to everyone's situation and pertinent to the space they were currently occupying. Yet sometimes his extraordinary ability to tune in to people's lives seemed to go beyond the realm of the 'normal.' In fact, sometimes his ability seemed uncanny.

"One night, I was in Shlomo's shul, attending a *shiur* (class) he was giving, when a woman—a stranger to us 'regulars'—entered quietly and slipped into a back seat. It was Shlomo's MO to greet everyone personally with a hug and a kiss, but as he was already in middle of delivering his remarks, he merely smiled pleasantly at the woman, called out something like 'welcome to our humble shul' and continued for a minute discussing the subject at hand. Suddenly, with absolutely no explanation or apology, he broke off in middle of his remarks and abruptly switched to an entirely different topic. Totally out of context, with no relation whatsoever to the evening's theme, he began reciting an *Ishbitzer* story about a woman who's been raised as a Catholic. When she's well into middle age, she stumbles upon the startling discovery that she's actually Jewish. All of us looked at each other in alarm. The story was inappropriate and not connected in any way to his previous remarks. What was the matter with Shlomo?

"As we worriedly considered his bizarre behavior, the stranger in the back seat began to cry. Shlomo jumped up from his seat and ran towards her side. He put his arm around her and asked, 'Darling, what's going on?' 'It's *me* you're talking about,' she sobbed. 'That story just happened to me! I was adopted by Catholics who raised me as one and they never told me that my natural parents—both my mother and father—were Jewish. They just told me the truth today. What a coincidence that you should tell that story just now.'

" 'Yes,' Shlomo agreed amiably, 'isn't it?'

" 'I was passing by your synagogue and came in on impulse. I was just about to leave when you started to recount the story. Now that you know my situation, maybe you could give me some guidance?'

" 'Absolutely!' Shlomo smiled."

———

After Shlomo Carlebach gave a concert in Efrat, Israel, one night, he was accosted by Rabbi Dr. Abraham Twerski, who bears the unusual distinction of being the only hasidic psychiatrist in the world.

"Shloimala," the psychiatrist shook his finger accusingly at Rabbi Carlebach. "Those melodies you sing . . . you know they're not yours!"

Shlomo, who was known as the father of contemporary Jewish music and had in fact composed thousands of original Jewish songs during his lifetime, responded with a startled look.

"What do you mean, they're not mine?"

Rabbi Dr. Twerski answered, "During the period of the First and Second Temples, the *Leviyyim* (High Priests) were known for the exquisite, spiritually uplifting melodies they composed. They were said to be so moving and extraordinary that whoever heard them was elevated to a different realm. After both Temples were destroyed, the melodies vanished. It was all very mysterious. No one could retrieve them, and no one could remember them. They were hopelessly lost. Together with the Jewish nation, they had gone into Exile, and no longer could the Jewish people uplift themselves spiritually through song.

"So, Shloimala, whenever I hear your compositions, I cannot help but recognize the truth. Those melodies are not yours—they belong to the *Leviyyim* of the Temple. God is bringing them back to the Jewish people through you. Your melodies are so spiritually rich and exalted. What other explanation could there possibly be???"

8

The Child Is Father
of the Man

"So everybody knows that nebech *what happened after the War was this: Some* yidden *lost faith completely and left* yiddishkeit *altogether, but others became* mamesh *ten times* frummer *than before! So how do you explain this? Open your hearts. The answer, my sweetest friends, is: what did they remember from their childhood? Did they remember a childhood where* mamesh Shabbos *was so sweet . . . where their tatta and mamma kissed and hugged them . . . where their* cheder Rebbe *gave them candies, a tender* glet *(pat) on their cheeks and told them they were special? If that was the childhood they remembered, they said, after the War: 'Ah, it's been so long since I had the warmth and beauty of* yiddishkeit, *ah, I remember it so well, I want it back in my life now!' So these people returned to their heritage, and became fire, fire! But what about those who remembered a different childhood? What about those for whom Shabbos was only 'NO!', whose parents tormented them, and whose Rebbes punished them with a strap? 'Hey,' they said, 'I've been beaten down to the ground, slapped around enough in concentration camp. I don't want that in my life ever again!' And these are the ones who* nebech *left* yiddishkeit *because they never saw its beauty and never knew its joy. So, my sweetest friends, always remember: everything begins in childhood!"*

—RABBI SHLOMO CARLEBACH

"*N*isht Vaat Foon Der Boim Haut Gefalen Dos Appela* (The apple doesn't fall far from the tree) is a favorite Yiddish expression that is particularly apt in Shlomo Carlebach's case," reflects Rabbi Itzik Aiesenstadt of Jerusalem, Israel. "Both his parents were extremely pious and philanthropic people, but his mother's saintly deeds were not as well known to the general public as his father's. The following story illustrates dramatically the level of *chesed* (acts of loving-kindness) Shlomo Carlebach's mother attained in her lifetime.

"In 1980 I attended an Alumni Dinner of *Ponovezher Yeshiva* (one of the most renowned yeshivot in Israel today, attracting the crème de la crème of Talmudic scholars, similar in status to Harvard or Yale). During the course of the dinner, which was held annually, it was traditional for the *Rosh Yeshiva* to cite the names of the yeshiva's benefactors who had died that year. Accordingly, midway during the program, Rabbi Abraham Kahaneman rose and, with great sadness, began to announce the names of those who had passed on. When he reached the name of 'Rebetzin Paula Carlebach'— Shlomo Carlebach's mother, who had died that year—he paused.

" 'I now have to let you in on a big secret,' he told the audience, 'one that may truly surprise you. I have to stop and pay special tribute to Rebetzin Carlebach, because the *yeshiva* owes its very existence to her.

" 'Before the Second World War, when the *yeshiva* was located in Poland, it was in dire financial straits and on the verge of collapse. I was sent to Germany to fundraise.

" 'In Germany, I stayed at the home of the Carlebachs, who were famous for their *hachnosos orchim* (hospitality to strangers) and *gemillat chasodim* (acts of kindness). During my first meal at their home, I poured out my heart to Rabbi Carlebach, while his Rebetzin, from a discreet, modest distance, listened intently. I brokenheartedly told Rabbi Carlebach that the yeshiva was literally bankrupt, and that we would be forced to close our doors if I were unsuccessful in raising a vital sum in Germany. The wealthier Jews of this country were our only hope. Rabbi Carlebach was shocked and distressed to learn of the celebrated yeshiva's misfortunes. Deeply engrossed in our conversation, neither he nor I noticed that in the midst of my bombarding him with the yeshiva's litany of woes, his Rebetzin had vanished!

" 'It was only some time later that we realized that the Rebetzin was no longer sitting at the table, nor could she be found in the kitchen—her most frequent habitat. Rabbi Carlebach seemed unconcerned by his wife's disappearance, and suggested that perhaps a neighbor had called on her for some help. She would show up soon, he suggested, and there was no reason for alarm.

" 'When she finally did appear, it was with a huge, battered suitcase that she lugged with difficulty into the dining room, panting heavily. "Reb Kahaneman," she announced excitedly, "your problems are over."

" 'The suitcase was filled and overflowing with cash!

" 'While her husband and I had conversed, Rebetzin Carlebach had quietly gone to her jewelry cases, her safe, and her silver cabinet, and collected all the valuables in the household. These she had taken to the local pawnbroker, and pawned them all for cash. She gave the entire amount to me for the *Ponovezher Yeshiva*, and thus the *yeshiva* was saved.' "

In recounting this story, Rabbi Aiesenstadt reflects, "People often debate about whether altruists are born or made. In Shlomo Carlebach's case, the answer is both! It's clear that even as a very young child, he was blessed with an altruistic spirit. But it's also clear, as this story vividly demonstrates, that both his parents helped mold and shape this spirit to a significant degree."

"Can you imagine a ten-year-old child giving up his bike for four years?" asks Shulamith Levovitz, Shlomo Carlebach's older sister, and last remaining sibling. "Yet this is essentially what Shlomo did for me when I was fifteen.

"We lived in Vienna before the War, and it was an era when differences between boys and girls were more pronounced. My parents kept my twin brothers—Shlomo and Eli Chaim—home all day to be privately educated by Torah scholars and pedagogues; in contrast I was sent for secular studies to the local Gymnasium, which was an hour away by foot.

"Perhaps it was because they viewed bike riding as immodest for a girl or perhaps it was because they viewed it as dangerous, but my parents adamantly refused to give me a bike to ride to school. I campaigned vigorously for a bike, to no avail. I felt the situation was grossly unfair, given that my twin brothers each had one of their own.

"One day I confided my distress to Shlomo. 'It's so hard for me to walk back and forth to the Gymnasium each day. By the time I get to school, I'm exhausted!' I bitterly complained. 'Take my bike!' he offered instantly. 'You can have it . . . gladly!' 'But Sh-Shlomo,' I stammered, 'I don't get back from school until around 3:00, so you wouldn't have the bike for most of the day.' 'It's all right, don't worry about it,' he assured me. 'But you use your bike when you have your study breaks . . . won't it be a hardship for you not to have it around?' I worried. 'You need the bike more than me,' he answered with a full heart. 'I insist you take it!'

"But how to circumvent my formidable mother? Shlomo and I choreographed an artful deception that was so thoroughly successful, that she never suspected a thing.

"Mornings were no problem because my mother was still asleep when I left for school. It was my return home that was the major obstacle. Sneaking into the house with the bike would be a tricky business; what if she just happened to be near the front door as I came in? For various reasons, leaving the bike outside was also problematic. What to do? Shlomo concluded that the best plan was for him to meet me every day at 3:30 at a certain street corner near the house. He then took the bike, pretending he had been riding it all along, and I tailed behind him by several minutes. He brought the bike back into the house, and somehow, my mother never noticed that our arrivals occurred within the same general time span.

"I never found out how Shlomo always managed to escape from the house at precisely the required time, because between both my parents and his tutors, he was under constant surveillance. Yet, there was never a period that Shlomo didn't show up at precisely the time we agreed upon. It didn't matter if it was raining, snowing, or sub-zero temperatures. For four years, ten-year-old Shlomo was unfailingly at the corner at the exact time patiently waiting for me to come home from school. He basically turned his bike over to me for four years, until I graduated Gymnasium at the age of eighteen.

"And the most amazing thing is—especially considering that he was all of ten when we first worked out this arrangement—that he never made me feel this was a sacrifice. He made it seem like it was the most natural thing for a ten-year-old boy to do. Sixty years later, his full-hearted 'Gladly!' still rings in my mind."

"Everyone used to marvel at Shlomo's extraordinary respect for all people," reflects Shulamith Levovitz. "People wondered from whence it came—who in the family, they often asked, taught Shlomo to be so reverential and loving?

"Both my parents were in fact unusual in the level of the *gemilat chasodim* (good deeds) and *hachnosas orchim* (hospitality) they performed, but there was one particular scenario involving my father that impressed itself upon Shlomo's mind, and which he often recounted as one of the examples that had inspired him through the years.

"As Chief Rabbi of the province of Baden ba Vien in Austria, my father, Rabbi Naftali Carlebach, had occasion to play host to many local and visiting dignitaries, and our large house was always filled with many eminent guests. The less fortunate—handicapped people, beggars, the mentally incompetent, widows, orphans—also made their way to our doors in a steady stream, petitioning my father for all kinds of help, financial and otherwise. When these people appeared on our doorstep, my father would engage in a ritual that little Shlomo watched with utter fascination.

"As soon as my mother would announce to my father—usually sitting in his study—that such and such petitioner was at the door, my father would retire to his bedroom, change into a freshly laundered shirt, put on a tie, and don a formal jacket. He would then proceed with a little toilette, running a comb through his hair and beard, and checking himself once, twice, in the mirror. When his preparations were completed and my father was satisfied that his appearance was impeccable, he would then move toward the dining room, where the humble petitioner was by now comfortably ensconced with a plate of pastries and a glass of tea.

"Not once did my father ever deviate from this routine. Considering the amount of respect he demonstrated toward these supplicants, is it any wonder that his son Shlomo became who he did, the type of person who would plead with his followers, 'Please, *chevra*, when a panhandler approaches you, always open your heart and give generously. And if you can only give a dollar, apologize! But never *chas v'sholom* give anything less, because that, my friends, is an insult and degradation!'

"Shlomo didn't have to be taught how to treat people. He just had to sit back and watch my parents in action. Thank God he absorbed these lessons exceedingly well!"

———

When the Nazis invaded Austria, Shlomo's father, Rabbi Naftali Carlebach, called a family conclave to discuss a plan of action. Soon, all the family members were assembled in the dining room, everyone that is but eleven-year-old Shlomo. Repeated calls for the missing twin elicited no response, and Shlomo's mother, Rebetzin Paula Carlebach, was dispatched by her husband to search for him throughout the family's spacious quarters.

A few minutes later, she returned breathless, her eyes wild with fear. "Shlomo's nowhere to be found," she reported in tense, clipped tones. "I've looked for him everywhere. He's definitely not in the apartment. Oh, my God," the Rebetzin clutched her heart in consternation, "he must have gone outside!"

Shlomo had been repeatedly warned by his parents that it was no longer safe to venture outdoors. He was a boy of unusual courage and determination, but he was also a respectful and obedient child, who almost always honored his parents' wishes. Could he have flagrantly flouted their authority this time? And for what purpose? Why would he have left the relative safety of their home? Where could he have gone?

Rabbi Carlebach instructed the family to disperse and check all of the rooms a second time. Once again, they returned emptyhanded. Shlomo had not been found, and panic was beginning to set in.

Suddenly, Shlomo's twin, Eli Chaim, had an inspiration. "I know where he is," he shouted triumphantly. "Follow me!"

"So Shloimala," said Rabbi Carlebach softly, as he ascended to the top of the house and spied his eleven-year-old son from a distance, "what are you doing on the roof?"

"*Tatta!* (father)" Shlomo turned to Rabbi Carlebach with burning eyes, "the roof is that much closer to *Hashem* (God).

"And at a time like this, shouldn't we try to be as close to God as much as possible?"

9

The Rabbi of Love

"You are born into the world, but until someone comes to you and tells you 'I love you,' you are still a stranger in the world. You feel like a stranger—you're not really here yet. The Zohar Kodesh says to take a stranger and invite him into my house means I am giving this person even more existence than God gave him. God sent him into this world and he is here, but this is not real existence yet. The real existence of a person has to be given by another person. What happens if I drink a Coca-Cola and make a brocha over it, what am I doing to the Coca-Cola? I am giving it existence! Because so far the Coca-Cola was like nothing. Or imagine I say hello to a little dog. What am I doing to the dog? I'm giving him existence. He was like a little stranger walking around in the world. And you know what my sweetest friends? Even God needs us to give Him existence! God is there, but until I really say He's there, He's not really there."

—RABBI SHLOMO CARLEBACH

They had all been rigorously trained in their youth to view the performance of *mitzvot* (good deeds) as the highest good, but they really couldn't help it. When this particular *shnorrer* (Jewish panhandler) walked through the portals of the yeshiva *Erev Shabbos* (Friday afternoon, before the Sabbath), they fled!

In the 1940s the *bochurim* (young men) of Lakewood Yeshiva were accustomed to their building being occasionally used as a sanctuary by society's rejects. Indeed, they welcomed the opportunity to do *chesed* (acts of kindness), which they performed earnestly and warmly for these lost souls. But this particular man . . . there was no way to put it politely . . . just stank! The odor was so venomous, in fact, that as soon as he entered the big yeshiva hall, one by one by one the *bochurim* slunk out of the room and disappeared until there was no one left but young Shlomo Carlebach.

Whether Shlomo was repulsed by the man's offensive smell one will never know. Perhaps, because by virtue of his own spiritual nature, he only inhaled the divine and sweet fragrance of every person's soul, he never even noticed. But whether he steeled himself against the fumes or was oblivious to them, he alone approached the *shnorrer* and gently said, "My sweetest friend, welcome! Let me give you something to eat, to drink. Please come up to my room and spend *Shabbos* with me."

The man was mentally confused, so Shlomo gently led him to his room, where he helped him bathe. As he disposed of the man's ragged and foul-smelling clothes, his glance fell on his bed, where that morning he had carefully prepared and laid out the one and only *Shabbos* suit he owned.

That *Shabbos*, everyone in Lakewood Yeshiva talked about how resplendent and proud the *shnorrer* looked, buffed, polished, gleaming in Shlomo's *Shabbos* suit. Young Carlebach, on the other hand, was dressed in his everyday clothes (an unheard of thing to do on *Shabbos*, a veritable desecration), but, nonetheless, he also shone . . . with the light of love!

———

L ate one night two years ago, I, a Bobover hasid from Boro Park, made a wrong turn off the highway and found myself in Harlem. Confident that I would quickly be able to get back on the main road, I was not too concerned about my accidental detour until my car's engine sputtered and died on a dimly-lit, garbage-strewn street. Leaving the safety of my car to open the hood, I saw three menacing figures step out of the shadows, moving quickly toward me. The street was deserted, and there was no one to call for help. I was sure that my end was near and began to recite the *Shema*. As the three young toughs threateningly encircled me, a fourth man—a big, burly, sinister-looking fellow—appeared out of nowhere, and yelled at the three, "Hey, brothers! Wait a minute before you attack this Jew. I want to ask him a question." The man approached me, looked me up and down, pulled a small white rectangle out of his pocket, shoved it under my nose, and asked, "You know this guy?" My heart palpitating, I looked down at the rectangle and saw to my shock a business card that read: RABBI SHLOMO CARLEBACH. "Yeah, sure I know Reb Shlomo," I stammered in confusion. "He's the greatest, the holiest." The tough looked at me appraisingly for a minute, and then smiled. "Relax," he advised and then turned to the other three and yelled at them to beat it. "He's a brother; leave him alone, he's under my protection now."

As the three men moved away in disappointment, the fourth man helped me fix the car and told me this story: "I'm helping you, because Shlomo always helped me. Years ago, I was among the homeless who live in cardboard boxes in Riverside Park near Shlomo's shul. I used to live on the handouts I got begging. The biggest handouts were always from Shlomo Carlebach. Every time I met him he gave me no less than $10 of his money, and five minutes of his time. He always greeted me with a 'Hey, holy brother, what's happening?' salute, and tried to help me change. I've never forgotten him, and I carry his card with me always. It's because of Shlomo Carlebach's love that I saved your life tonight!"

———

"Thirteen years ago, my husband was scheduled to undergo serious surgery at Mt. Sinai Hospital. The operation was considered so risky that doctors told us they couldn't guarantee he would survive it, but we had no recourse but to take the chance.

"During this time, my sixteen-year-old son had begun a sporadic telephone relationship with Shlomo Carlebach, whom he had never met but whose music he adored. Neither I nor my husband had ever made Rabbi Carlebach's acquaintance, but we knew that he had been warm and accessible to our son.

"On the eve of the operation, my son called Shlomo and asked for a favor. 'My father is undergoing surgery tomorrow and he loves your music. Would you come play for him a few minutes before he goes in?' 'It would be my honor,' Shlomo agreed instantly. 'Just tell me where and when.' Because the operation was scheduled for 11:00 A.M., my son asked Shlomo to come at 10:30. Shlomo promised to be there, and my son proudly told his older siblings about this great coup. They were not impressed. 'You are so naive!' they mocked him. 'Do you really think the famous Shlomo Carlebach is going to drop all his plans and come running to Mt. Sinai Hospital just because a young boy whom he doesn't even know asked him? He'll never show up!' 'You're wrong!' my son vehemently insisted. 'You don't know what kind of human being he is. He'll be there for sure.'

"The next morning, my son strode up and down the hospital corridors, waiting impatiently for Shlomo's arrival. At 10:35 he had still not arrived, and a sad, dejected look began to replace the eager one on his face. His siblings began to taunt him rather cruelly. 'So where's the famous singing Rabbi?' they teased.

"Just then Shlomo's celebrated figure burst into view as he breathlessly hurried down the corridor, guitar in hand. 'So sorry I'm late,' he panted, as he hurtled into the room. As he greeted my husband warmly, a nurse came by to announce that the surgery had been postponed one hour. 'Wonderful!' exclaimed Shlomo. 'That will give us more time together.'

"Before beginning his concert, however, Shlomo first honored the other two occupants in the hospital room, a black man and a Hispanic. He walked over to each of their beds, introduced himself, asked their names, inquired about their health, kibitzed around with them, and just made them feel great. Then he gently closed the door and played to my husband for one full hour.

"The risky, delicate operation was an unqualified success. We were deeply grateful for God's intervention and the surgeon's skill and expertise. But we also firmly believed that one of the major reasons my husband lived was because he went to surgery singing!"

———

"I was an American college student studying at The Hebrew University in Jerusalem when the Yom Kippur War broke out. I was petrified. My friends, my family, everyone I was really close with and could turn to for strength and comfort were thousands of miles away. I felt very much alone.

"Like many other Americans who found themselves caught in the middle of another country's war, I tried frantically to return home. Frustrated by my inability to make any headway with local travel agents, I decided to take matters into my own hands and go directly to the airport. There I found the place swarming with hundreds of hysterical American tourists, all scrambling to find a way back to the States. My heart sank. I didn't know at this point whether there were any flights still departing Israel, but what were my chances of getting a ticket anyway? I felt greatly discouraged.

"Suddenly, in the distance, I saw the familiar figure of Rabbi Shlomo Carlebach, guitar in hand, striding purposefully across the room. Instantly, my spirits rose. I knew Shlomo from New York, and just seeing a familiar face amidst the chaos of the airport made me feel better. And, if planes were still flying, I was certain Shlomo could use his 'protectzia' to help me get on a flight.

"'Shlomo! Shlomo!' I screamed as I dashed across the room. His face lit up and he gave me one of his holy hugs. 'I'm so glad to see you,' I shouted. 'I'm all by myself and I've just been absolutely terrified. Are you leaving on the next flight? Can you get me a ticket, too?'

"As I rambled on, his brows knitted together in a perplexed expression until his face suddenly cleared. 'Oh,' he said in dawning realization, 'you think I'm leaving the country. My sweetest sister, I'm so sorry, you're making a mistake. I just arrived.'

" 'But Sh-Shlomo,' I stammered in confusion, 'don't you know there's a war going on?'

" 'My holy child,' he answered heartily, 'that's exactly why I came.'

"Subsequently, he calmed me down and convinced me to stay. He promised he would take me under his wing and take care of me until the war was over. 'But Shlomo!' I protested, 'I'm sure you'll be performing for the soldiers at top secret military bases. I won't be allowed to come.' 'Don't worry, I'll get permission,' he replied with the utmost confidence. And, incredibly, he did.

"Thus I was hurled into the most amazing adventure of my life! Throughout the entire Yom Kippur War, I found myself in the unique position of accompanying Shlomo Carlebach on his exhausting, exhilarating, and frenetic tour of Israel's military bases, where he performed for thousands of soldiers. We traveled in army jeeps, with a military escort, often with our eyes blindfolded. We were on the very threshold of the war and at great risk, but Shlomo's *bitachon* (faith in God) was so great it proved contagious. In fact, I felt calmer with Shlomo at the army bases than I had felt in the relative safety of Jerusalem.

"During this time, we encountered at the bases many famous Israeli entertainers who were also devotedly performing for the soldiers day and night. But there was one major difference between their performances and Shlomo's. While the soldiers were not obligated to attend the performances of these entertainers—only if they wanted to—the Israeli army had made Shlomo's concerts *mandatory*.

" 'Why are you requiring the soldiers to attend Shlomo Carlebach's concerts, and not any of the other entertainers?' I asked an officer. 'Isn't it obvious?' he rejoined. 'For the morale, my dear, for the morale. No one can uplift the soldiers' morale better than Shlomo Carlebach!

"'You see, my dear, the big difference between Shlomo and the other performers is this: The other performers *entertain* the soldiers, but Shlomo Carlebach *inspires* them!'"

———

"The summer before he died, Shlomo asked me drive him to an afternoon gig in Cherry Hill, New Jersey, approximately two hours away by car. When I asked him what type of audience he was performing for, he was very vague. I knew Cherry Hill has a relatively large Jewish community, but almost all of Shlomo's concerts are scheduled for the evening. Because afternoon concerts were rare, I was puzzled by the time frame. But when we got to the address he gave me, everything became clear.

"Our destination proved to be a 'Y' Camp for Special Children, our audience a group of six children with Down's Syndrome. I said nothing, but silently bit my lips in fury during the entire concert. When Shlomo's performance was over and we were headed back home to New York, I exploded.

"'Shlomo!' I fumed. 'I cannot believe you would waste your time like this! The whole day practically gone . . . and for what? A man like you— the Jewish counterpart to Jerry Garcia—should be performing to packed houses in Madison Square Garden, not to six retarded children in Cherry Hill, New Jersey!'

"Shlomo looked pained at my outburst. 'Faygela,' he remonstrated gently, 'you're wrong! If I caught one Jewish spark today . . . if I reached even one Jewish soul . . . then believe me, the trip was worth it! It was well worth it!'"

———

"Shlomo Carlebach was notorious for almost always being late. Wherever he was supposed to be—whether it was a concert he was performing at or a wedding where he was officiating, you could count on him eventually appearing, but not without him first being delayed, detained, and very overdue!

"One time, I was present at a wedding he was scheduled to officiate, and, as typical, he arrived late. The father of the groom was visibly upset. Even though he was already an hour late, Shlomo was still dilly-dallying around, saying hello to people along the way, hugging some of them, walking slowly in a very relaxed manner towards the direction of the *chupah* (wedding canopy). Suddenly, the father of the groom marched up to him and chastised him angrily for his tardiness. 'You're late! Do you realize that, Rabbi? You're late!' he virtually screamed. Shlomo handed his guitar to a woman standing nearby and seized the man with both hands and shouted back, 'It's never too late! Never!' The groom's dad remained standing in place for a long while with tears streaming down his cheeks. Shlomo hadn't 'yelled back' at the guy; he had given him a life message that had obviously hit home. Later, he danced with Shlomo liked a *hasid* who had just found a *Rebbe*. But it was a life message that hit me, too, at that time and remains with me to this day."

"The first time I saw Shlomo Carlebach," reminisces Aryae Coopersmith, "was at San Francisco State College, back in 1965. I stumbled onto the scene. There was this hippie Rabbi, standing on the campus quadrangle surrounded by hundreds of students, playing his guitar, singing, dancing, jumping up and down, and everyone was joyously singing with him, and I felt awestruck. At a certain point, Shlomo stopped singing and asked everyone to join hands. 'You know *chevra*,' he proclaimed, 'if everyone in the whole world would hold hands and love each other, I swear *mamesh* those hands would go straight up to heaven!'

"Standing there in a circle with hundreds of my fellow students, with Shlomo and his guitar in the center, our hands really did reach to heaven. God's oneness was real. So many of us standing in that circle had been searching desperately for this experience, in Eastern religions, in psychedelic drugs. What I learned from Shlomo that day is that for me, the path to God's oneness was not about exotic adventures in faraway places. It was already there, in the history of my own family and own people, in the roots of my soul."

———

" A s one of Shlomo Carlebach's managers in Israel, I had grown accustomed to his largesse of hand and heart. In charge of his finances, I found myself continuously doling out huge sums of money to him, which seemed to mysteriously vanish within a matter of minutes. Often, he would ask me for several hundred dollars, which he would stuff carelessly into his pockets, and then quickly dart out the door, muttering that he had to go somewhere. About an hour later, he would reappear, and, with a twinkle in his eye, wheedle me for more. I would exclaim in astonishment, 'But Shlomo, I just gave you $300 not less than an hour ago.' Shlomo would look a little sheepish and I would sternly ask, 'OK, where did you just come from?' 'The *Kotel* (The Wailing Wall, where all the beggars of Jerusalem congregate) my friend, the *Kotel!*' Sighing, I would hand over more money, and he would disappear again! This scene, with my variations thereof, was repeated countless times.

"One particular day in 1963, however, really stands out as an example of his enormous heart. It was the morning of *Purim*. The previous night, Shlomo had been featured at a standing-room-only concert at the old Mugrabi Theatre in Tel Aviv and was paid 3,000 American dollars. In 1963 that was a princely sum, especially when translated into shekels. When I saw Shlomo stuff the cash into his pockets with a broad grin on his face, I began to worry. 'Shlomo,' I urged nervously, 'please give me the money. Let me take care of it for you.' He shook his head so adamantly that I began to worry even more. During our entire trip back to Jerusalem—where we were based—I begged him to allow me to safeguard the cash. My pleas fell on deaf ears, and I began to wonder what he had in mind for *Purim*. Before we returned to our hotel, he asked me casually if I could accompany him on an expedition the following morning. Believe me, whatever it was I envisioned happening on *Purim* with Shlomo didn't even come close to the stunning sequence of events that unfolded the next day.

"On the morning of *Purim*, right after the reading of the *Megillah*, Shlomo hired a small truck and driver and asked to be taken to *Kikar Tzion* (Zion Square), which at that time boasted a pastry shop, a grocery store, and a wine merchant, all adjoining each other. '*Gut Yom Tov!*' he jovially greeted the merchants as we entered their stores. 'If it's not too much trouble, could I please buy your entire stock?' The merchants blinked. 'It's a *Purim* joke, right?' one said with a sneer. 'No, my sweetest friend, I'm serious. How much do you want for everything in the store? Name a sum and it's yours!' Soon, a long procession of gleeful merchants and their sweating helpers were loading cartons of groceries, pastries, and wines onto the truck, while dumbstruck passersby stopped and stared. When the truck could contain no more, Shlomo beamed happily and said in a tone of immense satisfaction, 'Now we are ready to deliver *shalach monos* (the gift baskets of food and wine that are traditionally given on *Purim* to both friends and those in need).'

"Inside the truck, Shlomo pulled out several sheets of paper that someone had given him, listing the neediest cases in Jerusalem. All day long we journeyed to the most impoverished sections of the city, distributing parcels of food to indigent families. Each time we entered someone's home, Shlomo also pulled out a wad of cash from his pocket and as he shook the *balabos'* (head of the household) hand, tactfully slipped him the money. We must have delivered *shalach monos* to close to 100 families that day.

"In middle of all this, Shlomo discovered that his cousin had been taken to the hospital and told me that we had to go there immediately. 'But what about the *shalach monos*?' I asked. 'We'll deliver some to the hospital patients,' he said, grabbing his guitar.

"In the hospital, Shlomo's presence caused a stir. *Purim* is probably the most joyous of all days in the Jewish calendar, but one of the saddest ones to spend alone in a hospital. After Shlomo had spent considerable time with his cousin, he visited the other patients. He went from hospital bed to hospital bed, delivering *shalach monos*, chatting, telling stories, sharing jokes, and giving each patient a private concert of his own. From one of the beds, someone shouted: 'Hey, Shlomo, how about a new *niggun* (melody),' and Shlomo obliged by making up, then and there, on the spot, his famous *Yomin Usmall Tifrotzi*. Soon, everyone was singing and clapping along with him, and those patients who were ambulatory began dancing in the hospital corridors.

"When we left the hospital, there were a few more hours left until sundown, so we resumed our deliveries to Jerusalem's poor. By the end of the day, Shlomo didn't have a *shekel* left to his name.

"This is how I spent *Purim* 1963 with Shlomo Carlebach. Never before and never after did I so authentically and wholeheartedly fulfill the *Purim mitzvah* of *matanos l'avyonim* (gifts to the poor) as I did that day."

"During a break between prayer services at the Carlebach Synagogue on Yom Kippur, I was at Shlomo's side when a young, earnest man approached him in a state of abject misery. 'Shlomo!' he bitterly complained. 'I don't know what to do. I'm fasting so hard, and I'm *davening* so hard, yet I have the uneasy feeling that my *teshuva* (penitence) has not been accepted by God.'

"Shlomo studied the man thoughtfully. 'But brother Avrum*!' he exclaimed, 'throughout the whole *davening* I didn't hear you once give me harmony. Don't you know you can sing and dance your way into the Book of Life?

"'My dear friend, if all the *davening* and fasting in the world doesn't help . . . use your feet!'"

———

$\mathbf{I}$t was the right prayer at the wrong time.

"*Shema Yisroel Hashem Elokeinu Hashem Echad!*" (Hear O Israel God is our Lord, God is One) the woman's voice proclaimed the liturgical passage loudly, once, twice, three times, shattering the silence of the synagogue.

Congregants looked at each other uneasily. They were just about to begin the recitation of *brochos* (blessings), which appears early in the morning prayer services. However, the woman who had just unobtrusively slipped into the Carlebach Shul, and was in fact a stranger, was chanting a prayer that appears much later in that day's liturgy. She was clearly out-of-sync.

Carlebach congregants were used to the uncommon happening in their synagogue, but the woman's dissonance was puzzling. Usually, new *baalei teshuva* (returnees to Judaism) or visitors to the synagogue who were unacquainted with the prayer service would make valiant attempts to follow it, mouthing the unfamiliar words in soft, stumbling, hesitant tones. Or, they would ask fellow congregants for help finding the proper place in the prayerbook. Or, they would remain respectfully silent. This woman, however, had done none of the three. Without embarrassment, with no awkwardness whatsoever, she just kept repeating over and over again in a loud, booming voice, "*Shema Yisroel Hashem Elokeinu Hashem Echad!*" A few of the female congregants tried to approach the woman to offer their help, but her eyes were clenched shut, and she was swaying back and forth with such intensity that they felt reluctant to intrude. So they shrugged their shoulders, returned to their siddurim, and continued their prayers.

"*Shema Yisroel Hashem Elokeinu Hashem Echad!*" It was now becoming difficult to focus. Everyone's attention was riveted on the woman, whose chanting of the prayer pierced the synagogue, as it slowly escalated into a shrill, high-pitched scream.

From across the room, Shlomo Carlebach approached the

woman and placed his arm around her shoulders. "My sweetest friend," he said gently, "what's going on?"

The woman began to cry. "This is my first time in a synagogue in more than fifty years," she sobbed. "I had no intention of going into a synagogue, but as I was walking by, I saw your open door and something pulled me inside. The last time I was in a synagogue, I was three years old.

"You see, I was a small child during the war, and my parents hid me with Gentile neighbors in Hungary, good Christians. They promised they would come back to get me after the war ended, but they never did. They died in a concentration camp. I was raised as a Christian and removed from everything Jewish. I've been fairly happy with my life, but there's always been a void in my heart. Today, when I saw your open synagogue door, I knew I had to come in.

"Everyone was praying and I wanted so badly to pray, too! I felt something in my soul stirring. But I can't read the Hebrew alphabet—my family was taken away when I was only three, and the only prayer I remembered from my childhood was the *Shema*, which is why I repeated it over and over again. It's the only prayer I know."

Shlomo hugged and kissed the woman and turned to make an announcement to his congregants. "*Chevra*, I want everybody to know that this woman's *kavannah* (fervor and devotion) puts us all to shame! Do you think it's the words that God cares about? It's the cry from the heart that opens the gates more than anything else! I have no question in my mind that if God is moved by anybody's prayers here today, it's not mine and it's not yours, but this woman's, whose simple *Shema* is the holiest prayer of all. We are indeed privileged to have her in our midst, and may we all be *zocha* (merited) to one day reach this level of heartfelt devotion."

"Although he was unconventional, Shlomo Carlebach was strictly halachic (adhering punctiliously to the letter of Orthodox Jewish law)," remarks Jeannette Goldberg of Los

Angeles, who participated in many 'Shlomo' events on the West Coast and was a member of his entourage. "However, because the homes of many of the people who hosted his events frequently were not, it was always interesting for me to watch how he navigated—with sensitivity and tact—the problem of dubious *kashruth* (observance of Jewish dietary laws). In all the years I knew him, I never once heard him outright ask a host if he kept a kosher home. He would never do or say anything to embarrass someone or put them on the spot. At the same time, he was also fearful of hurting their feelings by refusing the food they had lovingly prepared and insistently urged upon him. So, if he were unsure of the person's level of *kashruth*, he would circumvent the problem by using the following tactic:

"Before the unsuspecting hosts even had a chance to try to serve Shlomo some food, he would preempt them by gazing with rapt interest at the table—usually laden with delicacies—and exclaiming enthusiastically, 'Sweetest friends, that awesome-looking cake on the table is *mamesh* a *gevalt!* I never saw such a delicious-looking cake.' He would then shake his head mournfully. 'Why is it that when I come to L.A. I can never find cakes like that? Maybe you can do me the biggest favor in the world and give me the name and address of the bakery where you bought this cake, so when I have a chance I can go there too?' If the hosts would then obligingly name a kosher bakery that Shlomo was familiar with, he would, much relieved, partake of the food. If, however, the hosts would mention a nonkosher bakery, Shlomo would appear relaxed and unconcerned, but immediately divert their attention by asking for something they could indeed give him. 'Oh, my sweetest friends, could you do me the biggest favor in the world and get me a drink of water; I'm so thirsty!' When they would return with the glass, he would noisily and enthusiastically gulp the water, saying ardently, 'Thank you so much, my sweetest friends. You don't know, you *mamesh* saved my life, I was so thirsty.' The unsuspecting hosts would then beam in gratification, thrilled to have performed such a tremendous service for the famous Shlomo Carlebach. He would continue to divert them in this way, until they got to a point where they simply forgot to urge him to sample their food.

"I accompanied him on dozens of such expeditions, and each time he successfully managed, with great skill and sensitivity, to avoid embarrassing his hosts. To do this was sometimes quite a feat."

"It was 2:00 in the morning at a Ruach *shabbaton* (a Jewish spirituality weekend at which Shlomo Carlebach was a featured attraction), and my soul was in torment. My marriage was on the verge of collapse and so was I. I had decided to leave my husband. Shlomo had often said that we always reach into our deepest place of truth in the middle of the night. So, knowing that I need clarity before making a major life decision, I sought out my Rebbe. I knew he would be awake.

"I poured out my heart to him and then was still. His take on the marriage was brief but incisive. 'Does your husband build you up? Does he make you feel good about yourself?' I looked at Shlomo with surprise. It was an area I hadn't touched upon in my litany of woes, yet it was probably one of the most relevant issues of our marriage. I began to cry uncontrollably. All it had taken was Shlomo's two-sentence question to point up the true heart of the problem, and I immediately knew with conviction: the marriage was wrong, the marriage was finished. The truth could no longer be denied.

"Going to my Rebbe not only gave me an answer that resolved my immediate problem, but delivered a life lesson as well, one that I have since adopted as my motto: 'Help people grow, empower them to become the best that they can be.' But this message in effect also epitomized Shlomo's own personal mandate, the true essence of his mission on earth, the flavor of all his social transactions . . . to see everyone as divine— and act accordingly!"

———

"Have you ever been in the company of someone who lavishly extolled the virtues of a muffin?" asks Mendel Sternhull. "Then you didn't have the pleasure of accompanying Shlomo Carlebach to a coffeeshop for breakfast!

"We were in a small, dingy restaurant, presided over by a sour-looking cook/proprietress, who doubled as waitress as well. I am not usually aware of or affected by other people's looks, but this woman was so unusually homely, almost offensive looking, it was hard not to notice. Her attitude was unpleasant as well. She served our order of muffins and coffee with a brusque manner that bordered on the rude, and frankly, I was relieved when she left our table to return to the counter. After one taste of the muffin, however, Shlomo waved her back.

" 'Yes?' she asked sullenly, her hand on her hip in a confrontational stance, braced for trouble.

" 'My most beautiful friend,' Shlomo said gently. 'Are you by any chance the person who baked this muffin?'

" 'Yeah, I am, what about it?' she asked curtly.

" 'I just want you to know that this is the most delicious muffin I have ever tasted in my life!'

"A hint of a smile now began to form on the woman's lips.

" 'Thanks,' she said, preparing to move away.

" 'And I also want you to know . . . that I have eaten muffins all over the world, but none come close to this one.'

" 'Well, thanks again,' she said, less abruptly, her mouth beginning to pucker into a more visible smile, but still obviously itching to return to her place at the counter.

" 'And *mamesh* I have to thank you because I was so hungry, and you did me the greatest favor in the world by so expertly baking this muffin, which is surely a Taste of the World to Come!'

" 'Well, gee, thanks a lot,' she said, smiling broadly, now firmly rooted to the spot. 'It's very nice of you to say. Most people never comment when the food is good; you only hear from them when they have a complaint!'

" 'Oh, but no one could ever complain about your food; *gevalt* it has to be the greatest in the world. Tell me, what special ingredients do you put into this muffin to make it so delicious?'

"By now, the surly woman had actually begun to beam, and she launched into an extensive discussion of her cooking and baking techniques. Shlomo listened intently, and when she had finished, continued to heap her with accolades. He was very specific with his compliments too: the muffin's texture was not only light and airy, it was buttery and fragrant as well, and she had expertly warmed it to just the right degree of temperature. As I listened in mingled amusement and astonishment to the great spiritual leader sing a virtual paean to a muffin, I turned to look at the woman. Up until now, my eyes had been fastened on Shlomo, and I hadn't noticed the change that had swept over the woman. When I turned to gaze at her, I was taken aback.

"The homely woman was no more. A few minutes with Shlomo had done the trick. She was transformed. She had become beautiful.

"From Shlomo, I learned many things, but foremost among them was *hakoras hatov* (acknowledging the good) and how to give compliments. And maybe one day, if I really work hard at my growth and have the *zchus* (merit) to evolve to a certain level, I'll also be able to acquire Shlomo's blessed ability—to sing hymns to muffins and make people beautiful."

———

Douglas Jablon, Director of Patient Services for Maimonides Hospital in Brooklyn, had returned home from his grueling stint at the busy facility and was unwinding after a difficult day, when the phone rang. It was close to 11:00 P.M. and he was startled to learn that the caller was a nurse, Millie,* from the oncology ward.

Millie, a West Indian from Jamaica, was stern, serious, and tough-minded—in short, formidable. She brooked no nonsense and was one of the hospital's most level-headed employees. Douglas was therefore surprised to hear an unusual quaver in her voice when she spoke.

"Douglas, I'm sorry to bother you so late, but there's a hippie in David Rosenthal's* room singing and playing the guitar! I don't know how this man got into the room, or how he snuck past security downstairs. He seems to have appeared out of nowhere. But the point is, he's in the room singing, and David is singing along with him, so what should I do?"

David Rosenthal, a young man dying of brain cancer, was the darling of the oncology ward. His sweet and gentle manner had endeared him to every member of the staff, while his courage had won their admiration and respect. Hordes of people visited him daily, and many rules had been broken on his behalf, but Millie was a strictly by-the-book type. Yet now she seemed uncertain, almost helpless. Her usual strong resolve appeared sapped, gone. Jablon's curiosity was piqued. "I'll be right over!" he promised, struggling into his clothes.

When Jablon arrived at the oncology ward some thirty minutes later, he found Millie slumped in a chair, shaken, trembling, misty-eyed. "Douglas, I swear I tried to get that hippie out of David's room," she cried. "But every time I moved to chase him away, something . . . I don't know what it was . . . just stopped me. It was the weirdest thing . . . I just couldn't budge! There's something about that hippie I've never encountered before. He has this . . . this aura!" And then Millie dissolved into tears.

Gently, Douglas opened the door to David's room, and quietly observed the scene.

All along he had his suspicions, but he had to come to the hospital to see for himself. Sure enough, there was the beloved figure of Rabbi Shlomo Carlebach, strumming his guitar, softly singing his soulful melodies, as tears slowly trickled down his cheeks. And there was David, sitting up in the bed but with his eyes closed, swaying to the music, transported to a different world. A world where suffering, affliction, and pain were vanquished, a world where peace and serenity reigned instead. The inner world of the spirit to which Shlomo Carlebach's melodies, veritably Shlomo Carlebach himself, always spoke.

———

She wore a hood and a face mask, rambled incoherently, and was unquestionably mentally disturbed. During a taping of my ecumenical cable television show, which that day featured Shlomo Carlebach, the young woman—a member of the studio audience—had stood up to ask him a question, and had been babbling gibberish for well over fifteen minutes. As she droned on, everyone else in the audience became increasingly tense and irate. The cameramen gesticulated wildly to each other, and signaled frantically to me. Distressed, I tried to catch Shlomo's attention, but he was listening so intently and respectfully to the woman that I was unable to make eye contact. He was in fact *shukeling* (swaying back and forth) in his seat and nodding his head solemnly at the woman's endless stream of unintelligible jabber. Thus encouraged, the woman just wouldn't stop.

I felt disappointed and frustrated. Everything had gone extremely well during the hour-length show until the woman had raised her hand. I myself never would have even considered calling on the bizarre-looking woman attired in a hood and face mask, but Shlomo hadn't hesitated. Now, more than a quarter of an hour had passed and been wasted, and the show was effectively ruined. Finally, I couldn't contain myself any longer, and leaned over to Shlomo to whisper in his ear. "Shlomo, it's time to cut this woman off. Clearly, she's not well, and she's destroying what's left of the program."

Shlomo whispered back, "My sweetest friend, I cannot cut her off. I don't want to hurt her feelings. Obviously, she needs to express and unburden herself. She needs to be treated with kindness and with love."

"But Shlomo," I argued, "her outlandish behavior is

demolishing everything you carefully tried to build from the beginning of the show."

"Let me tell you something, Art," he rejoined. "I would much rather that she demolish me than I demolish her!" With that he returned his attention to the woman, *shukeling* and nodding with as much intensity as before, until the hour was finally up.

And deeply humbled and ashamed, I said to myself: "I am a Catholic and Shlomo Carlebach is a Jew, but he's certainly much more of a 'Christian' than I am!"

———

Everyone was always welcome at the Carlebach Synagogue. Young and old, rich and poor, educated and illiterate, hasidic and assimilated, professional and blue collar; the spectrum of souls attracted to Shlomo's warmth and charisma was wide and variegated, an eloquent testimonial to his largesse of spirit.

Among the pilgrims seeking refuge under Shlomo's wing were individuals who needed particular love, attention, and kindness, individuals whom others might call emotionally unstable. Seeing the divine spark in every person he encountered, Shlomo never differentiated between souls or created hierarchies. Every human being he encountered was worthy of his attention, respect, and love.

There was a particular individual who had emotional difficulties, and Shlomo fell into the habit of taking long walks with him in an attempt to soothe and reach him. He put hundreds of hours into this man, but the difficulties persisted. A year before his death, while giving a class in his synagogue, Shlomo was rudely interrupted by this same man, who began to heckle him in loud and abusive tones. Every time Shlomo tried to make a point, the man challenged him in an obnoxious way; every time Shlomo tried to return to the text at hand, the man would jump up and create a disturbance. Curses and epithets attacking Shlomo spilled in torrents from the man, who was wild and frenzied. A few people sitting near Shlomo urged that the man be ejected, but Shlomo shook his head no, absolutely not. Instead, Shlomo closed the text he was teaching, and attempted respectfully to engage in a serious discourse with the man about his intellectual objections.

The man, however, was beyond intellectual discourse. After several failed efforts to engage the man both rationally and emotionally, Shlomo finally said to him, "My dearest, sweetest friend. I want to ask your forgiveness publicly. I know why you're so upset. It is my fault; I have failed you. I am so sorry, please forgive me. I didn't take enough long walks with you."

"Two years ago, I had the privilege of accompanying Shlomo Carlebach on a shopping expedition to Brooklyn. The Jewish Holiday of *Succoth* (Feast of Tabernacles) was fast approaching, and Shlomo was in quest of the most beautiful, the purest, *essrog* (citron) in the whole world. Not content with the quality of *essrogim* available in Manhattan, Shlomo decided to take off for Boro Park.

"Now everybody knows that Shlomo was, to say the least, not a materialistic man. His apartment could only be described as spartanly furnished, his clothing modest, if not downright threadbare. He gave all of his money away, and his only real possessions were the 10,000 *seforim* (holy books) he owned. Shlomo was thoroughly indifferent to material things, but when it came to objects used in religious rituals . . . ah, that was an entirely different matter altogether. In this realm, Shlomo became totally transformed. He became zealous, passionate, and very discriminating. Thus, *essrog*-shopping in Boro Park, which I thought would be a quick adventure, became instead a rather long and laborious affair.

"We walked up and down Thirteenth Avenue (Boro Park's main shopping thoroughfare) for hours. Shlomo stopped at all the *essrog* tables lining the street, inspecting and probing each and every *essrog*. Slowly and deliberately, he would turn the *essrog* this way and that, scrutinize it for flaws, smooth his fingers over it, even inhale its fragrance. Then, he would sadly shake his head 'no'—this was not the perfect *essrog* of which he was in quest—and gently return it to its original place on the table.

"What impressed me the most about Shlomo that day was the gentle, loving manner in which he rejected the imperfect *essrogim*. Each time he rejected one, he gave it a soft and lingering kiss before tenderly returning it to its original site, and murmured a few words of apology. This ritual was repeated hundreds of times that day. Not a single *essrog* was rejected by Shlomo Carlebach that didn't receive the imprint of his apologetic lips. He had such a sensitive spirit that it was hard for him to even rebuff the life force of a humble citron.

"As I watched Shlomo select his *essrog* that day, I realized that I had learned a profound moral lesson. Shlomo gave more honor and respect to an *essrog* than most people ever accord each other.

"After many hours of trekking all over Boro Park, Shlomo finally found an expensive *essrog* that he rapturously pronounced perfect. Joyously, he lifted it up high for everyone to see, and addressed the surging crowds that had mobbed him as he strode along Boro Park's streets. 'My sweetest friends,' he shouted in elation. 'I want to bless everyone here that your lives should be as pure as the *essrog* I hold in my hand!' The crowd cheered and clapped and, utterly exhausted, I accompanied him home."

———

"When I was going through a bitter, long, and drawn-out divorce, I turned to Shlomo Carlebach for help. We spoke on the phone constantly, and I derived tremendous strength and courage from his wisdom and kindness. One day, he told me gently that he was going on a trip to Israel and would be gone for two weeks. 'Oh no!' I shrieked, feeling desolate and abandoned. 'How will I ever manage without you?' 'Holy sister Esther,' he reassured me, 'don't worry, I won't forget you for a minute, you'll hear from me continuously.' 'Sure, sure,' I laughed sarcastically. 'You're gonna be in Israel and I'm gonna hear from you continuously.' 'I won't abandon you,' Shlomo repeatedly softly, 'I give you my word.' Although I was skeptical that Shlomo would fulfill his promise, he did indeed live up to his word. Every single day, for the next two weeks, I got a long distance phone call from Shlomo Carlebach in Israel. He didn't miss a day."

———

"During the last years of his life, former '60s radical and Yippie leader Abbie Hoffman moved into my neighborhood, and we became friendly," recalls Art Stabile, a Catholic layman and Director of the International Student Hostel in Manhattan. "He was interested in the work I was doing with students and often stopped to chat with me whenever we met. He also liked to give me feedback on a cable television program I was producing and hosting at that time, 'The International Student Hostel Hour,' which was mostly devoted to ecumenical dialogue. His comments were always intelligent and thoughtful.

"The day after a segment was aired featuring Rabbi Carlebach, I was standing outside the Hostel when Abbie rushed over in a state of excitement. 'That Rabbi you had on the show yesterday,' he said with rare animation, '. . . he's something else! He's awesome. I never met a Rabbi like that. Tell me about him.'

"I obligingly told Abbie about Shlomo's ministry for lost Jewish souls, and his selfless devotion to his people. I told him that many years back we had struck a deal whereby I would send him all the Jewish students who passed through my place. Even though the student guidebooks all describe my facility as Catholic-run, one out of three students who come here ironically turn out to be Jewish. Long ago, Shlomo had said to me, 'Look, Stabile . . . be fair. If a Jewish kid comes to your hostel . . . do me a favor. Before you try to introduce him to Catholicism, first send him to me.' During the thirteen years I knew Shlomo, I had sent approximately 300 Jewish kids his way.

"Abbie was undeniably intrigued. 'Rabbi Carlebach stirred something in my soul,' he confessed wistfully, 'something that I thought was long gone. Could you introduce me to him? I must meet him.' Abbie seemed pensive and melancholy that day, and I grew alarmed. Feeling a sudden, strange sense of foreboding, I decided to telephone Rabbi Carlebach immediately and ushered Abbie into the Hostel to wait while I made the call. Unfortunately, the Synagogue secretary told me, Rabbi Carlebach was overseas and wasn't expected to return for some time. Abbie left, sorely disappointed.

"A few days passed and I encountered Abbie once again. I was distressed to see how dramatically he had deteriorated in such a short period. He looked weird and disoriented. I tried to talk to him, but he was barely coherent. His bizarre behavior unnerved me, and left me with a feeling of doom. Several hours later, he was dead, a suicide.

"Over and over again, I thought about how much he had wanted to meet Shlomo Carlebach. I have often felt, with the greatest of conviction and sincerest of regret, that if the meeting had indeed taken place, Abbie Hoffman would surely be alive today."

———

"Several years ago, I fell ill with a serious disease and despaired of recovering. I had met Shlomo once at a class or a concert, and as he was wont to do with everyone, he scribbled down my name and number on a scrap of paper with the assurance that he would definitely give me a call. One night, I was particularly hard hit by the bleakness of my situation, feeling desolate, lonely, and very hopeless. I tossed and turned on my bed in agony, when suddenly the phone rang. I looked at the alarm clock on my bedtable and saw that it was 4:00 A.M. Who could possibly be calling me at that hour? I picked up the phone and whose voice do I hear but Shlomo's! 'Holy sister Stephanie,' he begins without further ado. 'What's your favorite flower in the whole world?' 'Roses,' I answer, thinking what a bizarre man, what a strange call. 'Then I want you to know,' he says, 'I am sending you right now, this minute, 2,018 roses. Do you see their beauty, do you smell their fragrance?' he asks urgently. 'Yes, Shlomo,' I answer patiently, 'I see them, I smell them.' 'Good! Now what I want you to do in your lifetime is slowly give the roses away—one at a time—to other people who may need them. But be sure to keep at least one for yourself.'

"After that phone call, I completely recovered from my illness and am busy presenting individuals all over the world with imaginary roses."

"Ten years ago, my younger brother, stricken with an inoperable brain tumor, lay in a coma in a hospital in Manhattan. Although he had never met Shlomo Carlebach, my brother adored his music and owned many of his tapes and records. With the dim hope of eliciting some kind of response from my brother, I called Shlomo and asked if he could possibly come to the hospital for a visit. Day after day, Shlomo came loyally to the hospital room with his guitar, playing his songs to my brother. My brother never did recover, but I can never forget the sight of the celebrated Shlomo Carlebach, legendary singer and composer, valiantly playing to a lifeless form in a hospital bed."

Several years ago on a Friday night, Shlomo was taking one of his long walks along Manhattan's West End Avenue, when he was attacked at gunpoint. "Give me all your money or I'll shoot you on the spot!" screamed the mugger, waving his gun. Undaunted by the gun, Shlomo smiled good-naturedly at the man, and patiently explained, "Holy brother! *Nebech*, I feel so sorry for you that you have to do this. I would really like to help you out, but I'm so sorry, it's *Shabbos*, and I don't keep money on me. If you will please come tomorrow night to my synagogue after the Sabbath is over, I will be glad to give you whatever you need." After hearing Shlomo's gentle words, the mugger lowered the gun and let him go. Something about Shlomo must have convinced this mugger that Shlomo would not trick him or turn him in, because *Motzei Shabbos* (sundown, when the Sabbath is over), the mugger kept the appointment and showed up at the shul. Shlomo gave him some cash and the man vanished, never to be seen again.

———

"One *Shabbos* afternoon, a severely handicapped fellow with a grotesque disability walked into the Carlebach Shul while *Shalosh Seudos* (the third sabbath meal) was in progress. As soon as he entered, Shlomo exclaimed, '*Mamesh* such a privilege . . . my best friend is here. Brother, I'm so happy to see you. You know, you're the highest of the high, the holiest of the holy! Please come join us at the table.' Most of us tried to emulate Shlomo's example by warmly welcoming the man, but a few of us not on his *madreiga* (level) couldn't help but avert our eyes. Truth be told, it was hard not to be repulsed by the man's deformity.

"As soon as the man was seated, Shlomo turned to him and said, 'Would you please honor us with some *divrei torah* (words of Torah)?' And the man, who on top of everything else, also had a speech impediment, nodded and began to expound on that week's Torah portion.

"The man *nebech* stuttered, and his words were barely comprehensible. People started fidgeting in their seats, finding it difficult to concentrate. The moment Shlomo saw this, he lifted up his chair, carried it to where the man was sitting, sat down next to him, lowered his head, and put his ear up to the mouth of the man so he could catch every word. *Shukeling* intently, Shlomo listened with rapt attention until the man was finished.

" 'Thank you so much my sweetest friend,' Shlomo said. 'Your words are so precious to me!' "

"My experience with Shlomo Carlebach consisted of exactly two isolated incidents—eleven years apart—but both encounters were momentous," reflects Amy Haviv of Atlanta, Georgia. "In fact, I will never forget either of them for as long as I live.

"When I was a sophomore in high school in 1969, I was asked to perform a solo in a musical cantata for my confirmation at a Conservative temple. This performance marked my debut both as a singer and guitar player. Because the cantata would be commemorating a religious milestone, I felt it was only appropriate that I perform a Hebrew song and listened to several Jewish records until I found the one that made my soul sing. It was 'Am Yisroel Chai (the people of Israel live),' Shlomo Carlebach's famous anthem for the Soviet Jewry movement. I fell in love with his music, and it became an integral part of my repertoire.

"In 1972 I underwent a spinal fusion operation and was confined to my bed with a full-body cast for a complete year. During this time, I felt depressed, uncomfortable, and isolated. Even though my prognosis was excellent, it was still hard to keep my spirits up.

"One night, Shlomo Carlebach came to Scranton to perform at a synagogue concert, and several of my friends went to see him. At the end of the concert, they stayed to talk with him and in conversation mentioned that they had this friend with scoliosis, who was in bed for a year. 'Oy, nebech, I must go see her right away!' Shlomo exclaimed and ran with a scrap of paper bearing my number to the nearest phone booth to give me a call.

"Twelve o'clock at night, the phone rang, and my mother, frowning angrily at this rude invasion, picked it up with a scowl. 'Absolutely not!' I heard her shout. 'It's totally out of the question. She has an early morning appointment at the hospital tomorrow, and she needs her sleep. No, it can't be done!' And she angrily banged down the phone.

" 'So what was that all about?' I asked. 'Can you imagine the nerve,' she fumed. 'Some nutcase says he wants to come over right now and meet you.' 'Did he give you a name?' 'Shlomo Carlebach,' she answered nonchalantly, not knowing him from the man in the moon. 'Shlomo Carlebach!' I shrieked in despair. 'Oh no, I don't believe this; you turned away Shlomo Carlebach! You have no idea what he means to me.' And tears slowly started to trickle down my face, as I brooded over this missed opportunity.

"About twenty minutes later, there was a furious pounding at the front door. It was around midnight, and my mother was alarmed. 'Now who could that be?' 'May I come in?' Shlomo Carlebach beamed, walking confidently towards my bed, followed by an entourage of fans. 'Amy!' he exclaimed familiarly, as if we were old buddies. 'Sorry it's so late, but I just had to meet you!' Shlomo apologized to my mother, who was not placated and was wringing her hands nervously. 'So,' he turned to me with a broad smile and a mischievous glint in his eye, 'Where's your guitar?' 'Wh-what do you mean?' 'I hear you're *mamesh* an awesome guitar player and singer; I want to have the privilege to play and sing with you.' 'You gotta be kidding,' I looked at Schlomo in disbelief. 'Haven't you noticed my full-body cast?' 'No problem!' he merrily rejoined.

"Very gently, I was rolled over on my stomach, face down, hanging over the bed sideways. (By now, my mother was wringing her hands full force.) A chair with my guitar was brought over to where my head was hanging, and I leaned over. Thus situated, I was able to pluck the chords and play with Shlomo until 2:00 in the morning, having the time of my life. I was no longer conscious of the shackles of my body cast, because my spirit—unfettered by Shlomo's love and music—was floating heavenward! The next morning, when my doctor pronounced me recovered and removed my body cast, I could not help but think that Shlomo's presence the night before had been an auspicious sign, an omen that new beginnings in my life were about to unfold.

"I never thought that I would see Shlomo Carlebach again, but we were indeed destined to meet a second time in 1983, eleven years after the first encounter. I was now living in Atlanta and heard that he was scheduled to perform in a local synagogue one night. I thought it would be nice to see him again and introduce myself to him in a vertical position! When I arrived at the synagogue, he had not yet begun the concert. He was milling around in the crowd, kissing and hugging everyone, so I made my way over to him, wondering if there was any chance he would remember me. 'Amy!' he shouted exuberantly the minute he glimpsed me. 'This is unbelievable; this is *mamesh* awesome. How are you?' We spoke for a little while and then he asked, 'So where's your guitar?' 'My guitar?' I repeated dully, uncomprehending. 'Whatever for?' 'Because, Amy,' Shlomo answered jovially, 'it would be my greatest honor and privilege if you would please join me on stage. Do you live far from here?' 'I'm about fifteen minutes away.' 'So, please, do me the biggest favor in the world, and go home and get your guitar. I'll wait for you; I won't start the concert without you.'

"So once again, I had the privilege to play with Rabbi Shlomo Carlebach until the wee hours of the morning. Once again, my heart expanded and my soul danced, radiant in his light. And once again, my spirit soared to celestial heights, flying to holy places it hadn't known for years. Everything in fact was almost identical to the first time I met Shlomo, eleven years before. The only real difference was that this time I was in an upright position and would continue to stand tall and proud for a long time to come."

———

At a *Ruach* (Spirit!) weekend, an annual *Shabbaton* (Sabbath get-together) that featured Shlomo Carlebach as its centerpiece, Cecelia Sacharow of Long Island had a strange dream. "Hordes of rough-looking men emblazoned with sinister-looking tattoos all over their bodies were coming and going in the dream," she recalls, "seemingly looking for something or somebody. Suddenly, both Sammy Intrator (Shlomo's manager and assistant rabbi) and Hadassah Carlebach (Shlomo's sister-in-law) appear, making an announcement that whoever wants their tattoos removed should go straight to Shlomo's room. In the dream, the room is a large amphitheater. Shlomo is sitting in a rocking chair, rocking gently back and forth, waving a pen of light over the people as they pass before him, instantly removing all the tattoos.

"As soon as I woke up, I went to find Shlomo to tell him about the dream. He listened intently, and then asked me what I thought the dream meant. The dream wasn't difficult to interpret.

"'The men in the tattoos,' I told him, 'represent the people who come to you with *teumah* (impurity) inscribed in their flesh. Some physicians of the soul attempt to expunge these marks by cutting, operating, and causing overall great pain and suffering, but not you, Shlomo. Not you. You take all these marks away with your sweetness and light, by accentuating the positive and beauty that resides in each soul.'

"Shlomo looked at me for a long moment," recalls Cecelia, "and finally murmured gently, 'Ah, I see you understand . . .'

"Then he lowered his eyes, put his face in his hands, and began to cry."

———

One week after Shlomo Carlebach's death, I met a woman sitting forlornly in his shul, weeping copiously. She seemed so bereft, that forgetting my usual inhibitions with strangers, I was moved to put my arm around her and awkwardly try to comfort her in her grief. After a few minutes, her sobs subsided and we quietly spoke about the terrible sense of loss and bereavement she was experiencing. "How long did you know Reb Shlomo?" I asked her softly, expecting her to respond ten years, fifteen, twenty . . . "Two weeks," she replied, her eyes once again welling with tears. "Two weeks," I echoed in shock and surprise. "Please forgive me, but how is it that you are grieving so profusely for someone you knew for such a short while?"

"Let me explain my situation to you," she replied. "I'm from Denver, fairly recent to New York, with no friends or family here to speak of. I have been feeling isolated and lonely for a long time. I started to explore different synagogues in the neighborhood a few months ago, and only found out about the Carlebach Shul three weeks ago. I had never heard of Shlomo Carlebach before and didn't know he was this famous Jewish personality. An acquaintance merely said to me one day 'Go take a look at this synagogue on 79th and Riverside; maybe it's for you,' so I went. As soon as I entered the shul, this radiant-looking man sitting in the back jumped up and welcomed me warmly. He immediately began to ply me with all kinds of questions and asked 'Do you have any family?' 'No, I'm all alone in the world.' I told him. 'Oh holy sister,' he said, 'then it would be my very great privilege and honor to adopt you!' 'What does that mean?' I asked perplexed. 'You shall see,' he promised, as an elusive sense of belonging enveloped me for the first time in many years.

"The next two weeks were wonderful. True to his word, Shlomo literally adopted me. He invited me to all the *Shabbos* meals, and took me everywhere with him, introducing me to hundreds of people and dozens of new experiences. It was not until he took me *essrog* shopping in Boro Park, however, that I began to realize that this kind, wonderful man was a celebrity! Everywhere we went in Boro Park, people jostled and crowded around him in admiring crushes. 'Shlomo, I didn't know you were a rock star,' I kidded him. Despite his fame, he was totally there for me. For the first time in my life, I felt that I finally had family, someone who really cared about me, and that I belonged. Even though I eventually heard from others that Shlomo had 'adopted' hundreds or even thousands of 'strays' like me during his lifetime, it didn't matter. For the two weeks that I was his 'adoptee,' Shlomo gave of himself to me 1000%.

"You ask me why I'm grieving so painfully for a man I only knew for two weeks. I feel like I've lost my father all over

again. Those two weeks were the most enchanted and wonderful two weeks of my life!"

———

I was on a bus carrying Shlomo and the *chevra* to a concert
stop in Poland, when I happened to overhear the following
lighthearted conversation between Shlomo and another rabbi
on the subject of death and the afterlife.

"You know," Shlomo grinned impishly at his seatmate, a
glint of mischief dancing in his eyes, "I already have a pretty
good idea where I'm going . . .

"But what a privilege!" he twinkled. "It's where I do my
best work!"

They both laughed heartily and turned to a different
topic. But their repartee, rather than amuse, stirred me deeply.
I had accompanied Shlomo on his tours of both Poland and
Russia—a feat duplicated by no other Jewish envoy in the
world—and had constantly been witness to his near-miraculous
impact on people. Embarking on a flight of fancy, I thought to
myself: "You know, if Shlomo would ever—by some angelic
mishap—be accidentally sent to hell, he would unquestionably feel it incumbent upon him to stay. If a heavenly
messenger cried out 'Oops! Sorry, put you in the wrong spot;
let me get you to your rightful place in heaven,' Shlomo
would surely refuse to leave, fiercely demanding, 'Not without my precious friends!' "

Because after all wasn't that truly Shlomo Carlebach's
mission on earth during his lifetime . . . to descend to hell so
that we in turn could be raised to heaven?

10

Never Say No!

"There is a saying that everything in the world is here for the service of God. Somebody once came to Reb Alexander and asked him how can you serve God by being an atheist? Reb Alexander answered that you have to be an atheist when someone asks a favor of you. If you believe in God, then deep down you'll think, 'I'll pray for you, I'll bless you, but I don't have to do anything, because God will do it.' So when someone asks a favor of you, my most beautiful friends, you have to be a complete atheist because God won't do anything for him, you have got to do it!"

"Sometimes someone asks a favor which is very hard. We don't have the faintest idea what a favor the person is doing us by asking! At that very moment God is opening gates for us, giving us a chance to have the image of God on our face again. We have to wash and polish ourselves, but sometimes there is so much dirt that soap and water aren't enough, we have to rub and scratch the dirt off. Even that isn't enough sometimes, and we have to go to a sauna. You have to do a mitzvah on the level of a sauna, burning hot. Sweat it out."

—RABBI SHLOMO CARLEBACH

In the 1970s Shlomo Carlebach participated in a three-day ecumenical conference held at a prestigious university in Boston. He was scheduled to perform his soulful melodies on the opening night of the program, but because of the extraordinary reception accorded him, was asked to return the second and third nights as well. On all three nights, he was introduced by the same master of ceremonies, a prominent assistant bishop, a rising young star in the Episcopalian Church. Shlomo always interspersed his songs with hasidic tales that illuminated a deceptively simple, yet truly profound, insight into the human condition; one of his oft-repeated spiritual teachings was the gentle counsel, "You never know." Shlomo had a large repertoire of stories from which he drew, and on the first night of the program he arbitrarily chose to tell his audience the tale of "Yosele the Miser." This was the story he told:

"Everybody knows that Cracow in the 1500s was *mamesh* bustling with Jewish life. It had a large and vibrant Jewish community, consisting of holy Rabbis, scholars, and saints. But like any other community, it also had its share of colorful characters, amongst them Yosele the Miser—the richest man in town—but, let's put it kindly, not known for his generous ways. For decades the *yiddalach* (little Jews) in town had despaired of Yosele's miserliness. *Mamesh* even in the worst of times during famines, epidemics, and wars, when people begged him for help, he turned them away from his door empty-handed. *Nu*, time passed, and one day when Yosele was very old and near his end, representatives of the Chevra Kadisha (Burial Society) visited him at his home with one final plea for help. 'During your lifetime,' they rebuked him, 'you did not fulfill the *mitzvah* (commandment) of *tzedakkah* (charity), but you still have a last chance to redeem your soul. Give us a large sum of money to distribute to the poor of the town now, and we pledge to bury you. But if you do not give proper *tzedakkah* now, we won't give you a burial at all.' 'I'll bury myself before I give you money!' the miser yelled, chasing the Chevra Kadisha representatives from his home. A few days later, the Miser passed on from this world, and, true to their word, the Chevra Kadisha let his corpse rot for days in his home. Finally, some anonymous soul had mercy on the Miser and quietly buried him in the pauper's field.

"A few days later, a man comes knocking on the Rabbi's door crying 'Please Rabbi, help me. I'm unemployed and I have no money to buy food for my family.' The Rabbi comforts the holy brother and gives him some rubles, and the man leaves. A half hour later, another man knocks on the door with the same appeal. All day long desperate petitioners besiege the Rabbi, until it finally dawns on him that something very strange is going on. Suddenly, all the unemployed men in the Jewish community are descending upon him at once. Can't be coincidence, right? So when the next holy brother comes to the Rabbi, the Rabbi asks him 'Tell me, how long have you been unemployed?' The holy brother says two years. The Rabbi asks, 'Forgive me, I don't mean to pry, but how did you manage until now?' 'Every Thursday night for two years an envelope with money was slipped anonymously under my door. This money was enough to sustain my family for the week. I never found out who my anonymous patron was, but last week the envelopes suddenly stopped coming.' *Oy gevalt!* now the Rabbi *mamesh* sees the light. 'Tell me,' he asks the man, 'did you ever petition Yosele the Miser for help?' The man thinks for a minute. 'You know,' he says slowly, 'when I first lost my job two years ago, I did approach Yosele. At first he was very nice to me, asking me how much I thought I needed each week to sustain my family. But when I told him the amount, he started screaming at me that I was crazy to think he could afford to support me, and he chased me from his home. But come to think of it—I never put two and two together because he acted so mean to me—the envelopes started coming the very next week.' The Rabbi asked every-one who came to him that day for help the same questions and always the answers were the same. They had all once gone to Yosele for help, and after inquiring how much money they needed he had chased them from his home in a terrible rage. But the very next week, the envelopes started coming. And they stopped only with Yosele's death. Nu, so it turned out that Yosele the Miser wasn't a miser after all but a *Tzaddik*

Elyon, the Highest of the High, the Holiest of the Saints, who had practiced the loftiest form of *tzedakkah*, *Matan Beseisar* (hidden charity). The Rabbi commanded the entire community to converge upon Yosele's grave in the pauper's field and beg his forgiveness. And on the tombstone where it was written 'Yosele the Miser' the Rabbi added the word 'Hatzaddik'—the Holy One."

This was the story Shlomo arbitrarily chose to tell the first night of the program. When he walked off stage, he noticed the Assistant Bishop staring fixedly at him, all color drained from his face. Before Shlomo could approach him and ask him if he was ill, he was surrounded by a throng of eager admirers, and when he turned again toward the Bishop, he was gone.

On the second night of the program, the same Assistant Bishop was master of ceremonies again, and before introducing Shlomo, made an unusual request. "Please, Rabbi Carlebach, when you tell a story, could you tell the story of Yosele the Miser again?" Shlomo was taken aback. "I'll be glad to honor any request you have. But please forgive me, isn't this the exact same audience as last night? Wouldn't they rather hear a different story?" The Bishop's eyes beseeched Shlomo. "I beg you to retell the story!" Shlomo found the request a bit bizarre, but he shrugged his shoulders good naturedly and said "If it means that much to you my friend, I'll be privileged to honor your request," and true to his word, Shlomo told the story over again.

On the third and final night of the program, the Bishop master of ceremonies approached Shlomo again and whispered, "Please, Rabbi Carlebach, please retell the story about Yosele the Miser." This time Shlomo lodged a gentle protest. "My holy brother," he said softly, "I want so much to honor your request. But this is the exact same audience as last night and the night before. Don't you think everyone is getting a little tired of the story of Yosele the Miser?" "Please Rabbi Carlebach," the Assistant Bishop replied with an edge of desperation in his voice, "I beg you to tell the story one last time." Once again Shlomo shrugged his shoulders in acquiescence. "Holy brother, if it means so much to you, who am I to deny you?" After the story had been retold the third time, the Assistant Bishop approached Shlomo and said, "Let's go for a walk. I am ready to explain.

"As you know, the Church is my entire life. I have excellent prospects for a promising career within the Church hierarchy, and am in fact considered one of the young leading lights in the Church today. I was raised by devout Christians who groomed me for this life early on. I have never had any question or doubt about my true path and my life has been smooth and untroubled. Until . . .

"A few weeks ago, my beloved mother, who was dying of cancer, called me to her deathbed. 'I know that my time is running out,' she said, 'and I cannot die in peace knowing that I have lied to you about your heritage. I have hidden this secret from you all my life, but now I must tell you the truth. You are not a Christian, you are in fact a Jew.

" 'You see, I was a concentration camp inmate and your father an American soldier who helped liberate the camps. Perhaps it was because I was so starved for affection, perhaps it was because my whole family had been wiped out, and I felt so alone, or perhaps it was because I was so angry at God, but I fell in love with your father. When he proposed to me, he made me promise that I would renounce my Jewish heritage and lead a Christian life. He also made me promise never to reveal the truth about my identity, and to raise any children that would come along as devout Christians. I promised all these things, and all my life I've faithfully kept my promise.

" 'But now as I lay dying and finally search my soul, I know I've made a terrible mistake. I respect your father's faith, but if God ordained you should be born a Jew, you *should* be a Jew! In robbing you of your heritage and aborting God's divine plan, I've committed a grievous sin against you, against the Jewish people, and against myself. Especially because you come from such an illustrious Jewish lineage! You see, we are descendants of a very famous Holy Man, known in Jewish lore as Yosele the Miser. Telling you the truth is my act of repentance. It is too late for me, but it is not too late for you to return to your people and reclaim your heritage. This is my last request, my dying appeal to you:

become a Jew! Become a Jew in the tradition of Yosele the Holy Miser!' After she had uttered these words, my mother clutched my hand feverishly and planted upon it one last kiss. And then she died.

"I walked around in a daze. Not only was I trying to absorb the shock of losing my mother, but also my identity as I had always known it. All the certainties of my life were gone. I didn't know what to do. So I did what I knew best—I prayed to God. And I said to God: Give me a sign. If you want me to return to my heritage, send me a person who will publicly tell the story of Yosele the Miser. And to prove that this is no mere coincidence but that this is in fact providence, the person has to tell the story *three* times. This is my deal with you, God; the die is cast!

"That is why I begged you to repeat the story, to show me that your presence was indeed a fulfillment of the sign. So Rabbi Carlebach, how does it feel to be God's emissary?"

Stunned by the story, Shlomo spent the entire night speaking with the Assistant Bishop, who decided that the best course of action was for him to simply "disappear." His destination, he told Shlomo, would be the only logical place— Israel. He would keep in touch, he promised.

Five years after the fateful encounter, Shlomo received a letter from the Bishop postmarked Jerusalem. "I live in Jerusalem, dressed in the hasidic garb and long *peyos* of my ancestors," the Bishop wrote, "learning Torah full-time. Tomorrow I go under the *chupah* (wedding canopy). I thought you would like to know how life turned out for the descendant of Yosele the Miser, who crossed paths with the man who has made him immortal."

———

"About seven years ago, I was at the Toronto airport, waiting for an early morning American Airlines flight to New York. Judging from the enormous crowd assembled in the waiting area near the gate, the flight was heavily booked. As we were all only too soon to learn, it was in fact, overbooked.

"An airline representative stepped into the waiting area, with a mike in hand, and addressed the crowd, 'We apologize to all of you ticket holders,' he said, 'but there are two people who have medical emergencies and desperately need to get back to New York in a hurry. We are asking for two volunteers to give up their seats for the sake of these people. The next flight to New York is in three hours. We know it is a great sacrifice, and we are sorry to put you in this position. Is there anybody here who is willing to extend themselves to help out these people?'

"One hand immediately shot up in the crowd. 'I'm ready!' shouted a hearty voice. Everybody craned their necks to see the sole volunteer. He rose with his ticket in hand to approach the airline representative. I had already recognized his unmistakable voice, but turned, together with everybody else, to watch him advance towards the ticket counter. It was Shlomo Carlebach.

"Now mind you, this wasn't an El Al flight, nor was it a chartered flight for Jewish travelers. It was a regular American Airlines flight, with mostly non-Jewish passengers. There was no more reason for Shlomo Carlebach to have given up his seat than for anybody else.

"We had all looked uncomfortably at each other and shifted uneasily in our seats when the request had been made. But nobody, except for Shlomo, had volunteered. And rest assured, that out of all of us gathered there that morning, it was Shlomo Carlebach who probably had the most heavily scheduled day ahead and the most compelling need to get back fast. Guaranteed, he had the least time to spare.

"But as he had demonstrated so vividly over the decades in all his social transactions, miraculously, he also had the most time to give."

In the summer of 1982 I served as a counselor at Camp Sdei Chemed, an international Jewish boys camp located in Jerusalem. Late one night I was walking with my campers through

the Old City of Jerusalem, when one of them spied Shlomo
Carlebach across the street. Awed at their proximity to this
celebrity, they acted as any group of star-struck adolescents
would: their mouths gaped open and they gawked at him
shamelessly. Shlomo, who up until then had been oblivious to
the presence of my group, must have felt the intensity of their
stares, because he suddenly turned around, smiled beatifi-
cally, and waved. Then he crossed the street to greet and
embrace us. The boys were thrilled and started whispering.
One of them tugged at my shoulder. "We want you to ask
Shlomo if he would sing a few songs for us now." "Hey, c'mon
guys," I answered, "it's almost midnight and he has his guitar
with him; he's probably just finished giving a concert somewhere and must be exhausted. I can't ask such a favor of him
so late at night." But the boys wouldn't take no for an answer.
They persistently coaxed and cajoled me until I finally caved
in and nervously conveyed their request. My trepidation
proved unnecessary, however, because Shlomo's swift, spontaneous, and jovial "Sure! With pleasure!" dispelled my
discomfort. Right there and then, Shlomo pulled out his
guitar and gave us an impromptu concert for the next two
hours. The combination of the starry Jerusalem sky, the
ethereal slant of moonlight illuminating the ancient walls, and
the soaring, uplifting quality of Shlomo Carlebach's melodies,
made this one of the most transcendent experiences I can ever
recall.

———

Shlomo was the first and only choice. Because Michael
Ozair had returned to his heritage as a result of Shlomo
Carlebach's influence and had met his fiancee at Shlomo's
Moshav as well, it was only natural that he would want him
to be the one to officiate at his *tnoyim* (engagement) in Israel.
Shlomo agreed and a date was set: *Tu B'av*, a particularly
auspicious period in the Jewish calendar for love and mar-
riage, that harkens back to ancient times.

A few days before the scheduled *tnoyim*, Michael received a call from Shlomo. "Holy brother Michael, would you mind very much if we change the date of your engagement ceremony? I know you had your heart set on *Tu Ba'av* because of its historic and symbolic significance, but I find that I'm going to be a little busy on that particular day." Shlomo offered no explanation, and Michael didn't press. It was only much later that he discovered the truth.

"One of the *chevra* who was with him that day told me where Shlomo had been *Tu Ba'av*: conducting a dozen different weddings for Russian Jews all day long. From noon to midnight, Shlomo was on the run, sprinting from halls to synagogues to parks to the Wailing Wall, to lead and perform at wedding ceremonies held in both Tel Aviv and Jerusalem.

"For all his work and all his time, Shlomo didn't charge a *shekel*. But what impressed me even more than his generosity was his great humility. A lesser person would have self-importantly trumpeted his schedule of activities for that day; a lesser person would have seized the opportunity to explain his sudden unavailability. But when Shlomo Carlebach called me to cancel the *tnoyim*, he never told me what he was doing instead. Had it not been for the person who accompanied him on his rounds that day, I never would have known."

———

"I knew that Shlomo played in some pretty weird places, but I wasn't quite prepared for a Buddhist convention!" laughs Stan Fleischer,* as he recalls an incident that took place more than twenty years ago. "Whenever Shlomo was in L.A., he would ask me to accompany him to gigs, where I backed him up with my guitar. Once he called me from the airport and said, 'Stan, could you do me the biggest favor in the world and meet me at such and such address in an hour? Something just came up and I don't want to disappoint these people.' By now, I was used to the impromptu appearances and Shlomo's spontaneity, so the suddenness of the request didn't daunt me. But when I arrived at my destination, I was unnerved by

the sight of hundreds of Buddhists in full regalia filing into
the hall where I was awaiting Shlomo.

"'Shlomo,' I hissed angrily, when his panting figure
hurtled into view, 'what are we doing here? We don't belong
here!'

"'Let me tell you something, Stan. I try never to refuse an
invitation. You know why? For several reasons. First of all, if
somebody invites you somewhere or asks you for a favor and
you say no, you're probably hurting their feelings a little bit,
right? Even if you have the best reason in the world and you
say no gently, it's still no, right? Second of all, if God is
sending me the invitation—because it's really coming from
God, right—then there's a reason for my being invited.
Clearly, God wants me there. And third of all, on a personal
level, for myself, maybe just this minute I need the extra
mitzvah, and God is opening gates. You never know, right? So
don't be upset, Stan, we can do good work here.'

"Thus reassured, I followed Shlomo into the building
and, when our time came, performed the gig. Shlomo did his
usual thing: singing, telling hasidic stories, teaching Torah,
and the Buddhists were attentive and respectful. When the
performance was over, Shlomo was surrounded by Buddhists, who told him, 'Hey, we didn't know Judaism was so
beautiful!'

"'What's your name, brother?' Shlomo asked each one as
they approached. They identified themselves by their Sanskrit
names, but Shlomo shook his head no, that's not what he was
seeking. 'Before you assumed your new name,' he said gently,
'what was your name before that?' 'Oh . . . Katz!' laughed
one. 'Schwartz!' smiled another. 'Rosenbaum!' mumbled a
third, embarrassed. I stood in dazed disbelief at Shlomo's
side, as one by one, almost exclusively Jewish names were
ticked off. Seemingly unruffled by this experience and appearing nonjudgmental, Shlomo gave each one a hug, a kiss,
and his card. 'Hey, brother, give me a call!' he urged one.
'Listen, if you ever happen to be in New York and want to get
together,' he suggested to a second. 'Would you like to taste
Shabbos?' he asked a third. Finally, when we were ready to
leave, one Jewish Buddhist followed us to the door. 'You

know Shlomo,' he said shyly, 'the Jews are a very spiritual people. If there were more Rabbis like you around . . . the Swamis, Yogis, and Gurus would all be out of business!'"

"Everybody knew that Shlomo Carlebach was absolutely zealous and uncharacteristically punctilious when it came to choosing an *essrog* (citron) for *Succoth*. His forays into Boro Park to *essrog* shop were legendary, and had become something close to an event in the Brooklyn neighborhood every *Erev Yom Tov* (eve of the holiday). He would spend all day going from vendor to vendor until he found what he considered to be the most perfect—and usually it also turned out to be the most expensive—*essrog* he could find. He would search exhaustively until the purest, most flawless, and most ideal *essrog* was unearthed, one which invariably cost several hundred dollars.

"One *Succoth* right before services were about to begin, my wife and I were standing next to Shlomo, when a new congregant—a middle-aged woman who had just recently become religious—approached him excitedly. 'Shlomo,' she enthused, 'I just bought my very first *essrog* and *lulav* and I can't begin to tell you how thrilled I am. Want to take a look?' When she opened the box that contained her *essrog*, we saw with dismay that it was pitiful-looking—small, shrunken, bearing many different defects and flaws. The woman *nebech* wasn't well off, and she had probably bought the cheapest *essrog* on the market—which usually goes for about twenty dollars. Before any of us could react, she turned to Shlomo eagerly and said, 'And can I see yours?' Obligingly, Shlomo displayed in turn his own *essrog*—this one being round, full-bodied, gleaming, fragrant, unblemished, and very pure. The contrast between the two *essrogim* was stark and undeniable.

"Instantly, the woman's spirits sagged. 'Oh, Shlomo!' she said petulantly. 'I like yours so much better. Do you mind if we trade?'

"My wife and I exchanged startled looks. Was the woman brazen or merely naive? Perhaps she really didn't know how much the *essrog* meant to Shlomo in terms of religious commitment, emotional cost, and financial expenditure? She couldn't know what she was asking, could she?

"Shlomo didn't hesitate for a second. 'My pleasure!' he boomed heartily, promptly handing her his beloved *essrog*, with a hug and a kiss. 'Gee thanks, Shlomo,' she said, snatching it eagerly from him and then starting to move away. 'I really appreciate it.'

"'My most beautiful friend!' Shlomo called after her quickly departing figure. 'Just one thing!' She twirled around with a question on her face. 'Make sure you do a lot of *mitzvahs* with the *essrog*, okay?'"

―――――

Shlomo was exhausted, drained. It was *Motzei Rosh Hashona; Rosh Hashona* services (which he had led with great intensity and fervor both days) had just ended a few minutes before, and he was just beginning to tug at the *tallit* still draped around his shoulders. I looked at him in distress. "*Heilege Rebbe* (Holy Rabbi), you look bone-tired," I exclaimed, concerned. "Why don't you go upstairs and rest?"

It was two years before his death, and although many people knew about his pacemaker and the physicians' dire warnings, Shlomo had―against all medical advice―kept up his frenetic pace, his energy never lagging. He was the type who never complained, but at this moment he looked wiped out. "Go straight to bed," I firmly commanded. "You're right," he uncharacteristically agreed, "I'm going upstairs this minute."

Just then the shul door opened and a foreign-looking young couple, with whom I was not acquainted, burst into view. A handsome pair, they both sported the familiar uniforms of El Al Airlines; the man's hat was emblazoned with the captain's insignia, while the woman was wearing stewardess attire. I had never seen them at the shul before, but they clearly knew Shlomo, because they made a beeline straight toward him.

"Reb Shlomo!" they whooped. "We're finally here . . . and we're ready!"

His face crinkled into a broad grin. "Danny! Arielle!" he exclaimed warmly. "*Mamesh* such a *gevalt* to see you. What are you doing in New York?"

"We're here on a brief layover. Tomorrow we return to Tel Aviv. The last discussion we had with you really made a dent, and we finally decided you're absolutely right. So we're ready . . . are you?"

"Oh, *mamesh* such an honor!" Shlomo said. "I want to thank you so much for the *zchus* and privilege. I just need *mamesh* twenty minutes to pull together some preparations. Is that okay with you?" They nodded their assent. "Sister Chay," he turned to me while motioning to the people still streaming out the door, "could you please quickly call the *chevra* back into the shul? We're making a *chasuna* (wedding)." "Now?" I asked in disbelief. "*Mamesh* now," he replied with a twinkle and a grin.

Shlomo took me aside and explained the situation. He flew to Israel so often on El Al that he had become friendly with its crews. Danny and Arielle, who were not religious, had lived together for several years, but had never been formally wed. During the last few flights that Shlomo had taken with them, he had tried to persuade them to sanctify their union with a religious ceremony, but they had not been receptive. "Look," he had said, handing them his card, "if you ever change your mind and decide you do want a religious wedding, please come to me and I'll be happy to marry you at any time for free." Clearly, they had taken him at his word.

"*Heilege Rebbe* (Holy Rabbi)," I whispered frantically. "You seem spent, and you were just about to go upstairs to bed. Why don't you tell them to come back tomorrow? They have a lot of *chutzpah* (nerve) to come *Motzei Rosh Hashona* after a whole day of *davening*."

"Sister Chay," he said softly, "first of all, *nebech* they're so far removed from the religious world they probably don't even know what it means to sit and *daven* all day in shul.

Second of all, it would hurt their feelings terribly if I told them to come back tomorrow, and I don't want to *chas v'sholom* (God forbid) dishonor them. And third of all, I have to grab the opportunity now. Right now they're ready and willing, maybe tomorrow they'll decide it was a stupid idea after all and they're not going to do it. I can't take that chance."

Shlomo called the *chevra* together for a brief conference, and quickly issued various duties to each person. One was dispatched to round up food and drinks, a second was sent hunting for a makeshift *chupah* (wedding canopy), while a third was assigned the task of collecting the *chevra* who had already gone home and bringing them back to the shul.

Twenty minutes later, Danny and Arielle were under the makeshift *chupah*, and the ceremony was underway.

The wedding—like all the weddings Shlomo did—lasted until dawn. Throughout the night, I turned more than once to look at him with concern and see how he was holding up. And as well as I knew him, as much as I had come to expect from him, I was still a little astonished.

Weariness had long been banished from his appearance; Shlomo's features only radiated pure joy and excitement. Nowhere on his face was there etched a single trace of exhaustion or line of fatigue. No one would ever have suspected how spent and enervated he had been earlier in the evening; the tell-tale signs and obvious clues had completely disappeared!

11

The Right Place at the Right Time

"What is the whole question of being in exile or being free? Being in exile means I am not in the place where I am supposed to be. Free means I am in the place where I am supposed to be. It doesn't have to be a different address. If I am sick, I am really not in the place I am supposed to be, because I am supposed to be well. If I am crazy, God forbid, I am also not in the place I am supposed to be. If I am lost in the desert, or in prison, or in the waves of the ocean, I am not where I am supposed to be."

—RABBI SHLOMO CARLEBACH

I was *davening* at the Carlebach Shul one Yom Kippur, where Shlomo, of course, was serving as *chazan*. Anyone who ever had the privilege through the years of hearing Shlomo *daven* would attest to the enormous amount of concentration and intensity he poured into each word, his remarkable ability to shut out the world while engaged in rapturous prayer and, above all, his fervor as he transported both himself and his congregants to celestial heights.

It therefore came as a complete shock to everyone when Shlomo suddenly stepped down from the *omid* (pulpit) in middle of chanting a prayer, whispered to someone to take over, and stalked out the door.

To say this was irregular behavior is an understatement—it was downright odd, abnormal, unheard of! I had been attending Shlomo's services for years, and such a thing had never happened before, never. Everyone exchanged worried glances, very alarmed. What was going on?

Somebody, whose curiosity I'm sorry to say was greater than his piety, got up and peeked out the door. This is what he observed:

Shlomo stood outside on the shul's steps with an air of expectancy, looking about him right and left, scanning faces anxiously, almost as if he were waiting for somebody. About a minute later, the figure of a young girl appeared down the street. Her pace was brisk, and she was about to pass by the shul, when Shlomo stopped her. "*Gut Yom Tov* (Good Holiday)!" he boomed in his hearty voice. She faltered, turned around, and looked at him uncertainly. "How did you know I was Jewish?" she asked (she was carrying a pocketbook and wearing everyday clothes). "Ah, you have such a holy Jewish face," answered Shlomo. "So tell me holy sister, where are you *davening* today?" She grimaced. "Tell you the truth," she said, blinking back tears, "I've just about had it. I never went to synagogue before, but today I felt an overwhelming need to reconnect with my roots. I guess it sounds a little corny, but lately I've been feeling such a deep hunger for something more in my life. I've been to four synagogues so far this morning, and I walked out of each one. I found the experience in each one to be empty and meaningless, not spiritual at all. I give up; I'm going home."

Shlomo spoke to her gently and convinced her to give his shul a try. We all turned around to stare as he came back into the shul with the girl in tow, found a place for her up front next to a nurturing soul, and returned to the *omid*. After services, many of us approached her, and wished her *"Gut Yom Tov!"* She told us she had been greatly moved by Shlomo's *davening*, and that it was precisely what she had been looking for.

"Imagine," she exclaimed happily. "I've been searching for God all day, and found Him in the Carlebach Synagogue!"

Several years have passed since that incident took place, and this young woman is today a strictly Orthodox Jew, very devout and pious. If Shlomo had not left the *omid* in such an abrupt and bizarre way to reach out to her, who knows where she would be now?

Many people have speculated whether Shlomo possessed psychic powers or was simply blessed with a rich, deep inner sense. Whatever it was, he definitely had an uncanny way of perennially being at the right place . . . at the right time!

There are some people who slip so easily into the new personas they adopt in life that you can't even begin to imagine that they were ever anything else in the past. I had always thought that my pious friend Rochel was *FFB* (*frum from birth*—born and raised religious). I would never have pegged her as *BTF* (*baal teshuva frum*—a returnee to Judaism), never! Although we had known each other for years, Rochel had always been reticent about her background, and I had respected her need for privacy. Imagine my surprise, when two days after Shlomo Carlebach's *petira* (death), during our daily walk together in a Jerusalem park, she suddenly blurted out the truth . . . that she came from an assimilated Jewish home and had become *frum* through Reb Shlomo. His death had come as a stunning blow to her, and she seemed possessed by an urgent need to talk about her experience. It was as if she felt she would be acknowledging her debt to him by finally recounting the story she had hidden from me all these years.

"Typical '60s story," Rochel sighed. "Assimilated Jewish home . . . spiritual seeker . . . into every possible *ism*, except of course for Judaism. My specialty was Kundalini Yoga. I even wore the white robes and white turbans of the movement and was devoted to the group's guru. I thought I had found the meaning of life.

"One night I was studying late in my college library when I heard exquisite music coming from inside the student union building. The music was so spiritual that I left the library to find its source. When I entered the building, I found the campus cafeteria packed with hundreds of students joyously dancing around a hippie rabbi strumming a guitar. Of course, it was none other than Shlomo Carlebach. I was captivated by his music, spellbound by the Torahs he taught, enchanted by the hasidic stories he told. I felt spiritually uplifted and stayed the entire night, until the 'happening' broke up in the wee hours of dawn. But the next morning, I went right back to my Kundalini Yoga, as if the entire experience had never occurred.

"After college, I became a permanent resident of an ashram in upstate New York, where initially I was happy. After a few years, however, I began to feel restless and unfulfilled. An empty, hollow feeling gnawed at me. After voicing my complaints several times to my guru, he advised me to try the movement's branch in Amsterdam. 'Maybe you'll find more enlightenment there,' he suggested.

"But things got worse rather than better in Holland. My mind was no longer 'unquiet' as the guru had characterized, it was downright tormented. All the breathing meditations and yoga postures in the world couldn't ease my distress. Something, my spirit told me, was terribly wrong.

"One night, I woke up with a start, seized by a sudden inspiration. 'I know who could help me with all these questions,' I thought. 'That rabbi in the cafeteria . . . that singing rabbi . . . what was his name?'

"It had been seven years since that night in the cafeteria, but it had left an indelible impression. Using my meditation techniques, I was able to conjure up both the image of the rabbi and his name, too. Carlebach, that was it! And I suddenly remembered him mentioning a synagogue in New York that bore his name. I put in a long-distance call to the

States, and got the information I needed. Trembling with excitement, I dialed the synagogue's number, only to get an answering machine that informed me that Rabbi Carlebach was spending the summer at his *Moshav*. I made several more calls and finally tracked down the *Moshav*'s number. But that, too, proved to be a dead end, because the person who answered at the *Moshav* told me, 'Sorry, Shlomo was here but he's away on a brief trip and we don't know where he is.' By this time my sense of urgency had accelerated, and I was frantic. I hung up the phone without leaving a message.

"The next day the entire ashram population was scheduled to leave for an overnight retreat in the country, but for some strange reason I suddenly decided not to go. I didn't even exactly know myself why I was backing out, but some gut instinct urged me to stay behind. My friends tried to coax me into participating, but I could not be persuaded. Finally, having exhausted their supply of entreaties, the group got up and left me alone.

"About one hour later, the phone rang. Although I was not the person ordinarily assigned to answer the phone, I was the only one left in the Center, so I ran to pick it up. 'Good morning!' a hearty male voice boomed. 'I'm an American visiting Amsterdam for one day, and my wife, who is pregnant, isn't feeling very well and is in need of a herbal remedy. I was hoping that the ashram—which I know stocks holistic preparations—might have the remedy I'm looking for?' 'Sure,' I said, 'give me the name of the remedy and I'll check the cabinets. Yes, it's in stock.' 'Thank you so much,' the male voice said gratefully, 'I'll be right over.'

"Not long afterward, there was a gentle knock, and who appears at the door but none other than the very man I'm looking for—Rabbi Shlomo Carlebach! I nearly fainted. 'Shlomo Carlebach!' I practically shrieked, 'I can't believe this. I've been hunting for you everywhere.'

"I poured out my heart to Shlomo, and he listened with rapt attention. He closed his eyes and *shukeled*. He opened his eyes, studied me carefully, and *shukeled* again. Then his eyes rolled into the back of his head and he *shukeled* some more. Finally, after all this intense concentration, he gave me a deceptively simple two-sentence answer. 'Go to Israel. And everything will be OK.'

"I went to Israel, got connected to my roots, enrolled in a *baal teshuva yeshiva*, became religious, married, had five children. Shlomo had been absolutely right; everything had indeed turned out very OK!

"Years passed and I never looked up Shlomo to thank him. Finally, I began to feel guilty about my lack of *hakoras hatov* (acknowledging the good that someone has done) and decided to attend the next concert he would give in Jerusalem. After the concert was over, I waited for him backstage. 'Do you remember the Jewish girl in the Amsterdam ashram?' I asked.

"He remembered me instantly. 'Holy sister Rochel!' he shouted jubilantly. 'I'm so happy to see you. *Mamesh* this is a *gevalt!* I always wondered what happened to you.' Eager to learn all the details of what had transpired since the ashram, he plied me with many interested questions about my life, and we stood talking for a long time. I was finally getting ready to leave, when he said to me, very casually, 'By the way, do you know what I was doing in Amsterdam that day?

" 'The Jewish community had flown me in from Israel,' he said. 'They were having an annual meeting that day, and I was supposed to perform a concert at its conclusion. But as the meeting wore on, it *nebech* became ripped apart by terrible strife. Things became so heated and tense, in fact, that the entire concert had to be canceled.

" 'So there I was in Amsterdam concertless, with time to spend before my return flight to Israel, thinking . . . what a mystery! Because everything always happens for a reason, why did God send me here? It's almost time to leave, and God hasn't revealed the purpose of my visit. What's going on?

" 'Ah, but when you opened the ashram door, Rochel, and I saw your holy Jewish face, the answer was *mamesh* so clear, so clear. Obviously, Rochel, the only reason I was meant to go to Amsterdam in the first place . . . was just to meet you!' "

Shlomo Carlebach had probably amassed more frequent flyer miles than anyone in history; in his travels to Jewish communities across the world he literally crisscrossed the globe several times a year. He was a familiar and beloved figure to flight attendants and pilots on almost every major airline in the United States, and he knew many of them by name. (His friends and followers often kibitzed that Shlomo was always "taking off," and that it was probably most fitting that when he died suddenly of a heart attack—his soul just "taking off"—it was on a plane.)

On one such flight, Shlomo was attended to by a blonde, blue-eyed stewardess who evoked his curiosity because she radiated an unusual purity. He was impressed by her sweetness and wanted to find out more about her, but as the plane was extremely crowded, the attendants were too busy and rushed to do more than exchange a few polite words with their passengers. Consequently, other than her name—"Kathy"—he was unable to elicit any information about her.

An hour into the flight, Shlomo rose to stretch his legs, and passed the galley, where, to his shock and amazement he saw Kathy *davening* (praying) from a siddur (prayerbook). He waited quietly until she had completed her prayers, and then approached her. "Holy sister," he exclaimed, "you're an angel from heaven! What are you doing?" Kathy explained that she although her parents weren't Jewish, she had always been drawn to Judaism. "I have no idea where this love comes from," she told Shlomo, "but it has been so compelling in my life that I recently converted." Kathy told Shlomo that she had studied for years with an Orthodox Jewish Rabbi, had undergone a thoroughly halachic (Orthodox Jewish Law) conversion, and was now a practicing Jew. Shlomo and Kathy conversed at length, until a passenger called for her assistance and Shlomo returned to his seat.

Several minutes later, Kathy approached Shlomo tentatively. "You know, because you're a Rabbi, maybe you can help me with a pressing problem I have?" "It will be my

honor and privilege to be of service to you, holy sister,"
Shlomo rejoined immediately. "Well, here's my problem,"
Kathy stated hesitantly. "You see, I'm in love with a Jewish
man whose parents—although not religious in the slightest—
strenuously object to him marrying a convert. They've been
carrying on something terrible, screaming and crying and
threatening to disown him should we in fact marry. We love
each other very much, but he is also equally devoted to his
parents, and doesn't want to cause them grief. As a result, he's
terribly torn. The whole thing's incredibly ironic because I'm
much more of a Jew than his parents are! Nonetheless, I'm
fearful that he's going to cave in under the pressure and call
the engagement off. Can you help me?"

"I will indeed try my best to help you," Shlomo promised. "Give me the phone number of your fiancé's parents,
and I'll call them as soon as I get into my hotel. I will do my
utmost to convince them not to oppose your marriage."

When Shlomo reached the father of Kathy's fiancé, he
found him hostile and unreceptive. Despite his best attempts
to make the father listen to reason, Shlomo made little
headway. His pleas fell on deaf ears. As Shlomo persisted, the
man grew increasingly irate. Finally, he snapped, "Listen here,
I'm a Holocaust survivor, and because of what God did to the
Jews I hate *yiddishkeit* (Judaism), but if my son marries a *shiksa*
(non-Jewish woman), I'll kill him!" Shlomo soon realized that
meaningful dialogue with the father was impossible and bade
him goodby. He then reached for the phone to call Kathy and
report, regretfully, on his lack of success.

It was Kathy's father, however, who answered the phone,
and he too was antagonistic and contentious. He was angry at
Shlomo for attempting to mediate between the two families
and castigated him for his "interference." Silently absorbing
the torrent of abuse, Shlomo responded with a Talmudic tale.
Now that God has finished creating the world, the Talmud
asks, what does he do all day? The Talmud answers that God
spends one third of his time making *shidduchim* (matches).
"So," Shlomo said humorously, "I'm just trying to give God a
little help in his work. Obviously, your daughter and her

fiancé love each other very much. Wouldn't it be a terrible shame if they did not get married?"

Something in Shlomo's voice must have touched the man, because he began to cry. "I will tell you a secret that nobody else knows," he told Shlomo, "and until your call came, I thought I would never share it in my lifetime. My wife and I are not really Christians, we are Jews. We are in fact Holocaust survivors, and because of what God did to the Jews we came to hate *yiddishkeit* and renounced our heritage. We never officially converted, but we pretended we were Christian and raised our children as secularists. To this day, they don't know the truth about who they really are."

"But if this is the case," Shlomo responded, "and Kathy is Jewish by birth, then there is no problem. Her fiancé's father objects to her non-Jewish parentage. If you will tell her the truth, the obstacles barring the way to her *bashert* (destined one) will be removed." Kathy's father tearfully agreed, and Shlomo spent the next few hours on the phone, making a flurry of calls between the two sets of parents. Finally, he arranged for them to meet in his hotel room the next day.

When the two fathers were formally introduced and rose to shake hands, they blanched in shock and recognition. A series of varying emotions—confusion, astonishment, pain, and awe—flitted across their faces in rapid succession. "Herschel!" shouted one in jubilation. "Yankel!" yelled the other in joy. To the bewilderment of everyone present, they fell into each other's arms and cried.

"We were *chavrusas* (learning partners) in yeshiva together before the War!" they cried out in explanation to their wives and children. "We were best friends. But I thought you were dead!" they exclaimed simultaneously.

The reunion was tremulous and tearful. Floodgates opened, and reminiscences were invoked of a long-lost era, forever gone. And they spoke of their youth with sorrow, with nostalgia, and with yearning. Finally, one looked at the other and said with a crooked, funny smile. "Do you remember the fanciful pact we once made, as we dreamed about the future?" The other laughed delightedly in remembrance. "Why yes, I do! How strange, how very strange!" he murmured and turned to Kathy and her fiancé to elaborate.

"This is indeed curious, but I promise it is true. When we were yeshiva *bochurim* (boys) together, we promised we would forever be friends. And to solidify the friendship we pledged that when we would marry and have children, we would betroth them to one another. It seems that even though we forgot this pledge, God did not. Against all odds, you met each other and fell in love.

"I ask you Rabbi Carlebach, how do you explain this? Is this coincidence or is this providence?"

And Shlomo, who hadn't said a single word while the reunion was taking place, just leaned back in his chair and beamed.

12

Blessing the Opposition

"There is a passage in the Psalms, 'Let the sin go away, not the sinners.' If I see someone do something wrong, I am angry, not at the person, but at what he is doing. As the Baal Shem Tov once said, the real person is not involved in the wrong-doing. He is like half asleep. So gevalt I am angry! 'Why aren't you awake?' But I cannot really be too angry, because he was asleep. The question is, if you are getting angry, are you getting angry at the person, or at the evil? If you are a neshama person, there is no hatred. If you have hatred, then you are evil also."

"If God had given me two hearts, I could use one for hating and the other one for love. But since I was given only one heart, I have only room for love."

—RABBI SHLOMO CARLEBACH

Universally loved and revered, Shlomo Carlebach none-theless had his detractors in the ultra-Orthodox world, some segments of which misunderstood his nontraditional methods of reaching out to lost, lonely, and alienated souls.

His "New Age" flavor was unfamiliar to them and his bridge-building deemed alien and outlandish. But what really offended some in the ultra-Orthodox world and remained the major source of its distress about Shlomo Carlebach was his custom of hugging and kissing everyone who came in his path—men and women alike. Shlomo was often heard to say that "you can preach all day long to people and nothing happens, but give them a hug and a kiss, and in a second you've reached them," but his explanation was unacceptable. Thus Shlomo occasionally found himself the subject of righteous wrath and disapproval.

One such incident occurred about ten years ago at the Wailing Wall in Israel. Shlomo was praying at the Kotel with a group of his followers from Moshav Modiin, when one of the Elders of Jerusalem approached him. In furious tones, he said to Shlomo in Hebrew: "Zeh Mokom Kadosh—this is a Holy Place—v'atoh ish tomei—and you are an impure person—lech mepoh—leave!" And then he spit directly onto Shlomo Carlebach's face.

Frozen with shock, Shlomo's followers watched in horror as Shlomo carefully began to wipe off the thick rivulets of spittle streaming down his face and waited for him to speak. Turning to his group, Shlomo said, "Did you see the holy eyes of that man? We are privileged to have in our midst such a Holy Man!" And there was absolutely no anger, no rebuke, no bitterness in his voice, just a sense of awe and marvel that a Holy Man had crossed his path.

———

"In 1991 I was in Israel visiting the *Amishenever Rebbe* (one of the most pious, revered, and holy Torah Sages of this generation), when a hasidic man approached him with a question. 'Why,' the hasid asked, half-curiously, half-angrily, 'does the *heilege* (holy) Amshinever associate with Shlomo Carlebach, whom everybody knows violates halacha (Jewish Law) by hugging women?'

"The Amshinever looked at the man for a moment and

sighed. 'My dear friend,' he said, 'I should only have as many zchusim in shomayim (merits in Heaven) as Shlomo Carlebach!'
"The Amshinever looked pointedly at the hasid, shukeled (swayed back and forth) for a moment, and said no more."

The essrog (citron) had mysteriously vanished. During Hoshana Rabah (the seventh day of the festival of Succoth) services at his synagogue on the Upper West Side, Shlomo Carlebach had momentarily placed both his lulav and essrog on a chair while he tended to a congregant's need. When he returned to the chair to retrieve the two items necessary for religious rituals that day, he stared at the chair in mingled shock and disbelief. The lulav was still there, but the essrog was missing.

Distressed, Shlomo Carlebach looked around the crowded synagogue. His Hoshana Rabah davening, renowned for its passionate and pentecostal-like celebratory service, drew people from all walks of life and from all over the five boroughs. Additionally, in warm weather the shul door was left open as a gesture of welcome to all wayfarers, and because the holiday had fallen that year in early October, many curious bypassers had stepped in for a look. Consequently, when Shlomo looked at the sea of faces crowding into the shul that day, many of them were strange and unfamiliar to him. Satmar hasidim with long, curly peyos to their chins; tattooed bikers in studded leather jackets and nose rings; conservatively dressed businessmen in tailored suits and small black velvet yarmulkes; women with long, flowing dresses and kerchiefs on their heads; a few of the neighborhood's homeless, whom Shlomo had adopted, grateful for a seat in the sanctuary he provided them . . . the spectrum of visitors to the synagogue that day was wide and eclectic as it always was in the Carlebach shul. One of them had—mistakenly or deliberately—taken the essrog.

Shlomo stepped up to the podium and in a troubled voice asked, "Please, chevra, has anyone seen my essrog? I put it down on this chair just a moment ago, and now it's gone. I'm sure it's a mistake; somebody probably thought it was his, and accidentally took it. I beg of you . . . do me a favor . . . look at your *essrog* to make sure it's yours." Silence fell over the room as everyone inspected the *essrog* in their possession. After a few moments, Shlomo asked hopefully, "So, *chevra*, has anyone found my *essrog* yet?" The concern in Shlomo's usually even-tempered voice was so perceptible that congregants stirred in their seats in obvious discomfort, looking at each other with dismay. They waited for someone's voice to ring out with an affirmative answer, they waited for someone to triumphantly hold aloft the missing citron, and they waited for someone to break the ominous hush that had suddenly descended over the congregation. But no exultant voice of discovery was raised, and no one came happily forward. A search of the shul was then rapidly launched; the floor, the benches, the chairs . . . every inch of space was exhaustively covered. But the *essrog* was nowhere to be found.

Shlomo's face was sad and hurt as he ascended the *bima*, but not angry. "Listen, *chevra*, I'm sure that the person who took the *essrog* took it by mistake, and even if it wasn't a mistake, I'm sure he needed it more than me. So, whoever you are, if you are still here, I want to wish you a *Gut Yom Tov* (Happy Holiday) and bless you that you should enjoy the *essrog* as much as I have up until now."

And with that, Shlomo Carlebach turned around, the dejected look on his face rapidly replaced by a celestial smile, and resumed the service, praying and singing as passionately and joyously as he had before.

"What's a sure sign of someone's greatness?" asks Rabbi Simcha Hochbaum of Hebron, Israel. "Opposition!

"If somebody is doing nothing, well obviously, no one is opposed to it. It's only when somebody is doing something really significant, that the opposition comes out in full force!

"And so it was with Shlomo Carlebach. He had his ardent hasidim, of course, but he had some fervid opponents

as well. These were people who misunderstood his inclusion-
ary manner and 'New Age' ways, people who regarded
Shlomo's path of love, tolerance, and acceptance with suspicion and contempt. Usually, Shlomo was extremely good-
natured about the opposition he encountered, forgiving and
patient. He never bore a grudge, repeatedly teaching that
'because every thought takes up space, we should have better
things in our heads than remembering something bad somebody did to us. People are only little messengers from God,
anyway,' he would add, 'so if you hold anger against someone, it means you didn't really believe their behavior came
from God.'

"This was Shlomo's approach, and as a result he was
rarely offended by acts of antagonism. The year before he
died, however, an incident took place which left him wounded.
I happened to be with him when the episode occurred.

"A Lag B'Omer concert had been scheduled at a hall in an
ultra-religious enclave. When Shlomo and the *chevra* arrived
at the hall, we found it dark and locked. A note posted on the
door informed us that the concert had been relocated to a
synagogue in a different neighborhood.

"Shlomo didn't say a word, but he looked hurt. When we
arrived at the new location, he quietly walked over to the
concert organizer and asked him what had transpired. The
man apologetically told Shlomo that a rabbi had approached
him earlier that day, advising him to cancel the concert or else
suffer the consequences. If he did not heed his warning, the
Rabbi said, he would organize a boycott of the man's hall, and
he would effectively be put out of business.

"In addition to this, the concert organizer told Shlomo,
this Rabbi had single-handedly distributed flyers to school-
children in several yeshivas, warning them to stay away from
the concert. Although this Rabbi had never met Shlomo
personally or spoken to him even once, he seemed to have a
particular axe to grind with him and, over the years, had
given him much heartache.

"Taken aback by the intensity of the Rabbi's hatred,
Shlomo struggled to understand it. So he asked the concert
organizer to tell him everything he knew about this Rabbi.

"The man gave him a brief run-down. In the quick bio he provided, he noted that the Rabbi was extremely poor and had thirteen children to support. 'Oy, *nebech!*' Shlomo shook his head compassionately. 'Thirteen children to support and no money! That's just heartrending! *Nebech*, I feel so bad for him.' Excusing himself, Shlomo left the man's side, approached one of the *chevra*, whispered something into his ear, and ascended the stage.

" '*Chevra!*' he yelled, seizing the mike. 'I heard *mamesh* just a minute ago the saddest story about a *choshuva* (important) *rov* (rabbi) who has thirteen children and *nebech* no real means of support. So before we start the concert, I want to take up a collection for his family. Everybody should please please open their hearts and give as much as they can. Holy brother Lenny* is passing around a bucket right now, so please put in whatever is humanly possible for you to give. This is *nebech* a terrible story, and we have to try to help.'

"And so, right there and then, on the spot, Shlomo Carlebach took up a collection for the man who had persecuted him for years, and, on that particular night, ruined his concert. When the *tzedakkah* was delivered to the man via a third party, its origin was kept secret. The Rabbi never knew that his anonymous benefactor was none other than the man he had pledged to destroy: Shlomo Carlebach!"

———

"Shlomo was in middle of performing at a concert in Haifa in 1966, when a man wearing pajamas suddenly ran out onto the stage, brandishing an angry fist. He raised his arm as if to strike Shlomo but hit his guitar—which served as a shield—instead. When his hand made contact with the guitar, the blow of the impact was so strong the guitar splintered and broke. The guitar had been expensive and was one of Shlomo's old-time favorites.

"As terrified members of the audience watched the bizarre scene unfold before their eyes, pandemonium erupted in the auditorium. People screamed and shoved. Some scrambled toward the exits, convinced that a deranged lunatic was amongst them, while others pushed and jostled in the opposite direction—toward the stage—in an effort to collar the fellow and rescue Shlomo. Some well-meaning souls ran to the nearest phone to call the cops, while still others ran into the streets to flag down a cruising police car. Very quickly, the police appeared on the scene.

"Meanwhile, Shlomo had begun talking softly to the man in a soothing voice. 'My most beautiful friend,' he said to him sympathetically. 'I feel so sorry for you! *Nebech* something must be really upsetting you so much! What's going on in your life? Can I help you?'

"By this time, the man was beginning to look shamefaced and sheepish. He mumbled embarrassedly to Shlomo that his life was full of constant hardships, and that he had terrible insomnia because of all the anxiety they provoked. He had finally fallen asleep that night, he told Shlomo, when the crowd at the concert hall, which abutted his apartment, woke him with its boisterous singing. Practically insane with exhaustion, he had run onto the stage in a fit of fury, but was now aghast at what he had done and the fracas he had caused. During this point of his recital, the police arrived and, ascending the stage, cautiously advanced toward the man.

" 'Hey, what's going on?' Shlomo yelled in dismay as the police made their approach. 'Don't you want us to arrest this man?' a policeman shouted at Shlomo. 'Arrest this man?' Shlomo repeated incredulously. 'Because of me, a Jew should sit in jail? *Chas v'sholom* (God forbid)!' 'So what do you want us to do?' an officer asked impatiently. 'Give me a minute,' Shlomo pleaded as he looked at his would-be attacker. The man was bareheaded; he clearly was not religious, otherwise he would have worn a yarmulke. Shlomo walked him a few paces away from the police and whispered to him, 'Tell me brother, have you ever put on tefillin (phylacteries—a symbol of man's covenant with God)?' The man shook his head no. 'So, let's make a deal,' Shlomo offered. 'You start putting on tefillin and I won't press charges. A deal?' The man nodded. 'A deal.'

"One *mitzvah* (commandment) led to another, and the

man eventually became completely *frum* (religious). It's almost thirty years since that episode first took place, and I personally know that this man is still religious today.

" 'See Itzikel,' Shlomo once commented, in discussing this incident. 'People thought he was raising his arm to strike me. What he was really doing was raising his hands in supplication to *Hashem!* "

———

Shlomo was scheduled to give a concert near the Kotel (Wailing Wall) one night, and a tiny group of zealots had mobilized a demonstration against him. At that time I was working as his manager in Israel, and got wind of the upcoming protest rally. Without saying a word to Shlomo—who was oblivious to the whirlwind about to envelop him—I called his two elderly mentors, two of the most pious and revered hasidic rebbes in Yerushalayim. I quickly explained the situation to both of them, and outlined my dilemma: I didn't want to cancel the concert, but I also didn't want to expose Shlomo to the anguish a protest rally would surely inflict. What to do? They both listened intently and said they would call one another to discuss a course of action. Not to worry, they both individually soothed. They would do everything in their power to protect Shlomo; I could count on it!

The evening of the concert, I picked Shlomo up, and as he entered my car, he turned around to stare in astonishment at the two unlikely occupants in the back seat. *"Heilege Rebbes!"* he shouted in disbelief. "What are you doing here?" "Shloi-mala!" answered one of the august patriarchs serenely, "we're both getting old and never had the privilege of hearing you in concert. *Nu, nu* we decided it's time already!" Throughout the entire trip to the Kotel, an awestruck Shlomo kept staring at the two venerable sages seated behind him, a series of varying emotions flitting across his face. You could also see from his face that he suspected that something was afoot, but he didn't want to dishonor the famous Rebbes by asking.

At the entrance to the Kotel, my three passengers disembarked, and Shlomo quickly offered an arm to each Rebbe, both as a gesture of respect and to assist them in walking. Thus the scene, as I watched it in smug satisfaction from afar, was Shlomo Carlebach slowly making towards the Kotel, flanked on both sides by two of the most esteemed Rebbes of our time.

I was not the only one, however, observing the tableau with great interest. From a distance, I could see the small band of zealots who had already gathered in a corner, armed with pebbles and stones, gaping at Shlomo Carlebach's holy escort. One by one by one, the rocks fell from their hands and dropped to the floor. Then they slowly slipped away, melting into the darkness, their presence marked only by a pile of stones they had left behind. And Shlomo, who all this time had only focused his attention on the Rebbes—his erstwhile guardians, who had come so wholeheartedly to provide him with their loving protection and support—never even saw a thing!

Squatters had seized an empty house in Moshav Modiin, and residents of the settlement were alarmed. The calm of the tranquil, family-oriented community had been pierced one night by the foreign and disruptive sounds of drunken screams, rowdy music, and splintering glass. When a squadron of men had been dispatched to investigate, they had discovered the squatters.

Calling the police was not even a consideration. As disciples of Reb Shlomo's and imbued with his loving spirit, the *chevra* had instead first tried reasoning, then coaxing, and finally pleading with the two men who had invaded the vacant house to leave. But their gentle entreaties were in vain. Surly and churlish, the two squatters had snorted in response, and impudently gestured rudely at them.

"Gotta call Shlomo," the *chevra* concluded sadly, reluctant to disturb his night and embroil him in what threatened to become a fracas. Still, Shlomo's benevolent presence and special aura had worked magic before on the most recalcitrant types, and the *chevra* had faith that his warmhearted approach could defuse the most sensitive situation. Hesitantly, they approached his home and knocked on the door.

But this time, even Shlomo's soft supplications failed to achieve the desired effect. The two squatters continued to make rude noises, snickered contemptuously, and insolently taunted him. "You're such a *meshugenah* (crazy person), Rabbi Shlomo Carlebach," the first one jeered, "that you belong in a *meshugoyim* house (mental institution)!" "You're such a low-life," the second one snarled, not to be outdone, "that you belong in a jail!" Then they both brayed derisively, delighted with their pithy bon mots.

Shlomo disregarded their abuse and continued to ply them with sweet appeals. But finally even he became discouraged, and departing, advised the *chevra*, "I know it's hard, but just wait it out and you'll see, they'll leave of their own accord." Sure enough, a couple of days later, they were gone.

About a week later, one of the *chevra*, who had been to Tel Aviv for the day, returned to the Moshav with an interesting piece of news. "You're not going to believe this," he announced to the others. "Remember the two squatters and what they said to Shlomo? Well, you know what happened to them? After they left the Moshav, they went to Tel Aviv, where they created some kind of disturbance and were arrested. So now listen to this. The squatter who told Shlomo that he's such a *meshugenah* he should be in a *meshugoyim* house was shipped off to a mental institution, and the one who said Shlomo's such a low-life he should be sent to prison ended up in jail!"

With any other Rebbe, the story would end here. But remember my friends, we're talking about Shlomo Carlebach! So what did Shlomo do when informed of the news himself? He immediately went to Tel Aviv to find out where the two squatters were being held, and, after lengthy inquiries, learned their whereabouts. Then he promptly embarked on his mission. First, he traveled to one side of town to see the squatter confined in the asylum, and then he journeyed to the other side of town to visit the second squatter sequestered in jail!

13

Harmony to the World

"All of God's wisdom is encased in a garment: it is in the music. When we speak, you say 'yes' and I say 'no' and we are already opposed to each other. In music, what is absolutely unbelievable, is that I can sing a melody, you can sing different notes, and it's the deepest harmony. The greatest revelation of God's oneness in the world is music."

—Rabbi Shlomo Carlebach

When Mayer Appel of Brooklyn, New York, traveled to Israel in June 1995 on personal business, he knew he would make a trip to Shlomo Carlebach's gravesite on Har Hamenuchos in Jerusalem. No Rabbi had ever spiritually uplifted him the way Shlomo had, and he had felt his death keenly. For eight months since Shlomo's death he had experienced a deep void, and he knew he would feel comforted by visiting his *kever* (grave). However, when he made the trek up to the large, labyrinth-like cemetery on his first day there, he was sorely disappointed not to find a caretaker who could guide him to the grave. He searched the sprawling grounds for hours, but failed to locate the *kever*. Exhausted and despondent, Mayer Appel finally left Har Hamenuchos, his mission unfulfilled.

Two weeks later, on the last night of his stay in Israel, Mayer abruptly woke up at 1:00 in the morning in the hotel, startled out of his deep sleep by a strong sense of urgency. "My God," he thought to himself with a start, "My plane is leaving tomorrow morning, and I never even visited Shlomo!" A usually feisty and tenacious personality, he felt ashamed at his curious lack of determination in ferreting out the *kever*. "How could I have even thought for a moment of leaving Israel without paying my respects to Shlomo?" he wondered out loud. Suddenly, he found himself springing out of bed in a state of exhilaration, fired with newfound fervor and resolve. "It's not too late yet. I can still go tonight."

He pulled out his personal telephone book and called Amir, an Arab driver who chauffeured him around Israel during his frequent trips there. "Amir," he said, "Sorry to wake you, but this is an emergency. Can you take me right now to Har Hamenuchos to visit Shlomo Carlebach's *kever*?"

There was a pause. Amir then politely inquired, "What are you . . . *meshugah* (crazy) or something?"

"No, Amir, I'm serious. You know, in our discussions, I've told you how much Shlomo Carlebach meant to me, and I also told you about my unsuccessful attempt to find his grave two weeks ago. I don't know why I gave up so quickly or how I ever even contemplated leaving Israel without visiting his grave, but I must find it. My plane leaves tomorrow morning. Now is my only chance."

"But Mayer," protested Amir, "it's pitch black on Har Hamenuchos. It's not like American cemeteries with spotlights or anything that will illuminate the darkness. If you couldn't find the grave during the day, how do you expect to find it at night?"

"I know this sounds crazy, Amir, but I just have the strongest feeling that this time something's going to lead me to the *kever*. I just *know* I'm going to find Shlomo right away."

"Okay," Amir sighed, "I'll pick you up in a half hour. But

I warn you this is a wild goose chase, and I'm going to charge you an exorbitant fee."

"No problem," Mayer Appel agreed happily.

When they arrived at Har Hamenuchos, the cemetery was, as Amir had warned, shrouded in a heavy veil of black. They paused at the main gate, squinting at the darkness, at a loss. "Now what?" sighed Amir. "I told you this was a crazy idea."

"You're wrong," insisted Mayer. "I just know we're going to find him!" "Oh, yes?" teased Amir. "Who's gonna lead you to him . . . God, maybe?"

Mayer craned his head in all directions, looking for clues, when suddenly he saw what he took to be an unmistakable sign. "Look!" shouted Mayer jubilantly, pointing to a gravesite in the distance. "Look, Amir, just look. What do you see?"

The grave was surrounded by rings of flickering *yahrzeit* candles. There was no question in Mayer Appel's mind that Shlomo Carlebach's elusive *kever* had been found.

Shlomo had always been associated with light. In the early years, Shlomo had often distributed candles to members of the audience, and the magical quality of many of his concerts had been enhanced by the presence of sparks of light glowing in the darkness. Shlomo himself had been a candle in the dark, Mayer reflected in a stream of poetic fancy. He had brought so much light to the world during his life, it was now only fitting that light should bring the world back to him in death.

Confidently, Mayer (with Amir trailing) made his way toward the direction of the dancing flames. As he had instinctively understood, they were indeed encircling the grave of Rabbi Shlomo Carlebach.

Mayer stood and stared at the grave for a long moment, his heart lurching. "Ah, Shlomo," he thought with overwhelming grief, "can it really be that you—who gave so much life to the world—are truly dead? Will we ever know again the love, the joy, the unity you brought us?" His body racked with sobs, Mayer pulled out a small *Tehillim* (Book of Psalms), which he began to recite. When the recitation was completed, he closed his eyes and started singing.

He was singing Shlomo's *niggunim*, of course, dozens of exquisite, heart-rending, celestial melodies that for decades had animated world Jewry, uplifted them, inspired them, renewed them. The songs were songs of fire; they had kindled the dying embers of a demoralized Jewry in the aftermath of the Holocaust. The songs were songs of joy; they had strengthened Jewry's resolve to live again and go on.

So, through the night, Mayer Appel sang Shlomo Carlebach's *niggunim*. He turned towards Amir, his Arab friend, and sang, "Amir, give me harmony!!! (Shlomo's own frequent exhortation to his concert audiences.)" Amir put his arm around Mayer's shoulder, and slowly, tentatively began to sing the *niggunim* with him, softly at first, then louder and louder, until the entire cemetery reverberated with the echoes of Shlomo Carlebach's songs.

And as they sang together at Shlomo Carlebach's gravesite, the Arab and the Jew, with their arms flung around each other's shoulders, awaiting the first light of dawn, Mayer Appel thought to himself,

"Even in death, Shlomo Carlebach brings harmony to the world."

Epilogue

Once, when a great Rebbe was about to die, he gathered his hasidim around him, and gently told them that it was time.

"Oh no!" they wept. "What are we going to do without you—without your wisdom, without your counsel, without your inspiration? Who will infuse us with your vision, who will elevate us to the heights to which you alone helped us ascend? Who will motivate us, encourage us, and give us the strength to carry on?"

"Rebbe!" the hasidim cried out in despair. "Are you going to leave us in the darkness?"

"Never!" the Rebbe whispered with a tender smile. "I leave you . . . holding the light!"

———

Whenever the Holy Baal Shem wanted to intercede with God on behalf of his people, he would go to a special place in the forest, light a special fire, and chant a special prayer. And always, his petition was accepted and blessed by the Almighty.

When his disciple, the Great Maggid, wanted to effect a similar response, he said, "I no longer know the prayer, but I know the special place in the forest, and I know how to light the fire, and that will have to be enough." And it was.

The Great Maggid's successor was not only bereft of the special prayer, but knowledge of how to light the special fire had also, sadly, been lost over time. But he knew the location of the special place in the forest, and faithfully made pilgrimages there whenever he needed to achieve a certain miracle on his people's behalf. Always he would travel to the place in the forest and proclaim, "I no longer know the prayer, I no longer know how to light the fire, but I know the place in the forest, and that will have to be enough." And it was.

When Rabbi Moshe Leib, the disciple of the disciple of the Great Maggid, wanted to a work a similar cure, he would declare, "I no longer know the prayer, I no longer know how to light the fire, I no longer even know the location of the special place in the forest. But I still remember the story, and that will have to be enough."

And it was.

Glossary of Yiddish and Hebrew Words

Baal chesed—a charitable person, a Good Samaritan, someone constantly engaged in acts of kindness.

Baal Shem Tov—literally, "master of the good name." Title for Rabbi Israel Ben Eliezer, the Baal Shem Tov of Medzibezh (1700–1760), the legendary founder of a Jewish mystical revival movement in eighteenth century Poland, the antecedents of hasidism.

baal teshuva—a returnee to the faith, newly Orthodox.

balebos—boss, head of the household.

Bar Mitzvah—literally, "son of commandment." According to Orthodox Jewish religious law, a Jewish boy becomes fully responsible in all aspects of Jewish religious life when he reaches the age of thirteen. It is an initiation time. On the Sabbath of his bar mitzvah, the boy is called to the Torah for the first time and is expected to deliver a *drashah*, an exposition on the Torah portion, for the congregation.

beis medrash—literally, "house of study." A synagogue or yeshiva study hall.

brocha—a blessing.

challah—braided Sabbath bread.
chas v'sholom!—exclamation meaning "God forbid!"
chazan—cantor.
chevra—friends.
chilul hashem—defaming God's name by not acting properly, by not acting in accordance with the Laws and Principles of Torah.
daven—to pray.
eitza—advice.
essrog—citron used for ceremonial purposes on Sukkot, Feast of Tabernacles.
fahrbrenta—inflamed, passionate, zealous.
frum—religious, observant.
Gabbai—synagogue administrator or personal assistant to a Rebbe.
Gemora—part of the Talmud that consists of discussions of the Mishnah.
gevalt!—exclamation that can mean the best or the worst.
Godol—a Torah giant.
gonif—a thief.
Gut Shabbos!—salutation meaning "Good Sabbath!"
Halacha—Jewish Law.
hakoras hatov—the act of demonstrating appreciation and gratitude, an important commandment.
Har Hamenuchos—Ancient and celebrated cemetery in Jerusalem, where many holy rabbis and scholars are buried.
hashgocha protis—divine providence.
hasidim—followers of rebbes or charismatic rabbinic leaders.
Havadalah—literally, "separation or differentiation." It refers to the ritual of saying good-bye to the Sabbath or Saturday evening with the intention of bringing the spirit of Sabbath into the weekday. Blessings are recited on a braided candle, a chalice of wine, and spices.
heilege—holy.
hocking—hammering away.
ilui—Torah genius.
kavannah—direction of the heart toward God while performing a religious deed, or the act of concentrating on the meaning of prayers.

kever—grave.

kiddush—benediction pronounced over the wine at the commencement of the Sabbath and holidays.

Klal Yisroel—the people, the nation of Israel.

kovod—honor.

krechs—a pained and heartfelt sigh.

lulav—long, pointed plant used for ceremonial purposes on Sukkot.

machloikas—an argument, dissension.

matanos l'avyonim—literally "gifts to the poor." Giving charity to the needy and sending gift baskets of food to the poor is one of the observances of the Jewish holiday of Purim.

mamesh—really, or "it's awesome!"

meiselach—little hasidic tales.

Melave Malka—literally, "Escort of the Sabbath Queen." The meal taken after the departure of the Sabbath. This meal is understood as bidding farewell to the Sabbath Queen. It "escorts" her away.

meshugenah—insane person.

meshugoyim—plural of meshugenah.

minyan—quorum of ten Jewish adult men needed for formal prayers.

mitzvah—commandment or good deed.

nebech—exclamation of pity.

neshoma—the soul.

niggunim—songs, soulful melodies.

oy!—exclamation like the American "oh, no!" or "how terrible!"

parnossa—livelihood or payment.

peyos—sidelocks.

Rebbe—a charismatic hasidic leader who is part of a rabbinic dynasty.

Rebbetzin—the Rebbe's wife.

Rosh Hashanah—literally, "the head of the year." The Jewish New Year, observed on the first and second day of *Tishrei* (September or October), the days of judgment.

Shabbos—Sabbath, Friday sundown to Saturday sundown, after three stars are sighted.

skakoach—felicitous "thanks, you were terrific!"

shalom bayis—literally, "peace in the house," harmonious relations between husband and wife.

Shalosh Seudos—the third meal of the Sabbath, eaten after the Afternoon Prayer, and accompanied by community singing and an address by the rebbe or tzaddik.

sheitel—wig that married women don as a symbol of their married status and as an act of modesty.

shnorrer—a panhandler or beggar.

shtiebel—the village synagogue, a prayer room, or, in America, an informal, loosely organized, small and comfortable shul.

shukeling—moving back and forth in prayer or study, swaying in concentration.

shul—synagogue.

siddur—prayerbook.

siyyata dishmaya—with the help of the Lord, God driven, or, bearing God's stamp.

Sukkot—The Feast of Booths or Feast of Tabernacles; an eight-day holiday beginning on the fifth day after the Day of Atonement. It commemorates the wandering of the Jews in the desert before entering the Promised Land.

tallis—a rectangular shawl worn at prayers by Jewish males; its four corners have fringes attached.

tefillin—phylacteries, leather cubicles containing scriptural texts inscribed on parchment. Following the commandment in Deuteronomy 11:18, tefillin are attached to the left arm and the head during the weekday morning service. They are a sign of the covenant between God and Israel.

teshuvah—literally, "return," religious penance.

tikkun—the act of restoring things to their original harmonious state; a fixing of the world.

tzaddik—a righteous or holy person, the leader of the hasidic community, or, in mystical tradition, a saintly, enlightened person who is able to perceive the essence of each soul that comes to him and is able to impart and transmit a *tikkun* for this soul.

yarmulke—skullcap.

yeshiva—seminary for religious studies or rabbinical school. Can also be loosely used to mean any religious school, including elementary and high school.
yiddishkeit—Judaism.
yungerman—young man.
z'chus—merit.

Contributors

In addition to the people cited in the Acknowledgments section, I wish to acknowledge with deep gratitude and enormous appreciation the following individuals for recounting their stories and impressions:

Chaya Adler
Rabbi Itzik Aisenstadt
Shoshana Altman
Mayer Appel
Leonard Baum
Rabbi Auri Vishi Beer Chaim
Rabbi Saul Berman
Stephanie Berghesh
Joseph Blatt
Faye Bloom
Edna Braude
Yaakov Braude
Wendy Cohen
Dr. Aryae Coppersmith
Menachem Daum

Devorah Davi
Rabbi Yankel Dinnerstein
Art D'Lugoff
Suri Dymshitz
Dr. Yaffa Eliach
Jill Elias
Michael Elias
Rabbi Dr. Dov Peretz Elkins
Kenny Ellis
Chaya Farber
Rabbi Yisroel Finman
Mitchell Flaum
Stan Fleischer
Julie Frank
Sarah Frankel

Naama Frenkel
Jeanette Friedman
Myriam Fuchs
Rabbi Meyer Fund
Michelle Gardner
Rabbi Laizer Garner
Shmuel Zalman Gehrman
Sam Glaser
Seth Glass
Jeanette Goldberg
Dr. Robert Goldman
Ashira Goodfriend
Glicka Gottesman
Joey Greenblatt
Zelig Grossman
Baila Guez
Rabbi Yaakov Haber
Moishe Halberstam
Heidi Hamburger
Rivkah Haut
Amy Haviv
Chana Heller
Tuvia Heller
Assemblyman Dov Hikind
Adena Hochbaum
Rabbi Simcha Hochbaum
Rebetzin Miriam Huttler
Malka Ilovitz
Douglas Jablon
Rebetzin Esther Jungreis
Rabbi Jacob Jungreis
Rodger Kamenetz
Yanky Kessler
Rabbi Eliahu Klein
Sender Klein
Dr. David Lazerson
David Lefkowitz
Yehudis Leventhal
Shulamis Levovitz

Shimon Lichtenstein
Stanley Lieberman
Kalman Lipsky
Donna Maimes
Rabbi Tzvi Mandel
Jonathan Mark
Naomi Mark
Devorah Marvy
Henny Milworm
Ann Minkoff
David Montague
Michael Ozair
Helen Parness
Aaron Reichel
Dr. Josh Ritchie
Carol Rose
Darlene Rose
Malka Rosen
Charley Roth
Dr. Moshe Rothkopf
Miriam Rubinoff
Laya Rosenfeld
Cecelia Sacharow
Terre Martin Sanitatas
Denise Sassoon
Charlotte Saunders
Rabbi Zalman Schachter-
    Shalomi
Racquel Schraub
Miriam Schwartz
Olivia Schwartz
Dr. Hillel Seidman
Rabbi Moshe Shur
Dov Shurin
Shimmie Silver
Art Stabile
David Steinberg
Sarah Stern
Mendel Sternhull

Shimshon Stock

Abie Teitz

Rabbi Dr. Abraham Twerski

Varda Verstandig

Stuart Wax

Rabbi Uzi Weingarten

Rabbi Gershon Winkler

Minnie Winkler

Ronan Wolf

Avrum Wolpin

Esther Zimmerman

Rocky Zweig

Index

About the Author

Yitta Halberstam Mandelbaum is the great-great grand-daughter of the Sanzer Rebbe, a nineteenth-century hasidic master whose teachings were brought to the American Jewish public and popularized by Shlomo Carlebach. She pursued graduate studies in American Literature at New York University, and taught Literature of the Holocaust at Baruch College. She has also worked as a newspaper reporter, writer for a nationally syndicated radio program, public relations director, press aide, and high school English teacher. Published since the age of nine, her work has appeared in more than 50 Anglo/Jewish publications and secular magazines such as *Parade, Working Woman, Money,* and *New York.* Mrs. Mandelbaum is co-author of the New York Times bestseller *Small Miracles* and its sequel, *Small Miracles II.* Currently, she serves as Director of Programming, Education, and Public Affairs for a non-profit organization. She resides in Brooklyn with her husband and children.